D1270994

A Mission for Justice

THEY CAME

they came
by car, by bus, by way
into the newark
afraid, hoping, determined
looking, and looking on
redemption, despair, scattered dreams
lay and religious
some just laying, always laid by the way side
looking on a new curious thing

whites and blacks assembled, marching

folks passing through the bowels of newark
touched by history, hoping for justice
something human in the air
the newark has always given
a truer sense of where we are not
where we have been, where we cannot go

some sang
sometimes we whistle when we are afraid
don't know what singing does
but that day, people came, black and white and other
to this place where God spent a lot of His free time
to newark
walking this american dream not lived
filling the space this day thick
they came
i wonder
if they knew
could see the real thing
would they finally scream enough
or just take this day as another
on the way to what has always been
how far could they walk with the knowing
they were stepping on the footsteps
of people who had this dream before
what could be understood
the change had come, newark would never

ever be quiet again, pain never hidden
like before
what the residents always knew
the believers would come to know
and hopefully, remember

i'm not sure but jesus came
he was there in the faces of those who knew
that this would be the last walk
the very last time
truth can only be crushed so long
then of its own volition will rise
will come to pass
in a way we may not be ready for
but those who came
were changed forever
they could never hide from themselves again
they would always know
where God's priorities are
and who HE entrusts them with

[illegible signature], 1993

Twenty-fifth
Anniversary
of the
Walk For
Understanding

A Mission for Justice

The History of the First African American Catholic Church in Newark, New Jersey

Mary A. Ward

The University of Tennessee Press • Knoxville

First Edition.

The poem "They Came," which serves as a frontispiece, is by Clifton Carter, 1993. Used by permission of Joyce Smith Carter. The letter in appendix 3 is used by permission of the Seton Hall Archives and Special Collection Center.

This book is printed on acid-free paper.

Library of Congress Cataloging-in-Publication Data

Ward, Mary A., 1947–

A mission for justice : the history of the first African American Catholic church in Newark, New Jersey / Mary A. Ward.—
1st Edition.
p. cm.
Includes bibliographical references and index.
ISBN 1-57233-190-9 (cl. : alk. paper)
ISBN 1-57233-191-7 (pbk. : alk. paper)
1. Afro-American Catholics—New Jersey—Newark—History.
I. Title.
BX1407.N4 W37 2002
282'.74932'08996073—dc21 2001007158

For
Fredric and *Vina Belle Ward*
and
Adrian John Ward Dancy

Contents

Figures

Following Page 42

Following Page 140

Maps

Tables

Preface

This is a case study of a local experience that I hope will add to the overall history of African American religion and particularly to the African American Catholic experience. In this respect, I am answering the call of the African American Catholic historian Rev. Cyprian Davis, O.S.B.

This history of the first African American Catholic Church in Newark, New Jersey, was pieced together from a variety of sources. I drew on more than thirty oral histories of parishioners, pastors, curates, sisters, and others involved in the history of Queen of Angels and on written documentation from various contributors' private collections, including letters, sermons, newsletters, church bulletins, anniversary journals, photographs, parish records, minutes of meetings, newspaper clippings, and magazine articles. To place Queen of Angels in religious and historical context, I have visited other churches in Newark over the past nine years: Abbysinian Baptist, Clinton Presbyterian, Bethany Baptist, and St. James African Methodist-Episcopal Church, St. Mary's Abbey, Blessed Sacrament, and Grace Episcopal Church.

No human event or endeavor can be understood without knowing its history. On the other hand, even after exhaustive research we can never be absolutely sure that we have it right. I hope this history of one of Newark's best-kept secrets will edify all who read it and give us a vision for the future.

In regard to self-referencing terms for people of African descent, I have generaly remained consistent in my use of "African American," with the following exceptions. Within the appropriate historical period, I may use the words *colored* or *Negro* when the actors of my story use them, especially when combined with other terms. Ethel Wright spoke of a church for colored people and a colored priest; Martin Luther King Jr. discussed the future of the "new Negro"; and until the 1960s the Catholic Church's work for African Americans was called the Negro Apostolate. I have also employed the word *black,* particularly if my narration refers to or is inclusive of people from other areas of the world who are African or whose ancestors are from that continent.

Abbreviations for Catholic Religious Orders Used in the Text

C.P.	Congregation of Discalced Clerks of the Most Holy Cross and Passion of Our Lord Jesus Christ.
M.S.B.T.	Missionary Servants of the Blessed Trinity, also known as the Trinitarians, a religious order of sisters who helped found Queen of Angels Parish.
O.P.	Order of Preachers (commonly known as Dominicans).
O.S.B.	Order of St. Benedict, also known as the Benedictines, a Catholic religious order of priests and nuns.
O.S.P.	Oblate Sisters of Providence, order of African American sisters who first operated Queen of Angels School in 1963.
S.J.	Society of Jesus, also known as the Jesuits, a Catholic religious order of priests.
S.S.J.	Josephite priests.

Acknowledgments

Two groups of people have contributed to this project: those I have interviewed, studied, and thought about for the past nine years, and others outside of the parish community who have sustained, enlightened, and encouraged me. I am indebted to the many people of Queen of Angels and the Newark community who allowed me to delve into their lives and memories and who often offered me spiritual sustenance and motivation as well.

I am grateful to all those who spoke with me informally or in taped interviews, but there are a few I would like to name. Elma Bateman and her sister Bennie Fields made me a part of their family; their unconditional love is both extraordinary and transformative. Valerie Smith, Ruby Jones, Gertrude Messer *(in memoriam),* and Joyce Smith Carter are women of tireless energy who never cease to give of themselves; I benefited by their wisdom and memories. Deacon Albert Bradsher and his wife, Regenia, angels both, were invaluable resources for the African American Baptist Church and the history of Queen of Angels. Al Heath, musical director at Queen of Angels, was always willing to provide me with his perspective and made me feel welcome in the gospel choir. Queen of Angels' pastor, Fr. James McConnell, has kept a perpetual welcome mat out for me, no matter how long between visits.

Both Msgr. Tom Carey *(in memoriam)* and Tom Comerford went above and beyond—answering questions, taking my phone calls, and visiting with me innumerable times. Msgr. William Linder, recovering from illness, gave me a crucial phone interview and valuable documentation. Pat Foley of New Community Corporation shared her documents, photographs, and remembrances. Fr. Kevin Ashe provided crucial information about the beginnings of New Community Corporation. My continuing gratitude to all of them.

The Reverend James Scott, educator and former pastor of Bethany Baptist; Robert Curvin, former regional director of the Congress of Racial Equality (CORE); and Kenneth Gibson, the first African American mayor of Newark—all graciously agreed to discuss the African American community of Newark and its relationship to Queen of Angels. This study could not have been completed without their contribution.

Acknowledgments

The women of the Missionary Servants of the Most Blessed Trinity contributed much to the early history and development of Queen of Angels and to this work. Sr. Peter Claver Fahy, Sr. Francis Damien, Sr. Theresa Ahern, and Sr. Mary Mathew all happily granted me several interviews at their generalate (motherhouse) in Philadelphia, fed me, and prayed for me.

I am deeply grateful to the Fordham University community for their dedication to excellence. The Reverend Mark Massa, S.J., introduced me to the history of American religion and to the *Madonna of 115th Street,* which led to this local African American religious history. He thought my attempting this project was a good idea from the beginning, and I have great respect for his judgment. Two other Fordham professors, Dr. James R. Kelly and Dr. Ewert Cousins, shared their love of knowledge with great generosity of spirit; without their moral support and confidence in me as a writer, I could not have finished the manuscript. And a special thanks goes to Edie Mauriello, now retired secretary of the theology department who, in subtle but substantial ways, kept me together for the years of my life that this project consumed.

Professors and contributors in the field of American religion Albert Raboteau, Gary McDonogh, Randall Miller, Jon Anderson, John McGreevy, and Jay Dolan generously responded to my questions in the beginning stages of my work and when I reached an impasse. Dr. Jason Martin helped me break through my greatest block and pointed me toward the overall vision of this work. I owe them all an immeasurable debt and am deeply grateful. I cannot neglect to mention Wilfrid Harrington, O.P., Irish biblical scholar and author, and my mentor during my master's degree program at Gonzaga University. He taught me to rethink my theological presuppositions and gently challenged me toward a greater understanding in multiple areas of life.

This could not have been accomplished without the assistance of several libraries. My thanks to the staff of Fordham University's Walsh Library; they were always kind, professional, and helpful. Seton Hall and Immaculate Conception Seminary libraries both extended their services to me, the latter by special permission from the Reverend William Harms. Thank you. The Newark Public Library, a great library in a great city, was indispensable for its excellent general collection and its New Jersey documents. The librarians in the New Jersey Room were especially attentive and knowledgeable. Assistant director of Special Collections and Newark historian Charles Cummings donated copies of maps and photographs that I could not have obtained otherwise; he was there for me at the crucial last moments.

Acknowledgments

JoAnn Cotz of Seton Hall University Archives was instrumental in starting this project. In collaboration with Lucille Forman *(in memoriam),* the dedicated director of the Archdiocesan Office of Black Catholics, JoAnn mounted the exhibit on African American Catholic history that inspired the following pages. She assisted me in tracking down primary documents and photos.

The New Jersey Historical Commission honored me with a research grant that eased the burden in the early stages of the work. The American Academy of Religion, especially Judith Weisenfeld, were responsible to a great extent for this book. They gave me the opportunity to present my work at annual conferences; my paper "What's the Attraction to the White Man's Church" caught the attention of the University of Tennessee Press, which led to this publication. The Press's acquisitions editor, Joyce Harrison, has been a joyful and sustaining presence without which the process of going toward publication would have been unbearable. Thank you, thank you.

Much appreciation to those who read chapters: Bishop Curtis J. Guillory, SVD, Jody Susler, Kathy White, Phuong Tranvan, and Tony Tudisco *(in memoriam)*. A special note of gratitude to Tasos Georgakopoulos, whose belief in me and the project kept me going in the most trying times. In addition, his assistance with the photographs proved to be invaluable pragmatically and for my vision of the work.

Thank you to my parents for their steadfast belief in me, and to my brothers and sisters, Judy, Fred, Tom, Barbara, Joe, and Monica. I hold deepest gratitude to B. J. Dancy, Cecee, and Dahlia Bijou Ward, who are no longer with us, but are remembered fondly. To my son, A. John Dancy, who in so many ways is part of this work.

Thank you to Clifton Carter, now gone from our midst, who taught me to "stop apologizing" for who I am and the life decisions I have made. And, finally, to Emma Thompson of Queen of Angels, who told me not to forget my roots.

Introduction

> *We must come to see that human progress never rolls in on wheels of inevitability. It comes through the tireless efforts and persistent work of men willing to be co-workers with God, and without this hard work time itself becomes an ally of the forces of social stagnation.*
>
> *—Rev. Dr. Martin Luther King*

It has been said, "Christianity cannot be either described or understood without a knowledge of the history through which it became what it is."[1] But more broadly, no human event or endeavor can be understood without knowing its history. It is also a good rule of thumb for historians and biographers to avoid idealization of those whose lives they recount; however, although I fought against it, I am not quite sure that I am free of guilt in that respect.

After the death of former President John F. Kennedy's son recently, it struck me how much I am a child of the sixties and seventies. I have a stubborn desire to resist cynicism and to believe in the ability of human beings to change things for the better. When John F. Kennedy Jr. died, I realized that as the slain president's son, he symbolized the hope that the idealism of the 1960s lived on in spite of his father's assassination. That event in Dallas in 1963 was the first of many blows against the spirit of optimism and positive change that pervaded the 1960s and 1970s. True, it was an era of inanities, extremes, and mistakes, but at the same time, it possessed a faith that something could be done by ordinary people.

This is a story about many ordinary people who lived in the 1960s and 1970s, and many decades before that. Possibly they were naive in the 1920s, 1930s, and 1940s, but they tackled life with brio and determination. They failed; they succeeded; they fought; they got it wrong; and they made things right. Whatever they did, they were interesting because they were interested.

This story is about African Americans, West Indians, and black Portuguese. It is about the European Americans who both assisted and restricted these people in their enterprise to raise themselves to their full height as Catholic Christians and American citizens. It is a history in microcosm, but it applies in some ways to the larger picture of people who are black and Catholic. In some ways, it can be applied to all of us.

When I began my nine years of research on the history of Queen of Angels, a parishioner named Nina Williams asked me why I chose to write about their parish. At that time I had not articulated my motives, much less analyzed them; I could not answer her with any certainty. As a European American Catholic, I was not sure what I would discover at Queen of Angels. Compared to other areas of religious history, the amount of available scholarship on black Catholics in the United States, especially local parish histories, was minimal at best. Compared to African American Baptists and Methodists, African American Catholics are few in number—a minority within a minority, according to Albert Raboteau.[2] But I was much more familiar with the better-known African American Protestant history than the subject I had decided to examine.

Ultimately, much of what I found was enlightening and even surprising. For example, the "mission to the colored in Essex and Union counties" (as Queen of Angels was officially called by the archdiocese of Newark) was involved in the lives of the black community on an astonishing level in scope and intensity. And at times in its history, the small community of Queen of Angels had an outsized effect on the larger culture. But I knew none of this when Mrs. Williams asked her question.

Short-Term Explanations

As the many years unfolded, I had time to ponder the question, and it seemed to me that the events in my life led naturally to this topic. In particular, three events occurred in 1990 that influenced me significantly and led directly to the initiation of this project. The first was when I read *The*

Madonna of 115th Street: Faith and Community in Italian Harlem, 1880–1950, by Robert Anthony Orsi.[3] As a social history about ordinary laypeople, it concerns the people in the pew, specifically southern Italian immigrants of the late nineteenth and early twentieth centuries who were faced with a less than satisfactory place in a predominantly Irish and German American Catholic Church.

Orsi tells their story frankly and describes how they made their way in their new urban environment in New York. We learn how lay Italians continued their spiritual and cultural connection to their homeland with the *festa* of Our Lady of Mount Carmel. They introduced to their neighborhood in East Harlem a religious and social tradition that governed their lives in the villages they left behind. In so doing, they re-created a social, cultural, and religious space that made them more comfortable in their new surroundings. It was a way of remaining Italian and Catholic while becoming American at the same time.

When Orsi looked at religious practices particular to this group, he did not minimize or defend them, but explained and framed them within the group's own understanding and way of being family. He did not sanctify them, but humanized them. I found this approach refreshing and exhilarating. And on a subconscious level, I think I began to explore the idea for my own project.

Soon after reading Orsi's book, I chanced on a photo exhibit of African American pioneers of the Newark archdiocese.[4] I saw laywomen dressed in clothing of the 1920s who had formed a Catholic organization before the mission church began. There were men in splendid top hats and tails marching in the Holy Name Parade down Broad Street in Newark with their pastor, Fr. Cornelius Ahern. In one photo, I discovered children dressed in First Holy Communion dresses and suits and, in another, gathered in front of one of the missions in their winter coats with the Missionary Sisters of the Most Blessed Trinity alongside them. I looked at the faces of the people in the photographs, and they looked back at me with candid, forthright expressions. They all seemed so resolute and sure of what they were doing, and in a matter-of-fact way, they seemed conscious that they were engaged in something noteworthy. I was intrigued immediately; I wanted to discover who they were and why they were Catholic.

Almost as a confirmation, the third event was when I read Cyprian Davis's *The History of Black Catholics in the United States,* in which he pointed out the need for local studies of African American Catholics to provide material to build a clearer and larger account of their lives and contributions.[5] I had my mandate and was certain this was a project I wanted to tackle.

In the spring of 1991, I made my first trip to Queen of Angels Church at 44 Irvine Turner Boulevard in the Central Ward of Newark, New Jersey. I was not certain what to expect in terms of liturgical style. For years I had heard of black gospel choirs in Catholic churches from Seattle, Washington, to Washington, D.C., and I wondered if Queen of Angels had such a choir.

In the late nineteenth century, a German congregation originally constructed the church where Queen of Angels Parish has resided since 1962. The interior of the church was long and narrow and not overly bright. Beams arched upward and beautiful stained glass windows allowed only the softest sunlight. I saw that one side of the church was cordoned off, and when I cast my gaze upward toward the falling plaster of the ceiling, I realized why. Clearly, the church had seen better days.[6]

I found a place in the middle of the church and felt slightly awkward. I was one of the few European Americans there. The atmosphere was hushed, but quiet voices murmured occasionally when greetings were exchanged warmly between parishioners. I noticed that a tall woman in front of me, with a very large brimmed hat, stood often throughout the two-hour liturgy to shout words of encouragement as the gospel choir sang. As a parishioner mentioned to me at the end of the Mass, I enjoyed myself thoroughly. It was the beginning of an adventure into history, the lives of a people, and a journey into myself.

Converts and Differences

A second- and third-generation European American, I married an African American many years ago and gave birth to a son, which has placed me at the crucible of race, religion, and identity. My parents converted from Protestantism to Catholicism shortly before I was born. I was aware from an early age that we were different from our extended Protestant family, and possibly even disapproved of at times. The impact of that fact on my life cannot be overestimated.

In addition to the theological essentials, many things about being Catholic captured my imagination: the seasonal rhythms of a mystical Latin liturgy, the family rosaries that prayed for the "conversion of Russia," and the angel to whom I prayed to protect me from a very large dog as I pedaled frantically to parochial school. In those days we could not darken the door of a Protestant church or date non-Catholics. Being Catholic pervaded my entire existence, and it set us apart from family and friends. Being different was uncomfortable, but it sensitized me to other people's differences. Because of my background, I was at ease with the culture of conversion and difference I found at Queen of Angels Parish.

By coming of age in the late 1960s and 1970s, some anomalous events were added to my personal history, but they were commonplace to all baby boomers like me. The election of John F. Kennedy, the first Catholic president of the United States, made me proud. And his murder, along with Robert Kennedy's and Rev. Dr. Martin Luther King Jr.'s, were devastating awakenings to a brutal reality. The Civil Rights movement of the 1960s and 1970s, and, for me, the subtle but positive take on it by the Holy Name Sisters who educated me, fine-tuned an already existing sensitivity to diversity, injustice, and the moral necessity to take sides.

Race is not so much a biological category as a construction of the social norms and values of a given society. In other words, we label, categorize, and base our actions toward others on our notion of their gender, race, and ethnicity. We take the complexity of a group and render it monolithic, uniform, and constant. I found myself reflecting on the social construction of race in my study of this African American community in close interactive and dependent association with European Americans.[7] As a European American, I experienced the self-conscious dynamics of minority status within the community until I felt less and less conscious of that construction. Possibly, both my notions and theirs were altered by our close contact. In any event, Catholics—African American or European American—are not monolithic.

Products and Producers in Time and Space

From the time I met him in 1991 until his death in January 1999, Msgr. Thomas A. Carey would often tell me that people are products of their time. He said this to explain and defend those who criticized his radical behavior. As administrator of Queen of Angels from 1958 until 1970, he led the parish through the turbulent 1960s with the attendant tumult of the Civil Rights movement, the race riots of Newark, and the assassination of Martin Luther King Jr. I agreed with Carey, of course. Everyone knows about the nurture part of the nature versus nurture debate—that is, that our environment helps shape us. The extent of that influence is debatable, but not the fact of it. The following history contains patterns of behavior and instances where people behaved according to the prevailing beliefs of their day—but not everyone did so. Much of what happened at Queen of Angels, especially under Carey's watch, was the result of people going against the thinking of their particular group or taking the initiative to affect their environment rather than conform to it.

Martin Luther King Jr., whose influence at Queen of Angels was palpable, put a different spin on the subject of time and environment that may go more to the heart of the events at Queen of Angels. In his "Letter from a Birmingham Jail," written in 1963, King talks about the "myth of time." He was responding to those who admonished him for what they perceived as asking for change too soon. After all, freedom will come for your people eventually, as one letter writer predicted, but "the teachings of Christ take time to come to earth."[8] King argued that time is neutral; it does nothing of itself. And to speak of time as if it acts actually excuses the unwillingness of people to change inequities. This, said King, is the "tragic misconception." King believed that time "can be used either destructively or constructively," and often those of evil intent use time more effectively than those of good will. "Human progress," he said, "never rolls in on wheels of inevitability. It comes through the tireless efforts and persistent work of men willing to be co-workers with God."[9] Yes, our environment affects us, but we are not passive receptors of time or the times. Therefore, from this perspective, the question is, are we formed by the times in which we live or do we ourselves make the times what they are? Thus is the world, or thus have we made it?

There are people like Martin Luther King Jr. who leave a timeless imprint, forever altering the definition of time and space. These people are not so much products as producers. To some degree, I would argue that the preecclesial mothers of Queen of Angels Church were such as these. Theresa Lane, Ethel Wright, and Lucy Mulligan initiated, organized, and—unasked—assumed responsibility for the continuity of their religious faith among their people. Without their first steps, Queen of Angels would not have come into being. They initiated the lay movement that resulted in the first colored mission in Newark and its satellite missions. After them came clergy, laypeople, and women religious (also known as sisters and nuns) who subsequently responded and acted. Coworkers and producers all.[10]

Mission: Asset and Liability

Quite accurately, the concept of the missionary church is perceived as a tool of colonialism, and the status of Queen of Angels as a mission church did have its liabilities. But there is another aspect to mission that is valid here.

In *The Churches the Apostles Left Behind,* the late biblical scholar Raymond E. Brown distinguished between two different ecclesiological models of church leadership in the New Testament: the missionary and the institutional leader.[11] Both models are considered necessary depending upon the needs of the faith community.

Being a missionary is tricky business, and for Brown, the consummate missionary was the dynamic but less than diplomatic Paul. It was he who insisted upon an egalitarian interpretation of Jesus Christ's good news. "There is neither Jew nor Greek, there is neither slave nor free, there is neither male nor female; for you are all one in Christ Jesus" (Gal. 3:28)—decidedly a troublesome verse for chauvinistic and ethnocentric people of all stripes.

Queen of Angels is technically a mission even now. But its first fifty years closely followed a mission model, and as such used extraordinary means to draw members to the faith. Its leadership style and methods were more charismatic than institutional. As early as the 1930s, the mainly white clergy and women religious at Queen of Angels generally took their cues for methodology from the laity they served even more than from the hierarchy they were under. Their fundamentals were thoroughly Catholic, but their evangelizing methods were fluid and intuitive. This could explain the phenomenal success the mission enjoyed until the mid-1970s. Why were they able to operate so loosely? I believe it was because they were technically and canonically a mission rather than a territorial parish. Mission status had its liabilities, but overall it contributed to the custom-made quality of the church. By virtue of its status as a mission, they were able to be charismatic in their structure. I use the word *charismatic* in the Weberian sense of an organization dependent on the energy and innovation of its leaders rather than on a more conservative need to maintain the organization's structural and traditional integrity.[12] What could be characterized as a laissez-faire attitude on the part of the diocese actually gave Queen of Angels the freedom of movement it needed to grow.[13]

Missionary types are similar to the prophetic or resistant typologies described by C. Eric Lincoln and Lawrence Mamiya in *The Black Church in the African American Experience*.[14] Queen of Angels resisted the larger culture in the 1930s by constantly finding ways to circumvent race-based societal restrictions. During the early years, from the 1930s to 1940s, clerical leaders at times spoke prophetically, decrying what they perceived as an indifferent church and a hostile larger culture. They noted the systematic oppression and at times begged for justice while acting obliquely to change it.

In the more blatant 1960s and 1970s, Queen of Angels acted in radical attention-getting ways and *demanded* justice and change. Their prophetic stance was loud and irritating, and divisive at times, but so was the culture of protest with which it kept pace. In both eras, behavior was always grounded in a concern for the priestly or spiritual element. And depending upon the devotional and liturgical style of the time, the spiritual was an essential ingredient of resistance. The call to evangelize and convert was inseparable from the amalgam of resistance and prophetic Zeitgeist.

An African American Sacred Cosmos

Our Lady Queen of the Angels Parish began with one woman, Ethel Wright, who filled an educational and catechetical void by instructing children in the Catholic faith. Although possibly a cradle Catholic, baptized as an infant, I argue that she still was affected by the southern black Protestant culture that retained a more unified worldview. In other words, the line between the sacred and the profane was blurred, and every act, no matter how mundane, was informed by a sacred reality and meaning. As Mechal Sobel observed in her study:

> Blacks in America, under the enormous pressures and hardships of chattel slavery, came to achieve a new coherence which preserved and revitalized crucial African understandings and usages regarding spirit and soul-travels, while melding them with Christian understandings of Jesus and individual salvation. A coherent Afro-Christian faith was created, and its reality was reflected in a vibrant and known institution, a black Baptist church, the history of which goes back to the 1750s.[15]

That Afro-Christian faith permeated all of the mainly Baptist and Methodist African American culture, solidified during the post–Civil War years when the black church was the central measurement of status and unifying force.

The faith of Queen of Angels' parishioners was grounded in this *cultural* sacred cosmos, not borrowed from any European Catholic worldview. Most of the parishioners of Queen of Angels were converts from the black church and thus brought that sensibility and worldview of the African American church to the spiritual table and combined it with the Catholic ethos.[16]

Today Queen of Angels has both the European American and the more African American style of worship in their two Sunday Masses. One Mass has a traditional European American preaching and music style, and the other is a gospel Mass, where Fr. James McConnell's preaching is more exuberant in the mode of the traditional black church.[17] He encourages call and response between himself and the congregation, shouting, the lifting of hands, and the crying out of words of praise. The choir sings a wide range of liturgical music but clearly favors gospel hymns common to the African American Protestant church, along with its movements and presentation. This appropriation of black church music and ethos is a relatively recent development of the post–Civil Rights era and Black Power movement. Not all Queen of Angels parishioners prefer it, with roughly half of the congregation attending the more contemplative Catholic Mass.

The diversity of devotional and liturgical sensibility exemplifies the makeup of those who are African American and Catholic. Over time, multiple discourses have taken place among the African American people at Queen of Angels. They have occurred between African Americans and the mainly white clergy, women religious, and lay volunteers who ministered to them, and transpired between both of these groups and the church hierarchy and secular society that exerted control over them and established boundaries around them. With self-conscious determination, the parishioners persevered in their pilgrimage toward complete participation. By the 1960s they transformed themselves into a people who contributed solutions, even in the midst of need, and others looked to Queen of Angels as a model of social activism and civil rights.

Ultimately, my hope is that this is a story of the complexity of the black experience in the United States and of the ways religion and politics informed African Americans' choices. Conversion, the ethics and value of the Catholic mission to African Americans, and how Queen of Angels was affected by the Civil Rights movement, liberation theology, and the Second Vatican Council are all elements of the mosaic. The facts of its history set this community apart in its impact on the Newark community, an impact much greater than its size or resources have ever been.

1

Errand into an Urban Wilderness

True followers of Jesus should challenge and change prejudice, not accommodate to it by declaring it beyond the power of individuals to alter.

—Thomas Wyatt Turner

Newark before African American Catholics

This history of African American Catholics takes place in a city that, at its beginning, had not a trace of anything African or Catholic.[1] In May 1666, Puritans founded Newark led by their religious fervor, and their desire for the freedom, at least for themselves, to worship God as they wished, recognizing themselves in the mirror of their personal beliefs and vigilant practices. The choices, decisions, and actions of early Puritans were grounded in a self-conscious conviction that they were proceeding where others had not gone and were sustaining faith when others trod an easier path.[2] In Puritan William Bradford's words, we can hear this sense of mission fallen on hard times: "Our fathers were Englishmen which came over this great ocean, and were ready to perish in this wilderness; but they cried unto the Lord, and he heard their voyce, and looked on their adversitie."[3] Theirs was an "errand into the wilderness."[4]

Ironically, as far apart as they were in many ways, those first Puritans and the African American Catholics of our story shared a commonality. For even though the English attempted to purify their Christianity of all things Catholic, and the African Americans embraced it, they both possessed a self-conscious awareness and a sense of historical importance. And later, in the urban wilderness of Newark, African American Catholics carved their space in a different religious and cultural landscape filled with newer, white immigrants from Europe and black immigrants from the South.

In the late nineteenth and early twentieth century, the chronicle of African Americans and European immigrant Catholics begins in earnest due to major demographic changes that brought them in close proximity. That story is awash with a hunger to be fully American at a time when the larger white Protestant culture eyed both groups with suspicion, distrust, and animosity. And to further complicate the picture, European American Catholics were at best ambiguous in their attitude toward the presence of blacks. Somehow in the midst of this muddled state of affairs a small window of opportunity opened between black and white, and in that space Our Lady Queen of the Angels Church was born.

Catholicism in New Jersey—A Micro History

The first settlement of English Catholics in colonial America was in the colony of Maryland, established with a charter granted by Charles I to Lord Baltimore Cecil Calvert. To allay the fears of the Protestants who were both patrons and fellow settlers, and to ensure the success of their commercial enterprise in the new colony, the Catholics resolved to practice their faith quietly. The Maryland colony prospered under an agreement of toleration between Catholics and Protestants.[5]

It was not until after the Revolution of 1776 that a few Catholics settled in New Jersey, and they, too, practiced their faith privately to prevent the antagonism of Protestant government and neighbors. They had reason to be nervous. In 1698 the General Assembly of East Jersey declared at a meeting in Perth Amboy that freedom of religion "shall not extend to any of the Romish religion the right to exercise their manner of worship contrary to the laws and statutes of England."[6] The few Catholics who settled in New Jersey kept their religion a secret, sustained by infrequent visits from itinerant priests, joined other churches, or gave up religion altogether.[7] They were prevented from holding office until an article in the second constitution in 1844 admitted Catholics to full civil rights.[8]

It was not until the late nineteenth century that large numbers of Catholic immigrants came to New Jersey to fill the jobs created by industrialization and mass transportation projects.[9] New Jersey's foreign population increased to 12 percent in 1850, 21 percent in 1870, and 23 percent in 1890. By 1850 the state contained 31,092 Irish and 10,686 German foreign-born.[10] Immigrants were attracted to New Jersey for its job opportunities in manufacturing, iron works, and leather. Another attraction was the building of two canals in the 1830s: the first connecting the Delaware River to the Hudson and the second connecting New Brunswick to Trenton. In addition, the state needed labor to lay the hundreds of miles of railroad track necessary to keep pace with the industrial revolution.

Catholics struggled with discrimination and prejudice, especially in the 1850s, with the rise of the Know-Nothing Party that was organized around an antiforeign and anti-Catholic sentiment. Catholics were marked because of their increase in numbers, although Catholics were targeted in all sections of the country, even those where the Catholic population was minimal.[11]

On July 29, 1853, Pope Pius IX constituted the state of New Jersey as a distinct See and appointed James Roosevelt Bayley as its first bishop.[12] During his tenure, one of Bayley's top priorities was to provide a Catholic education to the children of the diocese. To that end, he secured teaching orders of women religious to staff the schools he built. He also successfully pressured the state legislature to pass a law allowing Roman Catholic churches to incorporate their property. This move centralized power on the episcopal level and weakened the lay trustee movement, which had been struggling with bishops from the beginning of the American church for the right to select their own priests and control church property.[13]

The Rise of National Parishes

A series of events called the Cahenslyan controversy played out to a certain extent in the Newark diocese under its second bishop, Winand M. Wigger, who was of German descent.[14] German Catholics felt strongly about perpetuating their language and culture, forming strong communities in Newark as they did in New York, Milwaukee, St. Louis, and Cincinnati. Their motto, "Language Saves the Faith," expressed their view of the reciprocity and interdependence between the two realities.[15] The movement became most powerful (and doomed to failure) when Peter Cahensly, a merchant from Germany, organized a group called the St. Raphaelsverein to protect German Catholic immigrants; and German priests formed the national Deutsch-Amerikaner Priester-Verein to promote German solidarity. Cahensly recommended that dioceses, including the appointment of its bishops and clergy, be structured according to nationality regardless of geographic location, and that parochial schools and catechetical instruction be carried on in the mother tongue of the immigrant.

The German organization attracted the attention of Irish American Bishops John Ireland and John J. Keane. Imagining a German plot that Ireland dubbed "Cahenslyism," the two bishops launched a public and powerful attack.[16] Bishop Wigger allowed the German Catholic Congress to be held in Newark in 1892 and was accused in the Catholic press of treason to church and state. After a vigorous counterattack, Wigger successfully defended himself, but being German proved to be a hardship. He had to continually guard against accusations of favoritism toward his fellow Germans.[17]

Ultimately, the Germans' efforts were quashed completely, but at the same time, the diocese of Newark invested a great deal of resources to provide for other groups much of what the Germans were demanding. Italians, Poles, Slovaks from the Hungarian section of the Austro-Hungarian Empire, Hungarians, Lithuanians, and members of the Byzantine Rite formed their own communities and requested priests, not only of their own nationality but also from the section of the country from which they emigrated.[18] All of them, to varying degrees and depending upon their numbers, obtained national parishes and priests.[19]

Fearing that Catholics would lose control of the curricula, Wigger withstood lay attempts to incorporate parochial schools into the public school system. In 1893 the diocese was over $1.2 million in debt and was hindered by the depression. Nevertheless, Bishop Wigger was able to increase the number of clergy and religious orders to meet the needs of an ever-expanding diocese. He opened forty-five more parochial schools, several orphan asylums, industrial schools and protectories, four hospitals, and began work on a new gothic cathedral.

Most of these institutions were owned and/or operated by orders of women religious, without whom none of these institutions would have existed. As authors Carol K. Coburn and Martha Smith point out:

> The expansion of American Catholic culture and identity and its subsequent influence in American society could not have occurred without the activities and labor of these women [religious]. The proliferation of schools, hospitals and orphanages boggles the contemporary mind. By 1920, Catholics sisters had created and/or maintained approximately 500 hospitals, 50 women's colleges, and over 6,000 parochial schools, serving 1.7 million school children in every region of the country, both urban and rural.[20]

In the late nineteenth century, much of what the Germans were demanding was as commonplace in Newark as it was elsewhere in the United States. National parishes and instruction in the native tongue of immigrants were provided as much as resources would allow. The mistake the Germans made was to insist on their own dioceses and bishops, and they did so in a very direct and confrontational manner, threatening the mainly Irish composition of the church's hierarchy.

However, it would take almost a hundred years before African American Catholics would enjoy unfettered admission to Catholic churches, hospitals, and schools. Access to them would be to a great extent by demographic default due to white flight to the suburbs. But the Catholic Church's acquiescence to ethnicity created a precedent that would prove tempting to African Americans who were Catholic or became Catholic.

The national parish came to define Catholic life in urban America, creating a form of religious nationalism. The melding of religion and nationality was a central part of the worldview of Irish and German Catholics who immigrated in significant numbers to the United States beginning in the early 1800s.[21] In their respective countries, the Irish and Germans each experienced conflict and hardship because of their religion.[22]

In *Parish Boundaries,* John McGreevy described the confluence of parish boundaries and ethnic identity that produced an ethnically territorial worldview.[23] Further complicating the state of affairs was the practice at that time of categorizing ethnic groups as races. As McGreevy put it: "American Catholics were accustomed to viewing the world as a series of loosely connected enclaves, with the various 'racial' groups staking out claims to different sections of the city and different parochial institutions."[24] And, similarly, as Jay Dolan has expressed, each ethnic group created its own cultural space, a "religious oasis in the city" and "cultural barriers that separated them from each other."[25] These barriers not only separated them from other immigrant groups but also from African Americans.

In the formative nineteenth century, Catholic immigrants adopted the native-born American attitude toward African Americans just as they latched on to other American values. Irish Catholics, who made up the greater part of the Catholic immigrant population, found themselves sharing the same impoverished environment and job market with freed slaves. After 1840 these Irish were mostly skilled and unskilled laborers fleeing the ravages of an oppressed and famine-ridden Ireland. With the memory of starvation and homelessness burning in their minds and hearts, the Irish even envied the food, clothing, and shelter of African American slaves. On the whole, they refused to join the ranks of the often explicitly anti-Catholic abolitionist movement, declaring that they would even trade places with the slaves if they could—a safe threat considering there was no possibility of it becoming a reality. Slaveholders, not wishing to waste their expensive slave chattel on building the country's new infrastructure of railroads and canals, preferred the cheap and expendable labor of the ubiquitous and desperate Irish.[26]

Some Irish, alienated by their treatment, refused to volunteer for the Union army and resisted the draft. The final and disheartening straw came with the $300 exemption clause in the 1863 conscription law allowing the more prosperous to buy their way out of the draft. The Irish poor, who barely made $300 in an entire year, felt that the burden of the war was on their shoulders. Historians speculate that this turn of events may have led to the draft riots of July 1863, when out-of-control whites murdered African American men, women, and children. It was one of the bloodiest and most brutal race riots in United States history.[27]

In spite of these difficulties, some Irish soldiers, like the Union's Fighting 69th Regiment at Gettysburg, distinguished themselves in Civil War combat. In New Jersey, Irish and German Catholics numbered 16,180, or 20 percent, of the total number of troops (79,348) who fought in the Union army from 1861 to 1865.[28] As historian Charles R. Morris has indicated, in the entire North "the Irish were the most *under*represented of all socioethnic groups in the Union Army, with German Catholics next."[29]

Putting it bluntly, Morris wrote, "Making all allowances, the Irish and their church were racist, even by the standards of the time."[30] And Dolan agreed, writing, "Catholics in general looked down on the Negroes and considered them an inferior race."[31] Irish Bishop John Hughes of New York, as the leading spokesmen for the church when it was emerging from Anglo-American obscurity, set the tone for American Catholics when he "did not condemn slavery and shunned any connection with the abolition movement."[32] This public policy left African American Catholics with no place in the Catholic Church to call home; they were, as Dolan characterized them, "spiritual orphans."[33]

Newark—History and Influences

At the turn of the twentieth century, Newark blacks lived in small clusters among or near working-class whites. Old-time black Newark residents looked upon that period as one of peace and racial tolerance, largely because they lived on the same blocks with whites, although often with blacks on one side and whites on the other. They had access to the same stores, and their children attended the same schools without organized white opposition.[34]

One of my interviewees, Walter P. Brown, attended Mrs. Wright's catechism classes as a small child; he lived in a predominantly white neighborhood near St. Bridget's Church on Plane Street. At that time, it was an Irish-Catholic neighborhood with only three or four black homes from Central Avenue to the end of Plane Street. "Everybody knew everybody, [even though] you had never been introduced to them. . . . My mother would give my [white] next-door neighbor girl, Kathleen Sherwood, 25 cents a week to take me to school. And I held her hand. And do you know, I think I am the first black boy she ever knew."[35]

Others, like the first black mayor of Newark, Kenneth Gibson, remember black children speaking German or Italian as a result of their close, positive interactions with whites.[36] Both Brown and Gibson admit that distinctions were made based on race, ethnic group, and class, but they recall a fluidity among the groups and an atmosphere more amiable than that which evolved in later years. To understand the ethos of this period, it is important to know something of the history that began three hundred years earlier.

Slavery and the Civil War in New Jersey

Although no one knows exactly when Africans arrived in New Jersey, we do know that as early as 1628 African slaves were in the colony.[37] The earliest documentation of slavery in New Jersey was that of Col. Richard Morris of Shrewsbury, who in 1680 had sixty or more slaves working on his mill and plantation. In the Northeast, slaves mainly worked small farms but were also owned by merchants, shopkeepers, professionals, innkeepers, widows, and gentlemen.[38]

The English colony that became the state of New Jersey after the Revolution of 1776 was initially divided into two provinces of West Jersey and East Jersey, where Newark was located. Each region's attitude toward slaves evolved in opposite directions and continued to do so when they were reunited in 1702. Explanations for this phenomenon vary. West Jersey, which was generally against slavery, had relatively few blacks and was also far from the slave-trading port of New York. West Jersey was, however, close to the port of Philadelphia, where white indentured servants entered the country in great numbers, reducing the market for African slaves.

More important, West Jersey was greatly influenced by the Society of Friends, or Quakers, who had taken a strong position against slavery by the end of the Revolutionary War. They established the New Jersey Society for Promoting the Abolition of Slavery and focused a tremendous amount of organized effort into accomplishing their goal through every legal means possible.[39] Quakers strove to keep their rhetoric to a minimum, believing that it would only flame the fires of opposition. They patiently accepted the delays, compromises, and defeats, certain that justice would ultimately prevail.[40]

On the other hand, East Jersey fought just as tenaciously to preserve the institution in a variety of forms and structures. They were so successful in this that the last eighteen slaves of the North to be freed were from New Jersey, released from bondage by the Thirteenth Amendment to the Constitution, passed after the Civil War.[41] Forms of gradual manumission of different age groups were mandated, but slavery itself remained until 1865.[42]

The Influence of the Historical Black Church

The main objective of African Americans after the Civil War was to throw off the effects of slavery and to take their position in society. At the end of the Civil War, 95 percent of blacks were illiterate—a major problem that was addressed by those more educated. To quote Evelyn Higginbotham, it was believed at that time that "[g]aining respect, even justice, from white America required changes in religious beliefs, speech patterns, and manners and morals."[43] To accomplish this, black ministers and reform leaders spread the "gospel of moral improvement among the northern black community."[44]

At the turn of the century, the more militant W. E. B. DuBois, who would discourse with the more conservative black leader Booker T. Washington, formulated the concept of the talented tenth, which reasoned that the leading college-educated African Americans should uplift the race by example and by influence.[45]

Of prime importance to the development of African American culture was the rise of the historical Negro or black church. As C. Eric Lincoln and Lawrence S. Mamiya unequivocally affirm: "The Black Church has no challenger as the cultural womb of the black community. Not only did it give birth to new institutions such as schools, banks, insurance companies, and low income housing, it also provided an academy and an arena for political activities, and it nurtured young talent for musical, dramatic, and artistic development."[46]

Itinerant Baptist and Methodist preachers in the South planted the seeds of the black church during the First and Second Great Awakenings (1734–1736 and 1770–1815). The Great Awakenings were periods of intense spiritual fervor that spread throughout the country appealing especially to slaves and those marginalized by class and gender.[47]

Previously, Anglicans (eventually called Episcopalians in the United States) sent missionaries to the slaves but made little impact with their catechism approach to faith and belief.[48] But when blacks were exposed to the revivals and camp meetings of the traveling Baptist and Methodists, they discovered a worldview or sacred cosmos that resonated with their African spiritual sensibilities.[49] They were particularly attracted to the publicly expressive nature of the evangelical conversion experience and the belief in visionary communication with God.[50] The two faiths appealed to slaves with their initial emphasis on equality in the church regardless of race, gender, or economic status, and the venue of the outdoor camp meeting was unreserved proof of that accessibility.[51]

The emphasis on an experience of conversion rather than a catechetical approach to doctrine threw the net wider to include people of any economic status, literate or not. The proscription against teaching slaves to read placed an obstacle in the way of conversion, but access to God through personal experience bypassed this difficulty. And in the very early times of the revivals, Methodists and Baptists aligned themselves with slaves and against the system that bound them. Both denominations reversed their position after confronting the intense opposition of slaveholders, but by then it was too late. Blacks who had been allowed to become exhorters and preachers quickly started their own churches and saw in the stories and fundamentals of Christianity what they wanted to see.

Newark Churches

Newark was at first mainly composed of Puritans but gave way to the influx of other Protestant denominations, Catholics and then Jews by the time of the Civil War. In 1822 a wealthy black Methodist named Christopher Rush organized the earliest African American church in Newark, which was the forerunner of Clinton Memorial African Methodist Episcopal Zion. An African Presbyterian Church was formed by slaves and freed people who had worshipped with the original Old First Church members for generations. By 1831, tired of sitting on windowsills and in the gallery, and impatient with their less than full participation in the church, they decided to separate themselves and met in their own homes for a number of years. In April 1835, with slaves still among them, they decided to "be known and denominated as the first Presbyterian Colored Congregation of the City of

Newark."[52] In May 1835 the First Presbyterian Church gave them permission to separate, and with the help of Theodore Frelinghuysen, a U.S. senator from New Jersey, they secured land and built a church, incorporating as the Plane Street Presbyterian Church.[53]

Bethel African Methodist Episcopal was organized in 1842 in a building on Green Street with a group of about fifteen members. They had several locations but eventually changed their name to St. James AME Church and moved to a church building at 90 Union Street, and then to their present location at 588 High Street. St. Philip's Episcopal Church was formed in 1848, and Bethany Baptist Church in 1871 by the Reverend Ebenezer Bird. Bethany was the largest and most influential of the black churches before World War I. Its members were among the city's traditional black establishment, including businessmen and those who held civil positions. Bethany was financially independent, having paid off its mortgage and indebtedness in 1921. The strength of its members' social status and the financial solvency it enjoyed sustained its position as a leading religious institution in Newark.[54]

Samuel Cornish, who organized the First Colored Presbyterian Church in New York City, resided for a time in Newark and pastored the First Colored Presbyterian Church there.[55] He helped lead the movement to prevent the colonization of blacks and their forced return to Africa.[56] He was also on the executive committee of the American Anti-slavery Society, founded in 1833, and was editor of the newspapers *Colored American* and *Freedom's Journal.*

Although African Americans numbered only 1,789 residents, or 1.7 percent of the total population, they had as much a sense of belonging as white residents.[57] By 1870 Newark's small black community had its version of the gospel of moral improvement. Their churches, which constituted the community's dominant social force, exerted strong social control over its members. As was customary in Baptist churches, members were scrutinized and publicly sanctioned by expulsion from the body of the church for immoral behavior or lack of financial responsibility toward the church.[58] Certain behavior was expected: obligatory regular church attendance, financial accountability from each adult member, and the responsibility to lead morally Christian lives.

Although blacks worked mainly as servants and unskilled laborers, their occupations often did not reflect their training, since well-educated blacks seldom had access to jobs for which they were qualified.[59] Newark's churches at the turn of the century had educated members and financial stability, and they tended to follow mainstream middle-class values.[60] In addition, Bethany Baptist, St. James African Methodist Episcopal, and St. Philip's Episcopal Church boasted that their preachers were men of scholarship as well as men of deep religious conviction. Church services in the larger bodies were orderly and controlled, with little of the emotionalism that characterized southern congregations.[61]

Concurrent with the evolution of the historical black churches, African Americans formed other self-assistance programs, including fraternal lodges, benevolent societies, literary societies, and temperance organizations. According to New Jersey historian Giles Wright, blacks took steps to "promote the race's general welfare and to ameliorate the harsh conditions of black life."[62] By the 1920s, Newark's African American community had become thoroughly northern and urban, achieving a zone of comfort and a sense of status with the city they identified as their own. During this time, the history of African American Catholics was evolving elsewhere.

African American Catholics

From the eighteenth century, refugees from the West Indies contributed to the population of black Catholics in the United States. The first large immigration of black Catholics was from San Domingo, or San Domingue, now called Haiti, when they fled the island after the successful slave revolution of 1791. Whites, freed people, and slaves entered the ports of New Orleans and Baltimore, as well as New York, Philadelphia, Charleston, and Savannah. "They took whatever boats were available and went where they could, later scattering to inland towns."[63]

On July 9, 1793, fifty-three vessels arrived in Baltimore, with San Domingan refugees of 1,000 whites and 500 blacks—all of whom were Catholics.[64] The blacks were ministered to by the Sulpician fathers and became one of the core groups of Catholics who grew and dispersed throughout the rest of the United States. The religious persecution in Maryland spread them along the Atlantic seaboard and Kentucky, where they accompanied their masters and were augmented in number by the San Dominican refugees.[65]

Until the late twentieth century African American Catholics lived predominantly in Louisiana and Maryland and later Kentucky and Mobile, Alabama. In 1890 no census data existed on African American Catholics, but a realistic estimate would be 100,000 in a total population of 7,488,676, or 1.3 percent.[66]

The key factor leading to the small number of black Catholics in the United States is the geographic separation, with few exceptions, of African Americans from Catholics. Ninety percent of African Americans lived in the rural Southeast, while most of the white Catholic population was drawn to and remained in cities of the Northeast. Of the large proportion of Irish immigrants, 80 percent came from the rural areas of Ireland, but only 6 percent settled in rural areas of the United States. In fact, at any given time throughout its history, only 15 percent of the total American Catholic population lived in rural areas.[67]

Largely for this reason, by the time the Catholic Church made any inroads into the American sociopolitical scene, the Protestant black church was already established in the North and the South. It was not until the twentieth century, when African Americans began to migrate to northern urban centers, that Catholics encountered them in any great numbers.[68]

During the nineteenth century, sporadic Catholic efforts were made to convert and minister to African Americans, but generally American bishops were preoccupied with building up the church using limited resources and dealing with the hostility of the larger society to things Catholic. Because the ministry to African Americans was seen by American bishops as one of missionary activity, they tended to hand over the work of the Negro Apostolate to religious orders rather than their own diocesan priests.[69]

The church's first organized effort on behalf of African Americans began when the English Mill Hill Fathers (renamed Josephites in the United States) committed priests to the work. They came to Baltimore on December 10, 1871, and were greeted by Archbishop Martin John Spalding, who had arranged their arrival and formally installed them in charge of St. Francis Xavier Church.[70] The Jesuits, who had begun this first church for blacks in the United States in 1864, turned it over to the new priests. The Josephites established missions and schools along the Atlantic coastline, through the south-central states, and into Texas.[71] In 1872 the Fathers of the Holy Ghost opened an industrial school in the diocese of Covington, Kentucky. The Society of the Divine Word established their apostolate to African Americans in 1906, followed by the Society for African Missions in 1907. Unlike Queen of Angels, which was founded by diocesan priests, the members of these four organizations or others like them did the bulk of the black work in the United States until 1960.[72]

The first order of sisters who ministered to black people was the Franciscan Sisters, who emigrated from Mill Hill, England, in 1881. Then came the Sister-Servants of the Holy Ghost and Mary Immaculate in 1888. The most well-known order formed for that purpose was the foundation of the Sisters of the Blessed Sacrament for Indians and Colored People in 1891 by the wealthy American heiress Mother Katherine Drexel.[73] Among the many institutions she established, Xavier University in New Orleans is the only Catholic university for African Americans in the country.

These efforts were in earnest, but they were so few and far between, and the financial resources so paltry, that Catholicism and Catholics, for the most part, remained foreign to African Americans.

African American Priests and Women Religious

After the Civil War some quasi-systematic efforts were made to encourage black men toward priestly ordination, but social and psychological impediments affecting both whites and blacks kept the number very low until the 1970s. Whites had ambivalent feelings regarding the ability of black men to fill the intellectual and celibacy demands of priesthood. Blacks who were courageous enough to seek a priestly vocation had to face loneliness, prejudice, and the stress of continually proving to bishops and clergy that they could measure up. Black priests struggled to find a bishop who would give them faculties to function within a diocese.[74]

The first black priests in the United States were three brothers born of an Irish father and an African American slave mother in the 1830s. Their father provided them with a fine northern and European education, and all three brothers were ordained in Rome. James Augustine Healy went on to become the second bishop of Portland, Maine, in 1875. Francis Patrick Healy, S.J., was named president of Georgetown University in Washington, D.C., in 1874. Alexander Sherwood Healy was a noted theological scholar who was the personal theologian to Bishop John Williams of Boston at the Second Plenary Council of Baltimore in 1866 and the First Vatican Council in Rome in 1871.

The three Healy brothers were exceptional men who, through their wealthy background and excellent education, were able to ascend to ecclesial heights. Undoubtedly, their light skin color made things easier for them to achieve in the white world, but there is evidence that they were seen as black by some who made decisions that affected their lives.[75]

In 1886 Augustus Tolton became the next African American priest; he was also ordained in Rome. Unlike the Healy brothers, he was from a poor family, looked more distinctly African, and was of a darker hue. Considered something of a celebrity by African American Catholics and Protestants alike, he nonetheless had great difficulty finding a niche for himself where he was accepted by laypeople and not resented by his fellow priests.[76]

John R. Slattery, S.S.J., and the Josephite priests made some headway into the area of black priestly ordination.[77] In 1891 Charles Uncles, S.S.J., was the first black priest to be ordained in the United States followed by a mere twenty-six by 1940, or one every two years. But, still, ordination was the easier achievement, compared to the difficulty in finding a bishop willing to grant them canonical faculties. In light of these circumstances and other societal pressures the priests encountered, the state of affairs for African American priests would remain extremely troublesome until the late 1960s and early 1970s.

The history of African American women religious in the United States began in 1824 in Kentucky when a Belgian priest, Charles Nerinckx, encouraged three black women to become postulants in his newly formed order of the Sisters of Loretto. Unfortunately, his departure to Missouri and subsequent death deprived the women of an advocate and resources to carry on, and the project was abandoned.

The Haitian refugee colony in Baltimore gave birth to the first successful order of black sisters in 1829. Elizabeth Lange was the first superior of the order, which ultimately assumed the name of the Oblate Sisters of Providence.[78] This is the order of sisters that Queen of Angels would ask to run their school in 1962.

The second order was started in 1842 by Henriette Delille and Juliette Gaudin in New Orleans, who struggled for many years against the constraints of poverty, segregation laws, and even an archbishop's aversion to seeing black women in a religious habit. Called the Sisters of the Holy Family, they functioned as a diocesan congregation until 1949, when they were finally granted canonical recognition as an order.

A third order, the Franciscan Handmaids of Mary, would be founded by Ignatius Lissner, S.M.A., and Mother Theodore Williams of the Sisters of the Holy Family in Savannah, Georgia, in 1916.[79] Over the years, African American women religious have persevered in their charitable and educational work for their race in spite of the prejudice against them as African American women and as women religious.[80]

African American Lay Movements

Although some black men and women aspired to the clerical and religious life, African American Catholics claimed their faith mainly as laity. Daniel Rudd, a newspaper editor from Bardstown, Kentucky, initiated the black Catholic congresses. They held five congresses from 1889 to 1894 in Washington, D.C., and other cities. Rudd's goal was both to bring the attention of the church to the presence of black Catholics and to present the Catholic Church as the universal church to other African Americans.

In 1917 an organization called the Federated Colored Catholics was founded by Thomas Wyatt Turner, a Howard University professor from Virginia, who wished to address the place of blacks in the Catholic Church. Originally called the Committee against the Extension of Race Prejudice in the Church, its members initiated a letter-writing campaign to the hierarchy. Their main concerns were "discriminatory practices in the Church, the lack of proper educational facilities for black children or their higher education, and the urgent need of a black priesthood."[81]

Turner felt that the bishops who catered to the prejudice of white parishioners caused one of the biggest obstacles for blacks in the church. For example, he was particularly unnerved when bishops refused to place a black priest in a parish for fear that whites would leave. Turner insisted that "true followers of Jesus should challenge and change prejudice, not accommodate to it by declaring it beyond the power of individuals to alter."[82]

The Federated Colored Catholics attracted several thousand members of blacks and whites and held national conventions around the country until the early 1930s. The organization was weakened and eventually divided by a controversy between Turner and two Jesuit activists for interracial justice, Fr. John LaFarge and Fr. William Markoe. The priests initiated a sustained effort to change the character of the federation from one of lay-centered black activism to one with an essentially interracial character aimed at attracting and educating whites on the status and problems of African Americans.[83] Further developments found Josephite priest and historian John Gillard and LaFarge at odds. Gillard, who wrote the first serious work on the social and historical condition of African American Catholics, bristled at the audacity of the federation's tactics. Displaying a contemporary paternalism and clericalism, he believed that laypeople had no business requesting meetings with bishops and appealing to Rome to pressure the American church to change.[84] LaFarge had no objections to those particular efforts of the federation, and, moreover, he openly criticized Gillard for his patronizing view of blacks.

But LaFarge's conflict with Gillard did not help the rift between him and Turner, and it continued to grow until the organization split in two. Turner continued to lead a smaller East Coast faction of the federation that survived until 1952, while LaFarge led an interracial Catholic movement. Both the federation and LaFarge were factors in Queen of Angels' development.[85]

Rudd and Turner's attempts at systematic lay involvement were short-lived, but they were testaments to African Americans' desire to assert their presence in the Catholic Church, even if it meant violating accepted propriety by questioning the hierarchy. Daniel Rudd and Thomas Turner wanted to remain Catholic and work within the church to challenge the prejudices there. Turner did not approve of segregating parishes for blacks and considered it accommodation to prejudice.

Their behavior is reminiscent of Presbyterian Samuel Cornish and African Methodist Episcopal Richard Allen in their struggles with their respective denominations. A fundamental difference, of course, is the inability of a Roman Catholic to form a separate church and remain part of the official Catholic body. African Americans established separate Presbyterian and Baptist churches but remained part of those denominational bodies. Even in the case of the African Methodist Episcopal Church that separated from the Methodist Episcopal Church in 1787, its first bishop, Richard Allen, was consecrated bishop of the newly founded church by Bishop Francis Asbury of the Methodist Episcopal Church in 1816. If a group of Catholics formed a church outside the jurisdiction of the local bishop, they would not be in communion with the Roman Catholic Church and no bishop would ordain their priests or consecrate their bishops.

What qualifies, then, as accommodation? Is it in the act of becoming Catholic or remaining Catholic when one perceives prejudice? Is it resistance when a person refuses to leave a less than perfect church, or is it accommodation to seek a separate Catholic church for blacks to experience church more fully within that context? This centuries-old dilemma faced the pioneers of Queen of Angels Church in their efforts to endure as Catholics.

2

A Priest of Our Own

My work in the interest of our people began during wartime in 1916.

—Ethel Wright

In 1916, when Ethel Wright, the mother of Queen of Angels, began teaching her home catechism classes, Newark was just beginning to feel the impact of the Great Migration of African Americans from the South. Blacks headed North in such large numbers that, by the time the exodus was over at the end of the 1940s, it was the largest migration in United States history.[1] From 1865 to 1873, 35,000 blacks migrated to the northeastern part of the United States, mostly from South Carolina, Georgia, Alabama, and Mississippi. In the decade between 1910 and 1920, 300,000 migrated; from 1920 to 1930, 1.3 million; the next decade, 1.5 million; and from 1940 until 1970, 5 million blacks left the South seeking employment and fleeing the apartheid laws known as Jim Crow.[2]

In 1920 Newark's population was 414,524, of which 16,977 were black (4.1 percent). This was an increase of 7,502 (79.2 percent) from the previous decade. From 1920 to 1930 the black population increased from 16,977 to 38,880 (129 percent).[3] Most migrants followed the train lines to their points North, settling in the cities they passed through. Newark drew on those blacks that were from the southern seaboard states of Georgia, North and South Carolina, and Virginia.[4]

Several factors drew blacks away from the rural South: World War I caused the cessation of emigration from Europe and the return of great numbers of immigrants to their mother countries. This depleted the United

States of the unskilled labor force that had previously been filled by immigrants. War industries were opened and expanded at the same time that the army drafted all eligible white men. These factors created a deficit in the labor force that needed filling.[5]

While these sociohistorical circumstances were occurring, other factors came into play to influence the migration of African Americans. The improvement of the infrastructure of the nation and the concurrent invention and mass production of the automobile opened up the rural backwaters of the South for both black and white. In 1944 the invention of the mechanical cotton picker changed the lives of blacks even more because it rendered the sharecropping system economically obsolete, a system that had been in place since the end of the Civil War.[6]

The migration caught Newark unprepared to provide housing and social services for the new residents. The historic old churches of Newark experienced an increase of membership, but they were unprepared to cope with the social problems that developed. The immigrants were southern in culture, rural in conditioning, and great in number, making their adjustment difficult. The problems were larger than the resources the small middle-class black community possessed.[7] Many of the new arrivals joined the existing churches in Newark, but many turned to storefront churches for spiritual support and a link to a more familiar emotional style of worship.[8] Many of these were sanctified or holiness churches that began in 1867 when a group of Methodists formed the National Camp Meeting Association for the Promotion of Holiness, thus initiating the Holiness movement.[9] Individuals who felt the call established tiny churches in rented stores to cater to the displaced southern émigrés. And as New Jersey historian Clement Price has so aptly characterized: storefront churches acted as cultural brokers or mediating institutions that acted as acculturation tools for rural migrants attempting to adapt to the urban environment.[10]

From the middle of the nineteenth century in Newark, housing was a pressing problem and became more so when an abundance of African Americans migrated from the South. But the problem began earlier when European immigrants entered the city to fill the much needed labor demand for canals, railroads, and industry. City officials lacked the foresight and political will to plan and build housing for people who seemed to be considered a necessary evil. Irish laborers lived in shanties thrown together without adequate sanitary conditions that led to outbreaks of cholera and tuberculosis, and for which the immigrant inhabitants were blamed.[11]

By the 1930s, when Newark began to feel the impact of black migration in combination with the devastation of the Great Depression, the area north of downtown that was referred to as the Hill District became a physical and institutional ghetto.[12] This is the area where the Third Ward was located, with the largest concentration of newly arrived poor, uneducated, and unemployed blacks.

Secular organizations like the Negro Welfare League, formed on January 8, 1917, by two ministers, one black and the other white, gained status and influence in the black community. The organization, which later was renamed the New Jersey Urban League, attracted church members socially aware and interested in assisting the newer black arrivals to the city.[13]

The established black churches of Newark, like those of other northern cities, did not formulate a program of social outreach. They did not identify with the new immigrant population and could not address their problems to any real degree. Many old church parishioners became members of organizations like the Negro Welfare League. According to Price, "Although the meetings of these groups were often held in the old churches, the black religious institutions had conceded to the emerging importance of secular groups."[14] The Urban League was the leader in the race movement in Newark when the city was trying to adjust to the newcomers. But their efforts were able to provide only minimal solutions to the many problems presenting a window of opportunity for the Catholic Church to evangelize African Americans by meeting their social welfare needs.

The Status of African American Catholics in Newark

By 1920 the total Catholic population of the Newark diocese grew to 542,000, an increase of 53.5 percent from 1900.[15] Of the 202 churches in the Newark diocese, there were 59 national churches: 25 Italian, 11 German, 11 Polish, 4 Slav, 2 Slovac, 4 Lithuanian, and 2 Hungarian. The remainder were territorial and served English-speaking Irish Catholics.[16] One hundred thirty-seven of the churches, or 67.8 percent, had parochial elementary schools.

The black population was small, and those who were Catholic were all but invisible to the official church. They were most likely immigrants from the West Indian islands, Maryland, or other parts of the country with small populations of African American Catholics.

There was also a small group of Cape Verdean Catholics. The Black Portuguese, as they were also called, maintained a strong presence at Queen of Angels.[17] They were mariners from the Portuguese colony of Cape Verde, an island off the coast of Senegal, who remained in the Newark area after their ships docked in nearby Port Elizabeth. They gravitated to Queen of Angels soon after its opening at St. Bridget's Hall and felt the church was tailored especially for them.

John Gillard, the Josephite priest and first historian of African American Catholics, conducted his own survey of black Catholics in the United States, sending a statistical survey to every parish in the country. The Newark diocese estimated 900 African American Catholics in the entire Newark diocese, but Gillard's survey, based on anecdotal responses from parish priests, indicated 700 black Catholics in Jersey City and 400 in Newark.[18]

St. Benedict the Moor Parish in New York City was the first black Catholic parish in the metropolitan area founded in 1883. According to George Coll, the church's historian, it served African Americans from Long Island and New Jersey until the dioceses of Brooklyn and Newark were able to provide their own places of worship.[19] But oral and written histories did not yield any evidence that African American Catholics from Newark traveled to St. Benedict's, felt any special attraction to, or owed any deference to New York. Rather, Ethel Wright and the other black Catholics of the preecclesial movement in Newark attended white churches. Some dissatisfaction with their experience in those churches led them to organize and catechize on their own.[20]

Ethel Wright's Mission

Little is known of Ethel Wright's life. It is believed that she was a Catholic from infancy who had immigrated to Newark at some point in her life. We do know that she and her parents were born in South Carolina and her husband, Owen, and his parents were born in Georgia. Possibly she and her husband came to Newark via Maryland, since it was believed that Ethel was a Maryland Catholic.[21]

In a brief history, Wright described the path she took toward her commitment as a home catechism instructor for the African American neighborhood children. Her sister-in-law, Zepora Wright, and her friend Hope Jones began asking her questions about the Catholic Church. Zepora lived with the Wrights, and Hope Jones was visiting from Thomasville, Georgia. Wright tried to answer their questions but ultimately decided to seek the counsel of her pastor, Fr. William Masterson of St. Bridget Church. Masterson arranged for the three women to attend instructions with Sr. Francis Xavier, probably a teaching sister from the parish school.

It is interesting that her experiences did not lead to the entrance of black children to the Catholic schools; rather, it convinced Wright that she should teach children herself. Why the latter occurred instead of the former is not documented, but clearly it was not because Wright lacked assertiveness or tenacity. Wright was noted both for her steadfastness for the Catholic faith and her ability to recognize racism and to honestly tackle it directly.[22] Something convinced her that she had to take on the task herself.

Walter Brown recalls attending Mrs. Wright's classes, the importance that was placed on the instruction, and the fact that it took place in an African American home.[23] For fourteen years Wright taught and evangelized autonomously while parochial schools were sprouting up like wild flowers in Newark's Catholic garden.[24]

The Theresa Lane Council

Miss Anna Theresa Lane was a domestic servant who began working for the wealthy Heller family sometime in the 1860s or 1870s.[25] She was admitted to St. Michael's Hospital for a serious illness and became interested in Catholicism through the influence of a visiting priest. After she recovered from her illness, Miss Lane took instructions in the Catholic faith and was baptized in 1889.[26] She appears to have had the kind of personality that inspired others and drew them together, and eventually she joined with other black Catholics, some of whom were from the West Indies or Maryland.

One of those women was Lucy Mulligan, who was a talented organizer with definite ideas about assisting other black women, especially those who migrated to Newark in search of work.[27] Lane and Mulligan decided to form an organization that would raise funds for that purpose.[28] In December 1926, Mrs. Lucy Mulligan and another of the original members, Mrs. Margarite Cheeks, approached Father Masterson and told him that they were trying "to start a movement for colored Catholics." They asked him for the names of all the black Catholics in the parish. He told them that they should see Ethel Wright, which they did.[29] On December 19, 1926, the three women met at Mulligan's home at 52 Second Street with about five other women to discuss a plan to form what they called a Catholic Council. When a quorum was not present, they decided to adjourn until they had a larger number of people.[30]

On January 8, 1927, the women met again at Lucy Mulligan's home, where they officially established their fledgling organization. Mulligan was elected president; Ethel Wright, assistant secretary; Mrs. Margarite Cheeks, secretary; and Mrs. Gene Parker, treasurer. The executive board was made up of Mrs. Bernadine Lee, chair; Mrs. Suzie Bell, vice chair; Mrs. Lucy Hutchinson and Miss A. Theresa Lane, members. Mrs. Doreen McClamey and Mrs. Rose Gibson were also present. Ethel Wright took over as secretary after the first two meetings and remained in that position until she left the council in June 1928.[31] Both Wright's history and the minutes indicate that the name, The Theresa Lane Council, was in honor of Miss A. Theresa Lane, "one of the oldest Catholic women in Newark" and one of the "pioneer members of St. Rose of Lima Parish." Evidently, she inspired a great deal of respect from the other women. The following is a list of the original members of the Theresa Lane Council:

Mrs. Lucy Mulligan
Mrs. Margaret Cheeks
Miss A. Theresa Lane
Mrs. Dorene McClammy
Mrs. Lucy Hutchinson
Mrs. Gene Parker
Mrs. Bernadine Lee
Mrs. Susie Belle
Mrs. Rosa Gibson
Mrs. Rosa Lewis
Mrs. Mary Thatcher
Mrs. Maude Cole
Mrs. Hattie Ridley
Mrs. Wahneatia Brown
Mrs. Katherine Parker
Mrs. Madeline Lewis
Mrs. Hattie (Meredith) Land
Miss Hilda (Brooks) Mendez
Mrs. Marcella Thompson
Mrs. Ethel Wright[32]

Why Theresa Lane was so revered is difficult to know with absolute certainty. At first glance, it is somewhat astonishing that she was a domestic, since she regularly contributed 75 percent more to the council's treasury than any other member. It was not uncommon for well-educated blacks to occupy service positions and prominent places in African American society. And Lane was a single woman with no dependents who had a stable live-in domestic position with a very wealthy family. In depression times, she was better off than many others.

She donated ten dollars to buy the charter because she felt so honored to have the council named after her, and she offered to donate one dollar at each meeting "to help swell the Treasury," sometimes giving two dollars or as much as five dollars per meeting—a large amount considering the average dues were about ten cents.[33]

The Theresa Lane Council also occupied itself during the first year and a half with fund-raising and taking steps to become a local unit of the Federated Colored Catholics.[34] The fund-raising activities consisted of whist card parties (a form of bridge popular among African Americans), dances, and picnics. Lucy Mulligan deposited the proceeds in a special bank account for the council.

On May 18, 1927, the council had its largest turnout for the appearance of Mrs. Maria Spriggs of Washington, D.C. Her son, Francis Spriggs, was editor-in-chief of the *Council Review,* the monthly publication of the Federated Colored Catholics. Mrs. Spriggs spoke on the aims of the group and urged the council members to be present at the Third Annual Convention to be held at St. Mark's Church in New York City on September 6, 1927. Ethel Wright and an unspecified number of other members attended the convention. As a result of this presentation, the Theresa Lane Council became a unit of the Federated Colored Catholics. Subsequently, the council raised funds to donate to the *Council Review* and the Cardinal Gibbons Institute, a school for black youth in Maryland.[35]

Wright's involvement with the federation is curious, especially considering her later emergence as the biggest proponent of a separate colored church. Turner's federation was strongly and publicly against separate Catholic churches and schools for blacks, viewing this practice as sinful and "not Catholic." They argued that it was the biggest impediment to black conversion, since it gave the impression of a disinterested Catholic Church.[36] The position of the Federated Colored Catholics on the issue did not seem to dampen Wright's enthusiasm for the organization or, at the same time, discourage her from doing all in her power to bring about a separate church for blacks.

Here it becomes more clear that the women of our story laid the foundation for the first African American Catholic Church in Newark fourteen years before Bishop Thomas J. Walsh officially established Our Lady Queen of the Angels Mission to the Colored in 1930. But this fact is not immediately apparent to the reader of institutional histories and the local newspaper accounts of the day. Both were written with a certain agenda and point of view that did not include the African American worldview, and certainly not that of Ethel Wright. To get at the real story, one has to take oral histories and the humble documentation of nonscholars seriously, because, to paraphrase historian Nell Painter,[37] if historians do not use this material, the history of the American Catholic Church is told from the perspective of white, male clergy.[38]

For example, one official history states that Bishop Walsh "headed a survey which disclosed 150,000 Blacks were living in the areas of Newark and Jersey City." Acting on these findings, Walsh established Christ the

King parish in Jersey City on July 3, 1930, and Queen of Angels parish on September 9, 1930.[39] Also, a *Jersey Observer* article from April 7, 1938, noted that an "extensive survey of the negro population of the Diocese of Newark" was conducted, after which Walsh commenced his "work among the negroes." The necessity of a survey is puzzling, considering the fact that the number of blacks in the Newark diocese was easily found in U.S. census records.

When Walsh was installed as the new bishop of the Newark diocese March 2, 1928, certain of the council members wanted to see him about their plans for a separate church.[40] A special meeting of the Executive Committee of the Theresa Lane Council was called on March 26, 1928, to determine how to welcome him. And at the last recorded meeting, on May 13, 1928, a "motion was made that [the] action taken on [the] letter to [the] new bishop be received."[41] Unfortunately, the letter to the bishop has been lost, and it is not clear what action the motion refers to, but it may be the visit that Ethel Wright's group paid to the chancery. Wright recounts that "we went down to St. John's church [on] Mulberry St. [I]t was our aim [to] find out how to reach the Bishop. [W]e were going to ask for Fr. Derricks, a newly ordained colored priest, but we were advised by the priest we spoke to not to ask for any particular priest but to take a census of all the Catholic families in Newark and present them to the Bishop and he would use his own judgement in appointing a priest for us."[42]

About the same time, a woman named Mrs. Mary Ward, of Jersey City, conducted a survey and arrived at a figure of 300 black Catholic families in Jersey City.[43] Did Mrs. Ward conduct a survey for her own personal reasons, or did she make a similar enquiry and receive the same instruction to conduct a census?

It is interesting to note the importance the diocese placed on determining how many black Catholics were in Newark before proceeding with any special ministry to them. They placed the responsibility for census work on the black laity themselves and then ultimately credited the bishop with a survey when a mission was finally established. His ambivalence on the issue is evident in his sermon at the dedication of Christ the King Parish, the first colored Catholic parish in Jersey City, when he stated: "We have this temple for the colored people of this district, but you are welcome in any Catholic church or institution in this city and of this diocese of Newark. There is one place in this world where you receive perfect justice and that is before the Catholic altar in the Catholic Church of God . . . We wish our prelates, priests and people to welcome and to encourage our colored people in the habit of the one faith in God."[44] He exhorts Catholics to welcome African Americans, but the action of allowing a separate church for colored people belies his tacit acknowledgment that the Catholic altar in the Catholic Church of God was not dispensing perfect justice. Walsh could not concede that a dichotomy existed between official church teaching and the practice in the pew.

Walsh's confusion was not limited to white clerics. African Americans themselves struggled over the issue in public and private discourse. The decision to self-segregate and the movement to bring it about in an official Catholic church in Newark was not the choice of all the first mothers of Queen of Angels, even those who were eventually extolled as working toward that goal. The question split their first Catholic organization in two.

Disagreement over Goals and the Little Flower Guild

Within a few months of the inception of the Theresa Lane Council, it became evident that Lucy Mulligan and Ethel Wright did not agree on the main goal of the group. The desire of Ethel Wright for a colored church met with strong opposition from Lucy Mulligan, and it seems that the clearer Wright's objective became, the more certain Mulligan was that it was a bad idea. It is possible that the disagreement began in a miscommunication or lack of clarity at the very outset, but whatever the reason for the misunderstanding, it eventually grew to an insurmountable problem, causing an almost irreversible break between the two groups of women.

Much business was transacted in the first year of the council, and they connected to the greater black Catholic community through an alliance with the Federated Colored Catholics. But the Standard Rules for the Council were not decided upon until March 3, 1928, more than a year after the group's inception. A disagreement over the fundamental objectives of the council was fomenting, as is indicated by the entry of January 8, 1928, that "a motion was made by Mrs. Lewis and carried that by laws [*sic*] submitted by the President be laid on the table until [a] special meeting of Executive Committee."[45] It appears that Mrs. Mulligan, as president, had drawn up bylaws that certain members disputed, tabling the discussion for a later Executive Committee meeting. From what Wright tells us in her history, the disputed issues were Mulligan's control of the group, and more importantly, whether to work toward the establishment of a colored church.

Rule 10 of the bylaws stated the goal of the council in general and hopeful terms: "Resolve that all members shall work in peace and harmony and for [the] honor and greater glory of God."[46] The motto was: "I shall pass this way but once, therefore what ever service I render my fellowman, or what ever good I can do, let me do it now, for I shall not pass this way again."[47] The objective thus stated seemed to be for "peace and harmony," but tension existed over what their real mission was. Wright desired a "church for colored Catholics" and believed that the purpose of the council was to make that goal a reality: "We were given to understand and it was our firm belief that our work was to be in the interest of a church for colored Catholics in Newark, but as time went on some of the members led by Mrs. Lucy Mulligan drifted from the idea of working for a church and directed their attention to a community house for our people."[48]

In the absence of any written documentation or even oral history on the subject, we will never know what motivated Mulligan's resistance to the idea of a colored church or why Wright agreed to join the Theresa Lane Council with such a disagreement in the offing. One can only conjecture. Possibly in the beginning the two goals of a community house and a colored church did not seem mutually exclusive. It is reasonable to conclude that both Wright and Mulligan, in their enthusiasm to begin the colored movement, would have hoped for unity and compromise on their separate goals. Essentially, Mulligan agreed with the Federated Colored Catholics that a separate church was unthinkable. Wright, on the other hand, hardened in her resolve to bring about that reality. It was too volatile a topic for the women to overcome. Finally, in June 1928, the council split into two factions, with Wright and twelve of the women forming a new organization. The remaining women, including Theresa Lane, continued meeting as the Theresa Lane Council. As we will see, even years after Queen of Angels had been established, the question did not go away.

Ethel Wright contacted Fr. Augustine Derricks, O.S.S.T., a native of Santo Domingo (Haiti), the priest she was going to request of Bishop Walsh. Derricks was ordained in Rome on June 11, 1927, as a member of the Order of the Most Holy Trinity for the Redemption of Captives, also called Trinitarians.[49] By the time he met Wright, he was at St. Ann's Parish in Bristol, Pennsylvania, and most likely the women traveled there to see him.[50]

Wright wrote that he convinced her that "if we were in the right that God would bless [our] efforts, and if he saw fit for us to have a church we would get one."[51] They took Father Derrick's advice and started over, calling themselves the Little Flower Guild, after Thérèse of Lisieux of France (also known as the Little Flower), a saint known for her simplicity and humble sanctity. A list of the original members of the Little Flower Guild follows:

Mrs. Marcella Thompson	Mrs. Susie Bell
Mrs. H. (Meredith) Land	Mrs. Wahneatia Brown
Mrs. Rosa Gibson	Mrs. Katherine Parker
Mrs. Mary Thatcher	Mrs. Madeline Lewis
Mrs. Maude Cole	Miss Hilda (Brooks) Mendez
Mrs. Hattie Ridley	Mrs. Ethel Wright[52]

Sr. Peter Claver

The pivotal person in this narrative history of Queen of Angels is Sr. Peter Claver Fahy, M.S.B.T.[53] She provided the necessary link between the two black Catholic laywomen's groups and the official church. Sr. Peter Claver had had a desire to work among African Americans for many years, and her discovery of the two groups of women gave her the opportunity for which she had been searching. Originally drawn to an order that educated the daughters of the wealthy, she changed her mind when she learned of the Missionary Servants of the Most Blessed Trinity and their work among those less fortunate. Because of her hope to work with blacks, she took the name of Sr. Peter Claver after the seventeenth century Spanish Jesuit who ministered to the slaves in Central America and became the patron of all missionary activity to blacks. Although Sr. Peter Claver was involved directly with Queen of Angels only from 1928 to 1935, her importance to the movement cannot be overstated.

Her order, called the Missionary Servants of the Most Blessed Trinity (M.S.B.T.), was the women's religious counterpart to the priestly order, the Missionary Servants of the Most Holy Trinity.[54] Both started as a lay movement in 1909. The Missionary Servants, commonly known as the Trinitarians, began in the mind of Thomas Augustine Judge, C.M., a Vincentian priest ordained in 1899. Judge maintained from the beginning of his priesthood that the Catholic Church would benefit from the active apostolate of laypeople. Through a long and difficult career, Judge developed the leadership and apostolic skills of laywomen and laymen.

Judge had a special devotion to the Holy Spirit and directed the lay group under his guidance to develop an awareness of the Holy Spirit for guidance and inspiration. "Judge's devotion to the Holy Spirit is intimately related to his love for the church because he perceived with an uncommon intensity that the one and the same Spirit is the bond of fellowship *(koinonia)* within the Trinitarian life itself, as he is the bond of fellowship within the communitarian life of the church."[55] Over the years, fellowship (or *koinonia* in New Testament Greek) became both the goal and the modality of the Trinitarian orders of priests, brothers, sisters, and laypeople that evolved under Judge.

On April 11, 1909, Judge gathered together a group of five women who had been under his spiritual direction and to whom he had assigned certain missionary activities.[56] He believed that laypeople, with training in missionary work, could become "work-a-day apostles," reaching out to people in their "every day life." And, anticipating the Second Vatican Council (1962–65, an event that revolutionized the Catholic Church), he believed that through that experience they would be taught to "realize that they are the Church and to be alert for its interests and the welfare of souls."[57]

Judge called the group the Cenacle Lay Apostolate to emphasize their reliance on the work of the Holy Spirit as demonstrated in the Acts of the Apostles.[58] But he also had a particular affinity for the "abandoned," as he called them, especially immigrants, ethnic groups, and blacks of any religious denomination. He viewed those that society considered to be of lesser status through a sociological lens in order to explain the reasons for their economic and educational poverty.

Judge's view held a striking resemblance to his Protestant contemporary, Walter Rauschenbusch, who directed his co-religionists to a this-worldly interpretation of the Gospels and to those less fortunate. There is no proof that Judge shared Rauschenbusch's critique of the "kingdom of God" vis-à-vis capitalist greed or a middle-class neglect cloaked in Christian pretense. But Judge's approach was amazingly close to Rauschenbusch's concept outlined in his *A Theology for the Social Gospel,* published in 1917.[59]

In his book, Rauschenbusch called evangelicals to go beyond a personal sense of salvation, while Judge, operating within the context of Catholic spirituality, wanted laypeople to evangelize through the avenue of a radical gospel love of the poor.[60] The two approaches were similar in that they added a practical dimension to their particular brands of Christianity, but Judge's goal was ultimately evangelization, while Rauschenbusch's was the creation of the kingdom of God on earth through the eradication of injustice.

Unlike many European Americans, bishops and clergy included, who regarded Africans and African Americans as inferior, Judge stated that there was "no reason inherent in the mental, moral or physical make-up of the negro [*sic*] race which would prevent its attaining its full stature as a component part of the American commonwealth if certain environmental conditions that handicap it at present were to be removed."[61] He believed that racial problems were national and had to be addressed on that level, but that whites were incapable of solving the "negro question"—African Americans "must solve it themselves." To this end they required their own "priesthood and their own sisterhood and, therefore, . . . their own Apostolate."[62] Therefore, the Trinitarians should only be involved until African American clergy and spiritual leaders were sufficient, and at that time, "the missionary's work must be considered brought to a happy close."[63] Father Judge's permission to allow Sr. Peter Claver Fahy to begin her work among African Americans in Newark was informed by this philosophy.

Sometime toward the end of 1928, Miss Theresa Lane was attending Mass at Sacred Heart Church, sitting in the back, when two French teachers approached her. Theresa Lane told the women about the council, where they met, and that their goal was to buy a house to take care of young black women coming up from the South in search of work. The two white teachers felt this news was important enough to pass on to Fr. Felix O'Neill, the pastor of St. Michael's Parish and a very good friend of Father Judge and the Trinitarian order. O'Neill advised the teachers to see Sr. Peter Claver at the Missionary Cenacle and inform her of the people and activities they had discovered.

At the time, Sr. Peter Claver was working among Italian immigrants in Newark, but after hearing of the council, she wrote to Judge in January 1929. She received permission to attend one of their meetings in April along with Sister Carmel.[64] At that first meeting, she observed that most of the members of the council were West Indians, specifically Jamaican, and learned that they were educated by the Dominican sisters there. She also observed that Mrs. Mulligan was the apparent leader of the council, and that great deference was paid to Miss Lane, who clearly sustained the group financially and contributed a measure of dignity and authority to the organization.[65]

The women, in Sr. Peter Claver's opinion, were pleased to have the sisters as visitors but conducted their meeting almost oblivious to their presence. A great sense of ownership prevailed in their manner. At the end of the meeting,

Sister Carmel, overcome with enthusiasm, expressed the excitement she felt as she observed the proceedings. She likened their group to the gathering of the first Trinitarian laywomen in Brooklyn in 1909 under the guidance of Judge and urged them to continue their work.[66] Sr. Peter Claver could only tell them to pray to the Holy Spirit. It seems a sense of identification developed immediately between the sisters and the laywomen.

Over the following weeks, Lucy Mulligan and Sr. Peter Claver spoke quite often, and at one point Mulligan asked if the two of them could try to contact other black Catholics. Sr. Peter Claver received permission from her superior to take one day away from her work with the Italians to work with Mulligan.[67] They walked through the tenements, going door to door or following up the leads that Mrs. Mulligan or other council members had obtained. When the two found other Catholics, they told them about the council and invited them to the meetings.[68]

Monsignor John A. Duffy

John A. Duffy, the vicar-general of the Newark diocese, was the person who possessed the will and the power to effect changes for the black Catholic community. As vicar-general, Duffy was immediately under the bishop and, in fact, was acting bishop during the long illness of Bishop O'Connor, who preceded Bishop Thomas Walsh.

For years Duffy had been searching for "a suitable Church for the colored people" and had asked his business contacts to keep him informed of any possibilities. In 1926 William J. Kearns, a counselor-at-law from Newark, had contacted a "Negro minister" who had been using a former Jewish temple to hold services. The building was "a sort of Community Center for Colored people known as the Roosevelt Memorial Temple." Kearns felt that "the Negro Catholics in Newark would like a church of their own, and it would be [a] fine [thing] to do in Bishop O'Connor's jubilee year and a real charitable way of crowning his Episcopate."[69] But nothing came of the lead at that time.

After Sr. Peter Claver attended the council's meeting, Judge advised her to discuss the group with Father O'Neill. O'Neill felt it should be brought to the attention of Bishop Walsh. Judge, upon being informed of O'Neill's response, suggested that she meet with Monsignor Duffy instead because, as it was well known, the bishop was focused on Italian immigrants, and Duffy was sympathetic to Judge's work and a friend of Brother Gufstason, one of the original members of the Trinitarians from New Jersey. Sr. Peter

Claver saw Duffy and requested a place for black Catholics to meet, and for a priest dedicated to them. Duffy immediately called Fr. William Masterson, the pastor at St. Bridget's, and secured their facilities for the Theresa Lane Council. They began to meet on Sunday afternoons for Sr. Peter Claver's catechism classes, which were held either in St. Bridget's hall or basement, depending upon availability.[70] The priest issue was left for another time.

In January 1930, six months after Lucy Mulligan and Sr. Peter Claver began their work together, Mulligan told Sr. Peter Claver about the Little Flower Guild and Ethel Wright. Soon after, Sr. Peter Claver met with Wright and then took her to speak to O'Neill. According to Wright, she "had to explain" to the priest what they were doing, after which O'Neill told Sr. Peter Claver, "Now you have the right group."[71] At the sister's request, the Little Flower Guild and Wright's catechism class also began meeting at St. Bridget's Hall, and Sr. Peter Claver added the Little Flower Guild to her schedule of instruction classes on Sunday afternoons. In a diplomatic gesture, Sr. Peter Claver held them separately from the Theresa Lane Council.[72]

At some point during the next few months, and apparently discovering the person who could do something for them, a group of women led by Ethel Wright approached Duffy to request a priest. As Wright recalled: "He was very gracious to us. [W]e were frightened almost out of our witts [*sic*]. [H]e assured us that he would appoint a priest for us immediately after ordination and that we should see him again in June and remind him."[73] This is another example of the resourcefulness, tenacity, and clarity of purpose Ethel Wright and her friends had regarding their desire to have their own church and priest. Although Wright admits to being frightened almost out of their wits, it did not stop them from asking for what they wanted.

In June 1930 Mulligan died suddenly, and with her death everything changed for the council and for the future church. At her funeral, Duffy called her "a light of Catholic zeal for her people throughout the diocese, [and] though she has not lived to see the cause accomplished for which she so generously spent herself, with God and His saints she will watch over the work of her people and still be a powerful help to it."[74] It is very possible that her involvement with Sr. Peter Claver softened Mulligan toward the idea of a separate church.

With Mulligan gone, the council lost its momentum and was not able to maintain its fund-raising activities.[75] But Mulligan's death motivated the council and the Little Flower Guild to let go of their old conflict and meet as one body. The reality of a colored church loomed so large that those who were against it began to change their minds, and the women decided to put their disagreements behind them and work toward that common goal.[76]

In the spring of 1930, Sr. Peter Claver arranged a trip to the Trinitarian's St. Joseph's Shrine in Stirling, New Jersey. She obtained a bus from the Overseer of the Poor (the prewelfare office in Newark, which dated to the eighteenth century). Duffy spoke to the gathering, and afterward he discussed with Sr. Peter Claver his motivation for helping blacks with their quest for a church. He explained that when he was ordained a priest in Rome, two black priests stood with him, one on each side. As they were ordained together, he was moved to make a vow to God that he would do something for black people when he returned home to the United States.[77]

He had been a priest a long time, but as vicar-general he had the power and the opportunity to accomplish what he had promised those many years before. He then spoke to Sr. Peter Claver's superior and arranged for her to devote herself exclusively to the "black work" with the aid of a cenacle (as the Trinitarians called their convent) in Newark. After months of sustained effort, Sr. Peter Claver was ready to collapse from exhaustion and had lost her voice. She was allowed to return to the generalate (motherhouse) in Alabama to recover and prepare for her new work.

In August 1930, after a rest of several weeks, Sr. Peter Claver returned to Newark, where Ethel Wright met her at the train station. She learned from Wright that Fr. Joseph Shovlin had been assigned as the priest in charge of the colored work in Jersey City. In addition to his duties in that town, he was to begin saying Mass for their group at St. Bridget's Hall in Newark.[78] Ethel reminded Sr. Peter Claver that September 9, the Feast of St. Peter Claver, was only a couple of weeks away. She suggested that they say a novena, nine consecutive days of prayer, to the saint for a priest to be given to Newark as well.[79] According to Claver, they did not have long to wait:

> On the feast of St. Peter Claver, on Stone Street, at Blessed Trinity Cenacle, a tall priest named Fr. Ahern punched the bell. And I answered it. [He was] looking just above me [and said], "I'm looking for Sr. Peter Claver." I said, "Well, Father, I'm Sr. Peter Claver." He said, "Look here." And he opened up and showed me an "obedience" that he got that morning with the date, September 9th, Feast of St. Peter Claver, Father Cornelius Ahern in charge of Essex county and vicinity of the black people.[80]

Finally, Ethel Wright and the Little Flower Guild obtained the priest they had desired for so many years. Her errand was, to a great extent, accomplished. But the question still remained whether their choice of a separate church was a negotiated compromise with the dominant culture, or whether it was an act of irrevocable accommodation. Would the people be able to act from a position of power to pursue their faith life? Or did they put themselves totally in the hands of the "white man's church"?

John LaFarge, S.J., a great fighter for racial justice, at the dedication of St. Peter Claver Church, November 5, 1935. Used by permission of Queen of Angels Parish Archives.

The Theresa Lane Council in front of Lucy Mulligan's house, 52 2d Street in Newark, 1929. Standing (left to right): an unidentified person, Mulligan, Sr. Peter Claver, and on the top step, standing on the left, Theresa Lane. Used by permission of the Sisters of the Most Blessed Trinity Archives, Philadelphia.

Missionary Servants of the Most Blessed Trinity (1940) serving Queen of Angels and her mission. Left to right, standing: Sister Mary of the Holy Agony (a.k.a. Sr. Kathleen Champion); Sr. Nativity Filce, Sr. Helen Dunlay, Sr. Francis Damien. Sitting: Sr. Marion Qualey, Sister Mary of the Precious Blood. Used by permission of the Seton Hall University Archives and Special Collections.

A Christmas probably at St. Peter Claver Mission in Montclair. Msgr. John Duffy, vicar-general, with supporters of the missions (mid-1930s). Used by permission of Queen of Angels Parish Archives.

The first First Holy Communion at Queen of Angels. Standing on the left in hat, Sister Mary of Mercy Comyn; on the far right, Sr. Peter Claver; center, Fr. Cornelius Ahern. Used by permission of Queen of Angels Parish Archives.

A visit to the Trinitarian's St. Joseph Shrine in Stirling, New Jersey. The event attracted hundreds of African Americans, Catholic and non-Catholic, from the New York metropolitan area (early 1930s). Used by permission of Queen of Angels Parish Archives.

Queen of Angels' Pageant (1930s). Used by permission of Queen of Angels Parish Archives.

Queen of Angels Band (early 1930s). Used by permission of Queen of Angels Parish Archives.

Holy Name Parade in front of the second Queen of Angels' Church on the right with the brick front (mid to late 1930s). Used by permission of the Sisters of the Most Blessed Trinity Archives, Philadelphia.

St. Thomas Third Ward Mission on Broome and Morton Streets. Ahern was afraid to send the Trinitarian sisters to this notorious area of town, but they went anyway. *Used by permission of Queen of Angels Parish Archives.*

Communion Breakfast, which became a staple of Queen of Angels parish life. Seated on the left, Ahern with Madame Johnson, the first organist for the parish. Behind Madame Johnson are Mrs. Elizabeth Houston and her husband, John Houston, the grandparents of singer Whitney Houston. *Used by permission of Queen of Angels Parish Archives.*

The ordination of Fr. Donald Potts, the only Queen of Angels' parishioner to become a Catholic priest (May 28, 1960). Used by permission of the Seton Hall University Archives and Special Collections.

Crowd at a Queen of Angels' presentation. African Americans got inside public spaces ordinarily not open to them (1930s). *Used by permission of Monsignor Paul Hayes.*

The one-thousandth convert, Charles Coles, baptized by Archbishop Thomas Walsh, the first time in the history of the American church that a bishop baptized a black person. *Used by permission of Queen of Angels Parish Archives.*

Holy Name Parade (early 1930s). Fr. Cornelius Ahern front and center. William O'Laughlin with trombone on right; John Houston, three people to O'Laughlin's left. *Used by permission of the Seton Hall University Archives and Special Collection Center.*

The inside of Queen of Angels Second Church on Academy Street. The two men standing are Fr. Paul Hayes (left) and Fr. Joseph Lenihan (1950s). Elma Thornton (Bateman) seated to the right of Lenihan. *Used by permission of Msgr. Paul Hayes.*

Msgr. Thomas Carey, December 20, 1964.
Used by permission of the Seton Hall University Archives and Special Collections.

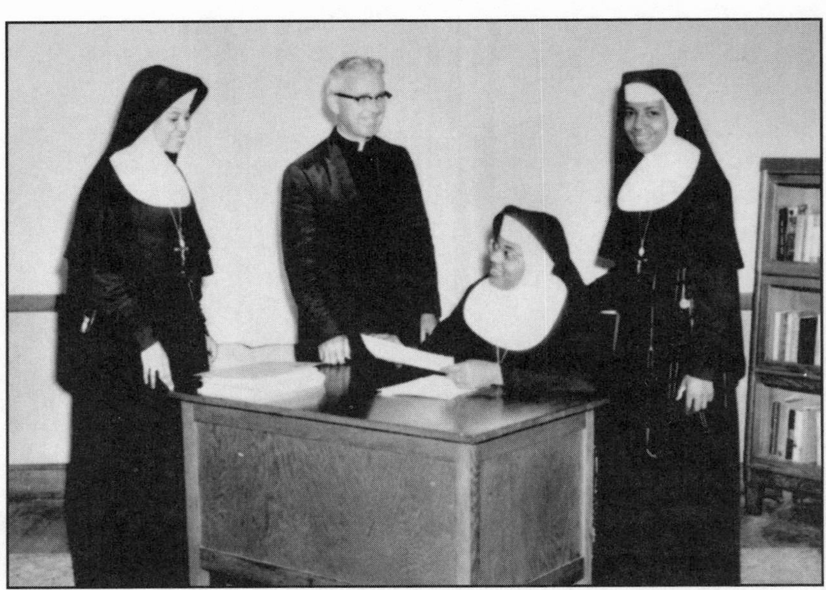

The Oblate Sisters of Providence with Fr. Thomas Carey. They were asked to run Queen of Angels' School in 1963. Left to right: Sr. Rose Ann, Mother Jonathan (seated) and Sr. Marie Cabrini. Used by permission of the Seton Hall University Archives and Special Collections.

Thinking big. The Queen of Angels Players' version of Guys and Dolls. Used by permission of the Seton Hall University Archives and Special Collections.

Queen of Angels' present church, formerly the German parish of St. Peter's, 44 Belmont Avenue, now called Irvine Turner Boulevard. Used by permission of the Seton Hall University Archives and Special Collections.

Inside the present church (1970s). Used by permission of the Seton Hall University Archives and Special Collections.

Center: Fr. Thomas Carey; to right of Carey: Bennie Thornton Fields; far right: Ruby Jones (1960s). Used by permission of Queen of Angels Parish Archives.

Rev. Dr. Martin Luther King Jr. on his last visit to Newark, March 28, 1968, one week before he was killed in Memphis, Tennessee. Used by permission of Queen of Angels Parish Archives.

The Walk for Understanding, April 7, 1968. *Used by permission of David Booker.*

The Walk for Understanding, April 7, 1968. The crowd listens to speeches in front of the courthouse. *Used by permission of David Booker, photographer.*

The Walk for Understanding. Banner made by David and Pat Foley's family. *Used by permission of David Booker, photographer.*

Stella Wright Christian Community meeting in the project apartment of the Rev. Thomas Comerford. Left to right: Mozetta Moon; James Lewis; Edward Satterfield; Father Comerford; Mrs. Louise Brummell; Sr. Maureen McDonough, a Sister of Charity. *Used by permission of the Seton Hall University Archives and Special Collections.*

Elma Bateman and Bennie Fields, daughters of Roberta Thornton—who taught them that church is church—at the wedding of Elma's daughter, Felicia, on August 19, 1999. *Photo by the author.*

3

A Mission with a Mission

With the drop of the hat, when we needed him he'd come. He could initiate all this . . . The sisters were on the firing line; we were working with the people.

—*Sr. Peter Claver, M.S.B.T.*

In September 1930, sixty-three African Americans gathered in St. Bridget's Hall on Plane Street in Newark as their priest, Fr. Cornelius Ahern, led them in the first Mass at Our Lady Queen of the Angels Mission.[1] In the congregation were Sr. Peter Claver, Ethel Wright, and Theresa Lane; the members of the two previously estranged groups: the Theresa Lane Council and the Little Flower Guild, and the children of Mrs. Wright's catechism class.[2]

The women and men prepared for their first Mass using egg boxes and a tablecloth to create an altar. As they worked, the adults instructed the children not to forget what they had done that day. They were making history; it was important; it was a story worthy to be passed on.[3] As African American Bishop Curtis J. Guillory affirmed, they expected, as did so many other African American Catholics, to have "a future in [the] Church even though much of their history bespeaks of a time when the Church overlooked their mission, their efforts, and their unique gifts."[4]

The Problems of Mission Status

For Queen of Angels, mission status presented three problems. Its boundaries were spread over two counties, several townships, and a large geographic area with pockets of black communities scattered throughout. It was common for neighborhoods to have whites on one side of the block and blacks on the other.[5] As director of a mission church, Fr. Cornelius Ahern was responsible for the Negro Apostolate in the entire area of Essex and Union Counties, and therefore the evangelization and spiritual care of all blacks in that area, regardless of the territorial parishes in which they lived.[6]

National parishes, on the other hand, normally served a particular ethnic group within a certain geographical area. Generally, the boundaries of national parishes coincided with the ethnic perimeter of the parish and encompassed an already existing cultural and religious space.[7] Where the national parish created a sacred space in the midst of an existing cultural space, the mission church had to create a sacred space across ethnic and parish boundaries. Queen of Angels was faced with the challenge of drawing the people into the church from every direction and making the services of the mission accessible to them.

The second disadvantage of the mission was that other pastors often felt relieved of their responsibility toward people of color in their parishes.[8] The creation of a mission church did not mean that a black person could not attend the parish in which he or she lived or that pastors were not responsible for their spiritual welfare.[9] There is evidence that white parishioners expected their priests to make an effort to keep colored people away from their neighborhoods.[10] Prior to the establishment of Queen of Angels, some pastors directed African Americans toward other white churches, and after Queen of Angels was established they sent them to their "own" church.[11] Sometimes the clergy were not sure if they had the right to baptize, marry, or counsel blacks on spiritual matters, even if they were inclined to do so.[12] Whatever success Queen of Angels and its missions may have had over the years, this dilemma left a legacy of confusion and conflict among the clergy and laity of Newark. It is a legacy they have grappled with continually and quite dramatically for many years.

The third problem area was the difference in culture between parish leadership and people. Gaining the trust and respect of the black community was a constant challenge for white priests and religious women who worked at Queen of Angels. Of course, the intuitive solution to the problem of cultural dissimilarity would have been to place African American priests in the parish, but in 1930 only four such priests existed in the United States.[13]

This condition was not present in the black Protestant church, where ministerial leadership played such an important role in African American culture. When African American Protestants formed their own churches, they freed themselves from white domination, influence, and scrutiny—an option not available to blacks who intended to remain Catholic. In speaking specifically of northern black religionists, historian Monroe Fordham makes clear that the separation "allowed blacks to come together in an atmosphere that did not challenge, or force them to compromise their dignity and self-respect."[14] But also, within the framework of the black church, in an atmosphere free from white influence, blacks could attempt to repair the destruction resulting from the "psychic burden" of racial prejudice and to uplift the people whose "spirit was trampled on."[15] According to Fordham: "The religious liberty made possible by separation afforded the reform-minded blacks the opportunity to use the pulpit, the sabbath school, and other facets and activities of the church for propagating the *kinds of religious beliefs which served those adaptive functions that blacks felt essential to their interests as a people* who were forced to remain outside the mainstream of American life" (emphasis mine).[16]

Could white religious leaders provide the "kinds of religious beliefs which served those adaptive functions" so their black parishioners could effectively negotiate with the same oppressive culture that white leadership represented? Certainly not in the manner that African American leaders could, but the history of Queen of Angels provides concrete examples of how this problem was addressed with varying degrees of success.

Any Advantages to Mission Status?

There was one possible advantage of mission status. Its roots date back to the early years of the Christian church as delineated by the late biblical scholar Raymond E. Brown in *The Churches the Apostles Left Behind.* Brown contrasts the models of church and leadership in the pastoral Epistles of I and II Timothy and Titus, written at the turn of the second century, and the earlier missionary model that emerges from Paul's letters. According to Brown, the pastorals called for church officials to possess "safe, institutional virtues" in order to ensure a "benevolent, holy, and efficient administration."[17] He observes that they may have been good, sound people, but they were not likely to be "dynamic movers who would change the world."[18]

Leaders like Paul (who, scholars agree, did not write, but to whom the authorship of the pastorals is ascribed) would have failed to qualify for the job. His "risky new ideas about Christ," his "untamable restlessness," and his "willingness to fight bare-knuckled for the Gospel" were qualities that lent themselves to great missionary work but would be undesirable if discovered in the behavior and personality of an institutional pastor.[19]

Missionary work has historically attracted those types of people who like the edge of life, being out on a limb; they are drawn to the innovative rather than the tried-and-true approach, and their untested strategies may bear ambiguous results. Adaptable, they are often comfortable with ethnic and cultural diversity. From what can be observed in the history of Queen of Angels, mission leadership was cast in this mold, and to a great extent, the hierarchy was willing to tolerate their customized strategies.

There were those white leaders who were aware of differences in worldview and were open to learning from the community. For example, Trinitarian Sr. Francis Damien identified an older parishioner who was willing to watch over her and keep her on track. She said to them: "I am new here; I have the best will in the world. I want to do the right thing, but I need somebody to help me. When you see me make a mistake, you tell me. And it worked; they owned you. They would call you over once in a while and say: 'you shouldn't have done that.'"[20] She had a built-in corrective from the community, but she also sent a message of respect for difference within the framework of a common faith.

Sr. Francis Damien's openness to another culture may not have been representative of all Trinitarian sisters. After all, they were subject to the same prevailing racial attitudes, paternalism, and clericalism as other whites of that era. A strong case can be made, however, that Father Judge's mandate to meet the abandoned "where they were" encouraged the sisters to go beyond whatever socially inculcated attitudes they may have brought with them. "It is very unlikely that a sister with a negative attitude toward blacks would have lasted long in the Negro Apostolate. They would have either left on their own accord or been transferred."[21]

It is also interesting to note that when parishioners were questioned about a paternalistic attitude on the part of Ahern or the Trinitarians, or, for that matter, any other priest or sister in Queen of Angels' history, they quickly attested to its nonexistence. People commented most often on the strictness of the sisters in connection with the behavior of the children or the teachings of the church. The sisters' strictness, incidentally, was spoken of with respect rather than resentment, which may confirm a perception of impartiality on the part of the sisters toward the people, as well as a coinciding of values in regard to child rearing.[22]

Just Another Good Priest Hoping for the Hopeless

The pastoral team of Queen of Angels consisted of Monsignor Duffy, Father Ahern, and the Trinitarian sisters. They each performed their own function: Duffy, vicar-general and liaison to the bishop; Ahern, central administrator of the work; and the sisters, missionaries, educators, and everything else. Every month the sisters drew up a required detailed record of all activities, revenues, and expenditures of the missions. Ahern forwarded this report to the vicar-general with his request for a subsidy based upon their expenditures.[23] Sr. Peter Claver perceived that the missionary role of the sisters was dependent on the administrative skill and magnetic draw of Ahern.

> When we got Father Ahern, we had a real organizer and a man that had many, many friends and he used them all. He was a real popular type of a man. He depended on us, and he thought his work was the financial and the business end of it mostly. With the drop of the hat, when we needed him he'd come. He could initiate all this. . . . The sisters were on the firing line; we were working with the people. . . . He was a parish priest brought up there in the city all his life, he had no missionary experience like we had. We were missionaries; we were schooled into it. We were missionaries from the beginning. He was a parish priest.[24]

Sr. Peter Claver characterized Ahern as a nonmissionary, which was true, but he was comfortable delegating responsibility to the sisters, who were missionaries in the sense described above. He allowed "each mission to set up their program, and he'd fit into it."[25] His concept of parish priest was innovative and adaptive to the needs of the people and the vision of the sisters.

There were two major philosophical influences that shaped Ahern: (1) the hero-priest of the mid-nineteenth century, and (2) the Irish liberator Daniel O'Connell.[26] At the funeral of a fellow priest, Ahern described the role of priest in detail. He referred to the parable of the prodigal son (Luke 15:11–32), where the father is overjoyed at his son's return from a profligate life. Ahern believed that the Catholic rectory was the father's house where his people could go when life became unbearable. There the father of Christ's prodigal son lived and waited for those who strayed from the path. He knew and loved them so well that he welcomed them home when the world and its people would cast them aside.[27]

According to Ahern, the priest is a conduit through whom God dispenses graces and gifts to his people. He must be all things to all people: an educated man possessing the sterling qualities of a gentleman; a theologian, philosopher, historian, and scientist; a doctor with doctors and a lawyer with lawyers in order to "lead them to their salvation." Since all strata of society must have the gospel preached to them, a priest must be as comfortable in the company of the "high" as with the "lowly."[28] But, most important, a priest must be a "father to his people. The wise father who builds with things material and who [counsels] with things spiritual. The father who loves his family an[d] knows his family loves him. To the world the lonely character possessing all and yet having nothing—but to his people the joyful father in their happiness, the helpful father in their sorrow."[29] How transparent was his desire to create family, to be father to his people. His paternalistic, larger-than-life, and somewhat unrealistic expectations of himself were not grounded in a racial ideology toward his black parishioners, as much as what he believed to be his mandate as a priest.

An example of a real-life hero-priest was Ahern's friend and role model, Harold Purcell, C.P., a Passionist priest who was the editor of *Sign* magazine and a famous orator who traveled the country several times preaching missions, a form of Catholic revival. Purcell possessed a particular interest in the injustices against African Americans, whom he observed lacked the educational and medical advantages afforded whites. In his desire to remedy the situation in some way, he conceived of a city containing a complex of a church, hospital, educational facility, and social center. He cast about for ten years seeking a diocese that would give him the support he needed to build his City of St. Jude. He dedicated the city to the apostle Jude, who is considered the saint of hopeless causes. He finally found such a diocese when Bishop Thomas J. Toolen of the Mobile diocese invited him to come to Alabama. On October 27, 1938, in Montgomery, Alabama, his dream was realized when the City of St. Jude was dedicated.[30]

Ahern was the homilist at the dedication, and his sermon that day tells us as much about Ahern as it does about Purcell. He spoke of Purcell as "just another good priest hoping, for the hopeless."[31] Good priests were those willing to risk the disapproval of others, even other Catholics, for those in society who had little power. Ahern gave this sermon after he had been at Queen of Angels for eight years. It seems that he could no longer repress the anguish, exhaustion, and disappointment that plagued him as he spoke to the crowd: "It is with a *mea culpa* that we of the Catholic Church must strike our breasts for the little [accomplished] in the past years. Credit should be given the few who have labored, but the cooperation of our Catholics has been found wanting . . . A thousand barriers are placed in the way of progress and the worst criticism comes from one's friends."[32] Although Ahern felt the criticism deeply and sometimes despaired in the face of the continuous barriers placed in the way, parishioners and coworkers remembered him more for his continually ebullient nature and consistent effort than for the difficulties he faced. He gave passionate sermons that instructed. They were not the chanted or folk sermons of some black Baptist churches, but were effective enough to capture the imagination of his black parishioners, who many years later remembered them as powerful.[33]

The other exemplar for Ahern was Daniel O'Connell (1775–1847). Known as "the Liberator," O'Connell was the leader of the Irish Catholic movement for home rule, or independence from the British Parliament. O'Connell, unlike other prominent Irish freedom fighters of his time, would not shake the hand of an American slaveholder or accept their money for the cause of Irish freedom, and he publicly criticized Irish American Catholics for not standing against slavery and for the slave. In so doing, he inspired the wrath of the formidable Bishop John Hughes of New York and the conservative lay Catholic Orestes Brownson. Both publicly called O'Connell an interfering foreigner on the issue of slavery.[34]

Counter to many of his fellow Irish Americans, Ahern honored O'Connell's fight against bigotry and his work as part of a series of events that changed the world. This indicates a similarity not only of mind but also of character, in that both men could "go their own way" in the face of opposition from their own people.[35]

In September 1930, when Ahern began his work, he brought enthusiasm and talent but had to learn some hard lessons. While tremendous resources were being raised and expended on European immigrant groups in order to educate and keep them in the faith, Ahern learned he had to do more with less. The American Catholic Church would have to emerge from years of preoccupation with its own survival before it would be able to turn its attention to those who were black and Catholic.

The Location of a Church: A Function of Class

Father Ahern's first objective was to find a home for the new mission, a goal that would prove extremely difficult to attain. In September 1930, immediately after Ahern assumed his position, he was instructed by Bishop Walsh to inspect a property on Court Street as a possible site for the church and to submit a report immediately. Ahern submitted his report to the bishop stressing his strong objections to both the property and, more important, to its location.

Ahern also immediately sent a letter and a copy of the report to Vicar-General John Duffy, asking him to use his influence with Bishop Walsh to prevent the church from being located in the Third Ward, "the scene of many a race riot," and continued: "Father [Thomas] Glover [vice-chancellor of the diocese at that time] informed me it was the Bishop's orders that we inspect the Ukrainian property on Court St. Before filing the report (demanded immediately) I was most anxious that you pass on my findings. However I was informed you were out of town and the enclosed is now in the hands of Father Glover."[36] Ahern's reasons for rejecting the property began with the extensive physical repairs that would be needed. But the repairs were not as important to him as the philosophical and sociological difficulties he felt the location would present to the mission. For one thing, he was concerned for the safety of the sisters who spent so much of their time with the people. The Third Ward would "hardly be the proper place to ask the Trinitarian Sisters to spend their evenings," since it was under Director Egan's curfew regulations and "[w]hite people are subject to arrest if seen in the vicinity."[37]

This was not the last time Ahern would play the role of protective father toward the sisters, and his appeal to the bishop on these grounds was probably an effective one. An examination of the facts, however, discloses a more complex picture.[38] The curfew Ahern mentioned in his report was directed toward white men who visited the area late at night to take advantage of its nightspots, pool, gambling, and prostitution.[39] But, according to Newark historian Clement Price, the ward's image stemmed more from "white indifference" and the area's "alienation from the larger urban community than efforts to stamp out crime or keep whites out."[40]

The Third Ward may have had a reputation as the "Roaring Third," but the inflammatory reactions of Public Safely Director Egan and even the protective concern of Ahern obscured the complexity of the landscape. The Third Ward was more than a troubled neighborhood. It was a vital community textured with the many storefront churches reminiscent of the rural southern churches the people had left behind.[41] These churchgoing folks avoided the nightlife of their neighborhood and instead focused their lives around their community churches the way African Americans had done since the eighteenth century. In Newark, with its segregated public spaces, the storefront churches offered the only social and emotional outlet outside the family unit.[42]

But the complexity does not stop there. The Trinitarian sisters became aware that the residents of the Third Ward participated in a kind of informal neighborhood watch system, observing the streets from their windows, noting the comings and goings of its inhabitants and visitors. They noticed when in 1929 Sr. Peter Claver and Lucy Mulligan walked through their neighborhood, going in an out of tenements and houses seeking Catholics. The sisters knew the people were watching them. "They'd hang out the windows. If they'd see us, one of them would keep their eye on where we were going and know what time we would come out."[43] But white priests would not receive the same reception in those areas of Newark. The reasons become clear in Sr. Peter Claver's narrative: "Father used to say to me, 'I'm going up to Broome Street to the tenement. Would you come with me? I'm taking the Blessed Sacrament.' And the hallway was black, just dark going up. But he was a man going into these apartments and they would be suspicious of a man going to a place, like a red light section. So he'd take a sister with him. But we didn't have anybody with us [when we traveled there]. I was never afraid, never."[44] Ironically, the women who were being protected from the infamous neighborhood by white male priests were in fact protected by that neighborhood, the same one for which the sisters acted as gatekeepers for their priest protectors.

Ultimately, Ahern's appeals to Bishop Walsh against the use of the property, in conjunction with Duffy's influence, worked: Queen of Angels Church was not located in the Third Ward.

But Ahern's objections to the Third Ward as a home for Queen of Angels Church were grounded in his view of the function of social and economic class in drawing and keeping converts. He felt that the church should be located in a middle-class neighborhood in order to "attract the middle or better class of negroes." Those were the people "upon whom we must build our hopes for success."[45] Ahern used Dr. E. Mae McCarroll as an example to prove his point. She was an African American medical doctor and graduate of Columbia University whom Ahern felt would never have converted to the Catholic Church if Queen of Angels was not using the downtown location of St. Bridget's Hall.[46] If that location changed to the Third Ward, he was convinced their prospects for converts would be destroyed.

Ahern believed that the middle class offered the financial base necessary to the viability of a parish, because they had the respectability of social class to attract not only more of the middle class but also the underclass and the working poor who aspired to something better.[47] The white Catholic Church could not, on its own merits (which were dubious from the African American point of view) create an incentive to either the upper or under class. Race leaders, or African American activists, community leaders, and blacks with social and economic standing in their own community would provide the magnet for converts.

The Reverend James Scott, former pastor of Bethany Baptist for more than thirty years, gave this powerful analysis of Newark's black community and history. A sense of respectability and class within the black community precluded the necessity for blacks to look to the white community for status. "They compared themselves, not to whites, but to other blacks," Scott said.[48] Newark's African Americans formed "a very small, insular community in which people felt very comfortable being themselves. And they weren't interested in being anybody else. They did want to have better contacts, more goodwill, easier communications with whites, but they were not willing to have it at the expense of being black."[49]

Illuminating the complexity of class further, Scott explained that even though most of the congregation of Bethany Baptist were domestics or worked in service occupations in the 1930s and 1940s (as did most of the members of all black churches in Newark at that time), "they thought they had it made" in terms of social class. They had very high aspirations for their children to get an education and better themselves economically, but this was to facilitate parallel movement across the racial chasm into the mainstream. African Americans at Bethany, St. Philip's Episcopal, and Queen of Angels "wanted to control leadership and they wanted to shape the black community in their own image."[50]

Ahern seems to have at least sensed this situation, as he immediately addressed the problems of both classes when he wrote the following: "After being over three weeks with the colored people I find we must (1) get them work (2) take care of the poor and deed them [get them housing] and (3) offer an attractive church and hall to compete with the wealthy Baptists and Presbyterians."[51] The wealthy Baptists and Presbyterians to which Ahern referred were those of the established black churches such as Bethany Baptist and the Thirteenth Avenue Presbyterian. They were harder to win over, as he observed almost three years later: "We may note here that to convince the better class of colored people is not going to be an easy task as the leading minds keep continually throwing conditions in the South at us."[52]

The established black churches in Newark, which by this time were outnumbered by the newer storefront churches, did not focus their energies institutionally on the social ills of the underclass. Instead, its members worked through the Urban League with whom Sr. Peter Claver and later others at Queen of Angels often collaborated. As time went on, Ahern sent figures of the mission's relief work to the African American newspapers and was invited on at least one occasion to speak to the Urban League.[53]

But in spite of the proliferation of storefront churches, they were able to offer "little more than spiritual comfort to the masses of black Christians" who crowded the Hill District.[54] Ahern reasoned that if the Catholic Church could demonstrate a commitment to the economic and social struggles of African Americans, a possibility existed that they could gain converts.

> Last Thursday, through the kindness of Mr. John F. Nugent, we fed one hundred and six very poor and destitute colored men, women and children, and I personally think that through this charitable endeavor we have prepared the way for some few converts. To me it seems that we are in a time in which the living conditions of the colored people of our City are at their lowest end and it would be far easier for us to make progress right now than at any time in the future. This is not that we are endeavoring to buy our way into their religious life, but through our charity our actions speak louder than words, and this I think is making a deep impression on the Baptist mind.[55]

But in order to convert African Americans, Ahern had to change their view of the Catholic Church.

4

Why Go to China?

We apologized for living and kept on singing.

—Fr. Cornelius Ahern

Expanding Public Space

Queen of Angels directed its efforts in several different directions to accomplish its goal of attracting African Americans. Those efforts consisted of devotional services, social events, missions, educational and leadership opportunities for adults and children, and economic relief to address every aspect of the people's lives.

When the Trinitarian sisters held rallies in the beginning of the colored work, they always attracted a large crowd of African Americans. They rented a hall and asked a prominent local citizen to speak to the gathering, distributed flyers, and advertised the event in the local newspaper. The speakers did not necessarily have to be Catholic, but the work of the sisters would be announced in the program. The halls would be packed with African Americans because the events provided the opportunity for them to access public space normally denied them.[1] One of the Trinitarians, Sr. Francis Damien, explained that "black people did not have entrance to a lot of places, whereas when we would run it [a rally] in a white center they would all come. If nothing else, they wanted to see the inside of that building. How could I get from the street into the inside of that [building] unless somebody asked me."[2]

Queen of Angels and its five missions afforded African Americans the opportunity to gather together for a variety of reasons. In an age without television, in the depression, when even in northern Newark blacks were compelled to sit in the balcony of theaters and enter through a back door, the parish created the opportunity for social events in a public space. The Christmas, Easter, and May pageants were great fund-raisers, as well as a chance for the children to perform for their proud parents. Although black churches of Newark may have offered the same kinds of activities, the sisters' proactive approach sought out and brought in those recent émigrés from the South who were making the adjustment from a rural to an urban environment.

Blacks were accustomed to finding their social and religious lives incorporated within the space of the black church. Queen of Angels followed the practice by providing the same space for both secular and religious activities.[3] The space was provided, but the people created the cultural environment by simply being who they were. They did not look to the priests or the sisters for leadership in their lay organizations. When the sisters attended their lay society meetings, the people did not defer to them or seek their counsel. Instead, they led their meetings and turned to the sisters for assistance in the things they could not provide, like access to public places for their social functions.[4] As Sr. Francis Damien saw it: "They ran their own thing. We were like the guiding light. We didn't call the meeting to order . . . They were making all the decisions . . . We used them to see what they wanted to do."[5]

Reserving public space for Queen of Angels' group functions would take a great deal of energy and cause constant anxiety and frustration to Ahern and the sisters. When Ahern attempted to book the children's summer camp in 1931, he reported to Duffy that the Knights of Columbus Camp at Culvers Lake, the Benedictines at Newton, and Monsignor Quinn's camp at Wading River, Long Island, rejected them.[6] In August 1932, with his parish still in a little temporary church with no hall for parish functions, his frustration became apparent in his correspondence with Duffy. Ahern pleaded with him to prevail upon the bishop for a space for his people. "Our Holy Name Society is planning for their Communion breakfast, but just where to go we know not."[7]

In 1934 Queen of Angels was still having difficulty procuring places for their parish picnic. Ahern lamented that it took a month to find "a place [that] would take us."[8] To get around the problem of discrimination against the African American children in summer camps, the church created a beach of sorts with an outside shower for the children donated by the city, transplanted Coney Island sand, and beach umbrellas donated from private citizens.[9]

Novena to St. Jude

A novena is a public devotion lasting nine days devoted to a particular saint or to Mary, mother of Jesus. It offers an opportunity for the faithful to listen to exhortations from noted preachers, to pray for particular intentions, and to spend time in prayer apart from the liturgy.[10] In October 1932, Harold Purcell preached the inaugural novena to what became the first continuous devotion to St. Jude in the country.[11] Rather than lasting for nine days, it became a perpetual devotion that continued for more than forty years under the leadership of the diocesan priests and ended when the order of priests, the Society to African Missions, took over the administration of the parish in the 1980s.

It was highly successful, attracting close to seven hundred people a day.[12] It is the only devotion to a saint that seems to have captured the imagination of the early black converts, but attracted whites even more. Ahern was amazed at the amount of white attendees even though "the old objection of whites mixing with the colored [in the larger society] will not be put down."[13]

To this day, former white novena attendees convey their fond memories to Queen of Angels' longtime parishioners. The St. Jude Novena provided a neutral ground where the petitioner's need for the impossible temporarily lowered boundaries. It increased goodwill by integrating white and black worshippers of different classes, attracted potential converts, and brought much-needed revenue into the parish.

Social Events

A great variety of religious and secular social events were sponsored by Queen of Angels and were open to Catholics and non-Catholics alike. These inclusive activities had a powerful effect on the African American community. Starting in 1935, and for many years following, the parish provided a pancake breakfast after every Sunday Mass, to which relatives and friends of the parishioners were invited. The annual pilgrimages to the Trinitarian's St. Joseph Shrine in Stirling, New Jersey, attracted blacks (1,000 in 1935) of every denomination from the entire metropolitan area; whites also were numbered among the attendees.[14] Queen of Angels parishioner Ollie Pierce, then ninety-six years old, stated that at times half of the participants at such affairs were non-Catholic. She told the author that non-Catholics "liked to go out with the Catholic people . . . Not only to the services, but anything that we would have, a breakfast or anything. There would be so many of them . . . The priest would stand and talk with them on Sunday morning, and stuff like that. And they liked that. Because they wasn't Catholic, they didn't push them aside . . . They was always welcome at the priest's table. Queen of Angels was known everywhere."[15]

As a matter of policy, Queen of Angels maintained the African American core belief that "everybody has a place, and by doing so, people found a place."[16] But places were hard to come by. White Newark was hesitant to share public space with blacks whether it was architectural or media space. The Trinitarians worked around the limitations by knowing their adversaries and their politics. Locating an appropriate and available space for the Easter, Christmas, and May pageants produced the following type of scenario.

> They didn't want to give a public school auditorium to a play. . . given by the Negro Mission. That was something new. So they kind of made you wait and wait. And they'd have to have another meeting, and they'd have to have another meeting. But see, we knew that we could get in there with a little push. So we'd have to ask and wait, and we were willing to wait, because we knew we had to wait. And we knew they had to say yes because the politicians and votes and things like that, you know, were important.[17]

Their efforts to publicize their activities at Queen of Angels presented difficulties as well:

> We could not get any pictures in the newspapers. When we would run affairs, they would tell us at the newspaper that we got our pictures in too late to publish it. So Monsignor Paul Hayes, who was in high school then, and a black boy by the name of Paul Seymour, built around my wash tubs in East Orange, a dark room, so we could take the pictures and develop them and get them to the newspaper office that afternoon. So they didn't have that for an excuse.[18]

Whites would not allow white nuns to see them as overt racists; therefore, they would have to give in when the nuns pushed or placed them in a position of not having an excuse.[19]

Music was important to Queen of Angels' parishioners and the Trinitarians included it as an important part of the liturgical and social life of the parish. The first organist was Madame Johnson, a woman who played for black Protestant churches for many years.

> [W]e needed somebody to play when we started Mass at St. Bridget's. Father said, "Go out and see if you can see somebody that can play. We have a piano." So I saw this woman coming up the street and I went up to her and said, "Excuse me, I'm Sister Peter Claver." She says, "I'm Madame Johnson. I'm on my way to church." And I said, "You know, I wondered if you played, do you play the piano, the organ?" She says, "Yes, Ma'am, I sure can. I was born to play." I said, "Maybe you'd come in; (I have the music), and help us." Madame Johnson comes in and she never left us 'till she died.[20]

The Queen of Angels' congregation participated in the singing so enthusiastically that Ahern, with characteristic wit, remarked, "great objection to our singing at Mass by Father Masterson. We apologized for living and kept on singing."[21]

Missions

While Queen of Angels was still using the temporary space at St. Bridget's Hall, Ahern and the Trinitarians founded several satellite missions connected to the mother church. Ahern constantly pleaded with Duffy for more funding and for an assistant to help with the work. Ahern estimated his territory to include "at least 80,000 negroes," making the field "vast" and the "harvest great." Within his grasp was a "golden opportunity," which he was sure Duffy would not want to lose.[22] The five smaller missions gave people in the surrounding area access to educational and spiritual services the sisters and lay volunteers provided. But there was a logistical problem for Sunday Mass: with only one priest, Mass had to be held in the larger space of St. Bridget's. In 1932 they devised a temporary solution by hiring a bus to transport the children from the missions to the church.[23]

Complaints about their singing were not the only frustration Ahern and Queen of Angels experienced. Its population was too large for its facility and resources. In September 1931, Queen of Angels' flock numbered 549 men, women, and children in Newark, 143 in Orange, and 108 in Montclair. In March 1931, Ahern provided a Portuguese priest to hear the confessions of twenty-eight men. The following year, thirty-eight black Portuguese made their Easter duty of confession and communion after being away from the church for as long as twenty-two years.[24] The parish was caring for twenty-three indigent families and Ahern expected three or four times that by the time "the real winter [set] in."[25] And they were still occupying borrowed halls, storefronts, and homes. "Our own churches" would be greatly appreciated so "we could do some good work," Ahern wrote to Duffy.[26]

In October 1931, the parish finally received an offer from Father McGinley, the pastor of St. Aedan's Parish, to buy their old frame church. It was a Sears and Roebuck prefabricated structure that the mail order company sold and shipped to customers who then assembled them. Queen of Angels could have the small structure if the parish could make arrangements to have it moved from Jersey City. Ahern hired contractor Edward M. Waldron, and in less than a month Cape Verdean men moved the church to 242 Academy Street near Wickliffe.[27] St. Dominic's Academy donated a heating system, plumbing, and a boiler that was installed without charge by plumber John Joyce. However, Ahern needed a note from Duffy to Mr. Bigelow, the superintendent of the Building Department, which promised that the frame structure would be a temporary measure. Duffy told Ahern to take the structure for one year, and then they would get their own plant.[28] On November 15, 1931, Our Lady Queen of the Angels Church celebrated its first Mass at its first church, inadequate and temporary, with no basement and no hall, but at least it was a start.[29]

At the end of 1934, well past the one-year deadline, the property the church rented at 242 Academy Street was taken over by a savings and loan company that could force the parish to vacate with only thirty days' notice.[30] The thought of an imminent and arbitrary eviction set Ahern's nerves on edge, in addition to the fact that the temporary structure was in need of extensive repairs amounting to $5,000.

In November 1933, a glimmer of hope appeared in the person of Mrs. Margaret Kelly, an attendee of the St. Jude Novena. She promised Ahern that upon her death she would bequeath $20,000 to Queen of Angels to build a new church. In December 1933 she signed her will in the presence of Ahern, donating that amount to the church. In December 1934, Ahern learned of available city property across the street obtainable for a twenty-year lease.[31] Rather than wait for assistance from Mrs. Kelly's estate, he borrowed $10,000 from the bishop to dig a foundation and build a frame-and-brick-faced church.[32] They said their first Mass on May 12, 1935, at 237 Academy Street. The structure was not as impressive as Christ the King Church in Jersey City and did not rival the architecture of St. Peter Claver's in Montclair, but it was attractive and provided the parish with a basement hall in which to hold their social functions.[33]

Queen of Angels was in desperate need of more funds and workers for the many converts they were attracting. They formed auxiliaries of white volunteers who donated their time, talent, and financial assistance to the missions. They transported children to classes, did clerical work, and after being trained by the Trinitarian sisters, taught catechism classes as well.

Two auxiliary guilds were formed in February 1931, a month after the St. Peter Claver Mission in Montclair and the Holy Ghost Mission in Orange were established.[34] The Montclair auxiliary guild membership included many wealthy women of the neighboring townships. With their contributions, St. Peter Claver Mission in Montclair obtained a space in a leased house on Elm Street.[35] After occupying a storefront for more than a year, in December 1932 the Orange Auxiliary donated the funds for the Holy Spirit Mission to move to a larger house.[36] In March 1934, the first Mass was said at the East Orange Mission Center. More than one hundred people, mostly black, were present, and of this number about twenty-five were non-Catholic.[37]

Queen of Angels founded the Mother Boniface Mission in Elizabeth, St. John's Mission on Albert Avenue in "Down Neck" Newark, and St. Thomas's Mission in the Third Ward, Newark. Initially, this only meant that the parish acquired some kind of rental property, or even the use of a house to begin minimal activities in the areas at some distance from Queen of Angels.[38]

In January 1932, the Mount Carmel Guild, the charitable and social services arm of the diocese established by Bishop Walsh, allowed Queen of Angels to use their house in Elizabeth to hold classes once a week for the seventeen young people ready to begin instructions. In March 1932, they held a rally in Elizabeth to launch the new Mother Boniface Mission Center, named for the Trinitarian Mother Superior who had died not long before.

Eventually it became clear that Queen of Angels was reaching only a few of the 25,000 African Americans in the Third Ward. Although Ahern did not want the main church located there, he did want to attract its occupants. He decided to go after them by opening St. Thomas Mission in a rented storefront on Broome and Morton Streets on May 12, 1934.[39] Ahern's goal was one hundred converts from this mission before the end of the year; by July 1934 forty-two people from the Third Ward were under instruction.[40]

The Potts were one of the families who took instructions at the St. Thomas Mission. Eleven of the Potts' twelve children were baptized in 1941.

Mrs. Potts was drawn to the Catholic faith after her friend Mrs. Eubanks invited her to the St. Jude Novena. One of the sons, Nathaniel, began attending St. Thomas Mission at the age of ten and served as an altar boy at the St. Jude Novenas for many years. His brother, Donald Potts, was the only Queen of Angels' parishioner to become a priest.

There were two elements that attracted the Potts family to the Catholic church: first, as Nathaniel Potts described, its highly organized structure and the strict discipline the sisters imposed on the children resonated with an African American manner of parenting. Second, the high level of involvement in lay organizations at Queen of Angels competed with the old Newark churches whose leadership positions seemed restricted to an elite and well-established few.[41]

This is an instance where, as a mission church, Queen of Angels had an advantage over established institutions. Queen of Angels dedicated all its resources to attracting converts, creating as many opportunities for participation as it could. It reached out with the material goods in short supply during the depression years and took the qualities of inclusiveness prevalent in African American culture to another level. The established, old-time black churches may have had a tendency to be careful and hesitant when faced with new arrivals to the city. They could not possibly absorb them all, and they did not have the resources to attend to their needs. Positions of status and authority in the church that had been held by people for years would not be easily opened to the newcomer. At Queen of Angels it was an open field, and there were plenty of opportunities to get in on the ground floor.

Educational and Leadership Opportunities

The era of the Catholic parochial school began in earnest during the New York public school controversy in the late nineteenth century, resisting the anti-Catholic tenor and curriculum of the public school system. Bishop John Hughes of New York became involved in a political fight for Catholic students to receive an unbiased education with state funding. When it became clear that public funds would not be approved for this purpose, the focus of the American Catholic Church was trained on creating separate Catholic schools.

In 1884, at the Third Plenary Council in Baltimore, the American bishops mandated that pastors must build parochial schools within two years of being appointed or face possible removal.[42] Bishop Thomas Walsh heeded the mandate of the Plenary Council to such an extent that his motto was "school room for every child," and he was widely known as an "Apostle of

Education."[43] When appointed bishop of the Newark diocese in 1928, he continued what he had begun as bishop of Trenton, addressing the parochial school issue and, most particularly, the high percentage of Italians in the public school system out of the reach of Catholic influence. He believed education was the key to stopping leakage of Catholic émigrés from the church. To that end, he dedicated a great deal of energy, funds, and personnel. He built parochial schools, staffing many of them with Italian sisters and American sisters trained in Italian.[44] He once said, "I'd rather lay the cornerstone of one Catholic school, than lay the cornerstones of 10 Catholic parishes."[45]

Ahern was aware of Walsh's efforts for Catholic schools, and he also knew of the lack of black students in those institutions. In 1928, one of Ahern's colleagues, the Reverend Ralph J. Glover, conducted a study on social welfare in the diocese of Newark. He discovered that the African American population in Catholic parochial schools registered at 0 percent.[46] In 1932, Ahern estimated that one out of every four pastors accepted black children into his school. He was continually rebuffed by pastors who refused to admit Queen of Angels' children to their schools and was at a loss to explain the situation when faced with the disappointment of hopeful parents.[47] He became more and more disheartened by his inability to provide a parish school for the African American children in his care. He insisted to Duffy, "We need a parochial school right now."[48]

But the Trinitarian sisters did not wait for the possibility of an official school building. Children and adults were encouraged to take religious instruction in the Catholic Church and toward baptism if they desired. The classes took place in homes, at St. Bridget's Hall, and in the various mission locations they opened in Newark, Orange, Montclair, and Elizabeth.[49] Thousands of miles accumulated on their car as the sisters drove from one location to another giving religious instructions, as well as offering sewing, choral singing, band, dance, cadet corps, and drama classes, to name just a few of their activities. In 1933, after the sisters logged 19,600 miles on their car and the clergy logged 14,908 miles on theirs, Ahern, in his inimitable fashion, asked Duffy, "Why go to China?"[50]

In addition to educational programs, they formed lay groups like the Rosary Society for women and the Holy Names Society for men. They also had Sodalities of the Blessed Virgin Mary for adults and children. Sodalities were pious associations founded by a Jesuit priest in 1563 and dedicated to the improvement of the layperson in virtue, prayer, study, works of charity, and evangelization.

Queen of Angels' parishioners responded enthusiastically to the call to lead these various organizations, spending long hours after work and on the weekends in meetings and on fund-raising events such as rallies, bazaars, pageants, picnics, and dances. Such great effort by laypeople and Trinitarians did not escape the attention of Ahern, who recounted their deeds in his reports to the vicar-general.[51] Mrs. Walker, whose husband was a dentist and a leading member of Queen of Angels, organized a Girl Scout troop for Queen of Angels' children. The women from the St. John's Mission on Albert Street formed themselves into a Mother's Club. Several of the parishioners received training to be catechetical instructors, often in homes when the distance was too great to travel to the mission.[52]

The laypeople of the parish continued their involvement with the Federated Colored Catholics. Evidently viewing the federation in a positive light, Ahern proudly reported the participation of 125 Queen of Angels' parishioners at the convention held at St. Patrick's Cathedral in September 1932.[53] In April of that same year, Sr. Peter Claver and Miss Adelle Lay attended an interracial convention conducted by the New Jersey Women's Clubs to keep the parish current with the thinking of the day on these issues.

In March 1932, Benedict Bradley, O.S.B., from St. Mary's Abbey in Newark began giving lectures on the Mass at Queen of Angels' various missions. Other priests, such as John O. Buchmann and David Kelly, lectured on diverse religious topics.[54] The mission held a course of lectures for non-Catholics that attracted as many as 260 people. Ahern hoped that these well-attended lectures would help convince the leading minds to embrace Catholicism, although he felt it would be difficult to do so.[55]

By April 1932, Bradley had published a missal leaflet containing an English translation of the prayers of the Latin Mass for the people to use. At Sunday Mass, a male parishioner led the congregation in the responses in English as the priest addressed them in Latin. In this respect, Ahern and Bradley were more than thirty years ahead of the Second Vatican Council that authorized the use of the vernacular in all liturgies. Another innovation was the mixed marriages performed between Protestants and Catholics inside the altar rail, which was against the directive of the Catholic Church at the time. According to canon law 1102 in the 1917 Code of Canon Law, all sacred rights were forbidden to mixed marriages between Protestants and Catholics. "Most certainly the exchange of vows are not to be done in church . . . If, however, a greater evil would come of this prohibition, then some ceremonies may be allowed, but always excepting the celebration of Mass."[56] As longtime parishioner

Walter P. Brown remembers: "We didn't have a vestibule, so Father Ahern [performed mixed marriages between Protestant and Catholic] in [the] church. Because I know, my brother married a Protestant, and it was inside the altar rail. I was the best man. We did a lot of firsts. We held dances in the church basement, which wasn't allowed. Father Ahern said he was glad to have the young people meeting in the church where they could be supervised."[57]

The Browns were among the few black children who attended a parochial school, and they, along with one other family, attended St. Patrick's School. Concerned that her children would be restricted to an all-white school experience, Mrs. Brown received permission from St. Patrick's School for her children to receive Holy Communion at Queen of Angels once a month. Mr. Brown felt that his mother "did not want us to attend that all white school thinking that that's all there was. She made certain that we would remember who we were, that we were black, African, whatever, and that we attended Our Lady Queen of Angels with the Angel Sodality."[58]

Spiritual and Corporal Works of Mercy: A Catholic Social Gospel

While Father Ahern focused his energy on obtaining a church building, raising funds, and other administrative functions, the Trinitarian sisters continued the work Sr. Peter Claver had begun with the Theresa Lane Council and the Little Flower Guild.[59]

The sisters divided their work between what they called the Corporal Works of Charity and the Spiritual Works of Charity. More commonly known in Catholic tradition as the Corporal and Spiritual Works of Mercy, they are traditional Catholic actions based on the admonition of Jesus in the gospel of Matthew, chapter 25, to care for those in need. "Truly, I say to you, as you did it to one of the least of these my brethren, you did it to me" (Matt. 25:40 RSV).

Consequently, the Corporal Works of Mercy mandated that Christians should feed the hungry, give drink to the thirsty, clothe the naked, give shelter to the homeless, visit the sick, ransom the captive, and bury the dead. To these, Catholic tradition added the Spiritual Works of Mercy, which are to instruct the ignorant, to counsel the doubtful, to admonish sinners, to bear wrongs patiently, to forgive offences willingly, to comfort the afflicted, and to pray for the living and the dead.[60]

The sisters were guided by the Works of Mercy and then added more of their own, such as posting bail for those accused in the courts, securing employment, and any other request that came their way. Nothing was off-limits.[61] As their name suggests, the Missionary Sisters of the Most Blessed

Trinity were members of a biblically charismatic organization—that is, they acted under the guidance of the Holy Spirit and followed where it led. At this early stage of their organization it could also be referred to as charismatic in the Weberian sense of being infused with the mission of their founder, Father Judge, and with the structure and modes of operation open to inspiration rather than solidified into routinization.[62]

Their main objective was to save souls, but they followed the gospel mandate to care for the poor, those in prison, the sick, and the helpless. This Catholic form of the Protestant Social Gospel did not strive to alter societal injustices on an institutional level but sought to alleviate the suffering of those who were subjected to them.

In a sense, there was a merging of, or at least a dialogue between, the priestly or otherworldly and prophetic or this-worldly in the sisters' actions. Their theological underpinnings were based on saving souls, but the result was achieved in quasiprophetic ways. They located the difficulties of African Americans in the discrimination they faced, improvising techniques to maneuver around them while attending to spiritual needs at the same time. When Catholics were still proving their American loyalty, they certainly would not have advocated anything remotely tainted with a socialist agenda, but they seemed to be acting, nonetheless, like unconscious adherents of the Social Gospel.

A case in point is that the lack of work for African Americans was perceived very clearly as caused by discriminatory practices. In the tenth anniversary journal for Queen of Angels in 1940, the authors charged the large companies of the city for unfairly denying work to African American men: "If the Prudential Insurance Company can house our people why cannot they hire him? And what we say of the Pru, may also be said of the other Insurance Companies, and of the Banks, the Public Service, the Department stores and other Public Institutions and Companies who are most willing to accept gratuities but offer none in return. Keep the Colored man working and keep him a good citizen—OR ELSE?"[63] The journal did not elaborate on what the "OR ELSE" meant, but it appears to have been prophetic considering the anger and frustration that erupted in the civil disturbances in Newark in 1967 in the midst of poor housing and high unemployment among blacks of the city. This would not be the last time Queen of Angels would warn the powerful of Newark to act justly for African Americans.

In 1932, the City of Newark's Overseer of the Poor (corresponding to today's welfare department) was so impressed with the efficacy of Queen of

Angels' relief programs that it dedicated one of its caseworkers to Queen of Angels to expedite the investigation of cases. After the caseworker determined assistance eligibility, the checks were then signed and sent to the sisters, who distributed them to the people.[64] Two years later, the City of Newark and the State of New Jersey went a step further and recognized Queen of Angels as a "distinct social unit" with "full charge of investigation and distribution of food checks."[65] At that point, 68 families, or 302 people, of the parish were "participating in every sort of charity the officials can offer," which saved "the church and [C]atholic charities a vast amount of money each month."[66]

At the end of 1932, Ahern felt that the "relief work [was] running along smoothly." The parish was "prepared to take care of most of [their] deserving families in case the city fails."[67] The white auxiliaries donated clothing, and the women from the parish cleaned, restored, and distributed or sold them.[68] At Christmas every child of the parish received a toy and, when needed, some clothing. Two hundred and seventeen baskets of food were given to needy families donated by white auxiliaries and benefactors. If all else failed, the bills to Bamberger's Department store for the first Holy Communion and confirmation clothing, and those for the small things the children needed from the five and ten were sent to Monsignor Duffy to pay.[69]

In the next two years the parish's collections increased with the greater number of parishioners, but Queen of Angels could not keep pace with the number of people on the relief roles.[70] At Thanksgiving and Christmas, organizations like the Elks, Eagles, Knights of Columbus, Newark Police, and the Mt. Carmel Guild helped distribute more than 300 baskets of food, clothes, and shoes to the needy of the parish. As Ahern wrote, "There is so much charity needed among these people we do not know where to turn."[71] This was in addition to the 100 loaves of bread donated daily for years by the A&P Company, and the 65 loaves the Fischer Baking Company agreed to donate daily starting in 1934.[72]

Ahern attempted to involve President Franklin D. Roosevelt's New Deal agencies like the National Recovery Administration (NRA) and the Emergency Relief Administration (ERA) in the relief efforts of the parish, but they proved more trouble than they were worth. Beginning in the fall of 1934, Ahern sat in on several meetings in the self-described capacity of "representing the colored of Newark."[73] (Why black leaders were not there to represent the people is not known.) From contacts at the meetings he was able to procure jobs for fifteen men, but the relief arrangements were less than satisfactory. The NRA donated bags of food left over from white community relief, and both the NRA and ERA promised relief to families "thrown back" on Queen of Angels because of "lack of funds." Ahern, "after much persuading and pulling wires," would have to get the families back on city relief.[74]

Medical and health issues were a great problem in the poor sections of the city. As in New York and other major urban centers where poor European immigrants and African Americans crowded into substandard housing, communicable diseases proliferated and medical care was in scant supply.[75] When the poor had to be hospitalized they were relegated to the city hospital. Death from tuberculosis for African Americans was four times that of whites in Newark in 1930. The most important causes of this high rate were housing with poor ventilation, heating, and plumbing facilities and lack of access to healthcare for early detection of illness.[76]

Hospitals discriminated against black medical personnel and black patients. No hospital in New Jersey would intern black doctors or train black nurses. Patients were turned away "because white patients and students would object."[77] Hospital accommodations were commonly segregated, and blacks were generally limited to ward beds and corridors. Hospitals often had separate visiting hours for blacks, and two hospitals limited black care to one four-bed ward.[78]

Sister Mary of the Precious Blood, M.S.B.T., who later became administrator of the Trinitarian hospital in Alabama, often told her fellow sisters that "when a colored person gets sick and they go to the hospital, they are going to die . . . They are so poor, they never get a doctor. When they get the doctor and the doctor orders them to the hospital that is probably the end . . . If you ever hear they are in the hospital, go right away."[79] So the sisters did. They visited them, and when a priest was not available, they baptized them and arranged their burials, often in the city's potter's field. But two things should be understood here. First, any Catholic may baptize if a person is in danger of death and no priest is available to do so; second, when orders of women religious worked with immigrants or blacks or anyone unaffiliated with a parish, the sisters evangelized, baptized, and buried them. Because the Trinitarians' work focused on the abandoned or unchurched in Newark, specifically Italian immigrants and blacks, such activities were not uncommon. So the sisters trained the laypeople of Queen of Angels to visit the sick also, and to tend to their spiritual and material needs as much as they were able.

In order to provide the much-needed noncatastrophic care to the community, Queen of Angels opened its first medical clinic in April 1932. Two

Protestant doctors administered the clinic on a volunteer basis.[80] This particular clinic operated until the 1950s, closing before Fr. Joseph Lenihan left the parish in 1957.

We Feel Like Abandoned Souls

On June 29, 1933, Queen of Angels lost its first and most powerful advocate when Msgr. John Duffy was elevated to the position of Bishop of Syracuse. Ahern's anguish is quite evident in his correspondence to Duffy; he was losing a mentor and, it seems, someone who was like a father to him in a difficult and lonely work.

But Duffy's relationship with the people of Queen of Angels predated Ahern's presence on the scene. Duffy's efforts for African Americans began as a promise at his ordination in Rome. We have evidence of his search for a church at least as early as 1926, and his relationship with the preecclesial group of black Catholics was warm and trusting. The Theresa Lane Council called on him to help them save their Wilsey Street House when they could not pay the mortgage. "Our little colored group is in distress," wrote Anna Kerwin in her letter to him. And Ethel Wright wrote "your little group of colored Catholics are having a procession in honor of our Blessed Mother. We want very much to have you come."[81] Ahern was not exaggerating when he told Duffy that Queen of Angels, with its congregation of 1,100 people, could have not come as far as it had without Duffy's efforts. "[T]he work was begun, has been carried on and has received [its] inspiration through your efforts."[82] And when he asked Duffy to personally say good-bye to his people at their request, he was conveying their true feelings.

With so much still to do, Ahern was devastated by the loss of his intercessor. How, Ahern wondered, would they be able to carry on without Duffy? He tried one more time to elicit Duffy's influence with the bishop in securing the resources he still desperately needed to carry on. He wrote, "We feel like abandoned souls right now with very little to show for three years work except the gathering together of this great number we now have and the spiritual advancement of our group. We cannot carry on as we [now] are, we must have a church, school, etc., and this very soon if we are to survive. May we ask you to use your good graces with the Bishop for St. Bridget's Church here in Newark?"[83]

Ahern continues in even more despairing terms, but this time the "we" was more likely a euphemism for "I": "We all feel that we are at the end of our rope and in order to perceive some sunshine we need larger tools with which to carry on our work."[84] Ahern had his heart set on St. Bridget's as the perfect place for the Negro apostolate; but then and later his pleas fell on deaf ears.

Ahern and the other priests involved at Queen of Angels, its missions, and Christ the King were diocesan or secular priests, not members of a religious order as were the priests who directed the great majority of black missions and parishes in the United States.[85] The common practice among bishops was to invite a religious order like the Society of the Divine Word or the Josephites to handle the Negro Apostolate, but for some unknown reason, Duffy turned to his own diocesan priests to head the work.[86] It was not until the 1970s that the Society for the African Missions would take over the administration of the parish.

Ahern relied heavily on Monsignor Duffy and Sr. Peter Claver for spiritual and emotional support, in addition to the very effectual deeds they performed for the parish. To carry on in such an unpopular and lonely work, one needed the bolstering of comrades, something the Trinitarian sisters had in their fellow sisters. Ahern's friend, John LaFarge, S.J., who was also director of the Catholic Interracial Council, stressed the following:

> No matter how painstaking was the spiritual care of the colored people, no matter how much energy was expended upon the education of their youth, the work was in great measure frustrated by the indifference shown toward the Church's apostolate to the Negroes by [white] Catholics themselves. Even where downright hostility was absent, mission work for the colored people languished from a general apathy. Those who devoted their lives to the Negroes' welfare did a job which for the most part made little or no appeal to the average American Catholic's sympathy or understanding.[87]

In addition to this persistent issue, Ahern was now uncertain that he would be allowed to carry on the work after Duffy's departure, so tied the fate of the parish seemed to be to the fate of his mentor.[88] But this fear was not realized, for in the next month he submitted a report, this time addressed to the interim administrator, Msgr. J. C. McClary, and he repeated his request for a better church facility. On July 25, 1933, Msgr. Thomas H. McLaughlin was installed as the first auxiliary bishop and new vicar-general of Newark. He took Monsignor Duffy's place as Ahern's director and would prove to be as devoted to the work as Duffy had been.

The Clergy Conference on Negro Welfare

Ahern took steps to join forces with other clergy in the field of the Negro apostolate when, sometime in late 1932, he and Harold Purcell met with John LaFarge and the Reverend Dr. Edward C. Kramer (national director of the Catholic Board of Colored Missions and the editor of *Our Colored Missions*) to discuss an organized interracial approach to the problems they were facing.[89] Possibly at this time Ahern and Purcell began formulating their own organization, the Clergy Conference on Negro Welfare, which they officially formed the following year.

In his autobiography, John LaFarge explained that Ahern and Purcell planned to "attack the problem directly and see if organized effort would not accomplish what individual approach failed to achieve."[90] At a conference meeting, Ahern said that the conference's goals were (1) to help the bishops, priests, sisters, and laity of the Catholic Church become more "colored conscious," and (2) to "create a more sympathetic attitude toward the colored people and toward work of the colored among the rest of the clergy and the Catholic people of the United States."[91]

Ahern and Purcell held their first meeting of the Clergy Conference on Negro Welfare on November 12, 1933, at Queen of Angels Parish in Newark. Intellectuals, editors of periodicals, writers, and parish priests attended. Among them were Fr. James M. Gillis, C.S.P., editor of the *Catholic World;* Fr. Wilfrid Parsons, S.J., editor of *America;* Fr. Leo E. Hughes, O.P., editor of *Torch;* and John T. Gillard, S.S.J., author of *The Catholic Church and the American Negro* (1929) and *Colored Catholics in the United States* (1940). Also included were Bernard Quinn of St. Peter Claver in Brooklyn, Michael J. Mulvoy, C.S.P., from St. Mark's Parish in Harlem, and Fr. Augustine Walsh, O.S.B., of the Catholic University of America, and others from as far away as Alabama and Virginia.[92]

The priests discussed ways of counteracting the apathy and prejudice of Catholics on every level. They formed committees to study and improve communication and understanding with bishops, seminaries, sisters, white Catholics, colored Catholics, colored non-Catholics, and Catholic colleges. They felt that even though priests were doing heroic work in the field, "very little encouragement or assistance has been offered to them."[93] It was recommended by one of the members that they suggest to the bishops that they "advise their clergy and people on the [economic] conditions of the Negro . . . housing conditions, unemployment, and their great religious spirit." Protestant Bishops were vocal on these issues, bringing them to the attention of their people, and "so should ours."[94] "The bishops fear of the white people is the crux to the conversion of the Negro to the Catholic faith. The bishops must lead the way but we must assist and convert them to our cause in a diplomatic [manner.] Our priests in the work should do all possible to [break down] the antagonism of our White people and this includes Priests and Sisters."[95]

The clergy at this particular meeting spoke of confronting their own fear of losing white students by admitting blacks to St. Benedict Preparatory School in the coming school year. They cited a case at an Ursuline convent school in Cleveland, Ohio, where two African American girls were accepted and the attendance increased.[96] Evidently, their fears were not overcome; St. Benedict's did not admit African Americans in any significant numbers until the 1970s.

In 1935, Ahern suffered another shock from which he may not have recovered. Sr. Peter Claver was transferred to Alabama to head another project for her order. When she told Ahern of her impending departure "it was a terrible blow, it was a terrible blow for me and for him. He said that he hoped that I'd save my soul. He thought that I wanted to leave and it was the greatest crucifixion that I've ever gone through for them to take me out of the black work. And he had no comprehension."[97] First Duffy and then Sr. Peter Claver left Ahern to undertake work that was fraught with difficulties on every side. Ahern was wearing down.

Ahern Leaves Queen of Angels

In December of 1935, at the end of his monthly cover letter to McLaughlin, Ahern suggested that it was no longer necessary to pass on such detailed mission reports. At that point, the comprehensive reports detailing the activities of Queen of Angels ended, and unfortunately none of Ahern's correspondence to the vicar-general are available after 1935.

The years from 1930 to 1940 were full of energy and purpose. The surviving tenth anniversary souvenir brochure of 1940 registered the sense of history and pride the people felt about themselves and their clerical and lay leadership. In that year, Gillard cited 4,553 black Catholics in the Newark archdiocese, up from a very generous count of 900 in 1928.[98] All five missions were operating, the novenas were overflowing as were the many lay societies, activities, and organizations. The Holy Name Society marched proudly through the Newark streets in the annual Holy Name Parade, with Father Ahern in top hat leading the men of the parish. Mr.

William O'Laughlin led the Queen of Angels' band, resplendent in the uniforms donated by the auxiliary guilds.[99]

The African American youth of Queen of Angels were involved in myriad activities and organizations, and young white men attended the novenas seeking involvement at Queen of Angels. A group of them sat on the stairs when the novena crowds overflowed the church; the sisters called them "the boys on the back stairs." They would linger at the mission after the novenas or come to the mission on their days off asking for things to do. The sisters formed them into a special auxiliary group and included them in the corporal and spiritual works of mercy. "It was Catholic. It was something we were doing for the poor," explained Sr. Francis Damien.[100]

Sometime in the 1940s Sr. Peter Claver received a letter from Fr. Joseph Shanley telling her that Ahern had left Queen of Angels, and he urged her to contact Ahern again. Sister recalled, "it was Shanley that tried to make the connection for us, to mend that big breach that [was] caused by my being sent away from the mission. And Fr. Shanley wrote me and told me that [Ahern] gave up the black work."[101]

Most likely at his own request, on December 26, 1940, Ahern was appointed pastor of the old and established Irish parish of St. Columba's in Newark.[102] Oral tradition indicates that he gave up the work in an official capacity but continued to work in the background, meeting at St. Columba's rectory with Fr. John LaFarge and other members of the Clergy Conference on Negro Welfare.[103]

Sometime in 1945 Ethel Wright died. The parish's records are unusually sketchy regarding the statistics: the exact month and day are not clearly noted, and only "60+" indicate her age. We are not given the date or place of birth. A widow (her husband, Osmond, died in 1935), she died at her home on Morris Avenue in Newark. Father Brendan noted in the church records only that she was the sister of Marcella Thompson, the first housekeeper for Queen of Angels.[104]

How ironic that the person who refused to give up on the idea of a colored church and was greatly responsible for Queen of Angels died in obscurity. I can only conjecture that Mrs. Wright was so self-effacing that her contribution was soon forgotten. The eulogy that Monsignor Duffy spoke for Lucy Mulligan at her funeral in 1933 applied much more fittingly to Wright. It was she who spent herself fighting for a church and a priest for her people, a struggle for which she was apparently never publicly recognized.

In 1945, the same year as Wright died and before Sr. Peter Claver could reestablish contact, Father Ahern died suddenly from a heart attack at the age of fifty-six. On September 13, 1945, fifteen years to the day after he baptized the first parishioner at Queen of Angels, Ahern was gone. He died fifteen years and four days after he appeared at Sister's door with his obedience from the bishop appointing him head of the colored work. It was too late to mend the fences, and it was too late for Ahern's dream church at St. Bridget's to become a reality.

5

On Pilgrimage to Justice

So our purpose comes to bother consciences, of witnessing and having your witness do its own ministry in the world.

—Monsignor John Egan

Struggling for the Dream

At Queen of Angels, the years from 1941 to 1957 were a time of staying afloat by selling off, closing down, consolidating, maintaining, and keeping the faith.[1] During that time, Queen of Angels and its new pastor, Joseph C. Lenihan, had to contend with financial constraints, the closing of several missions, and a relationship between parishioners and pastor that was often strained. Despite these problems, the population of Queen of Angels increased, and two missions, St. Peter Claver in Montclair and Holy Spirit in Orange, became independent parishes. From 1946 through 1954, the total population of Queen of Angels and its satellite churches numbered around 3,800 adults and children, or approximately 650 families.

The Novena of St. Jude had a consistent attendance of 3,000 per year until 1954, when it dropped to 700, and by 1958, to only 250. Many blacks were faithful to the novena, but whites accounted for more than fifty percent of its attendees. As Newark began to change when whites, and particularly Italians, moved to the suburbs in the 1950s and 1960s, the novena numbers dropped considerably.[2] Under adverse circumstances, Queen of Angels baptized close to 200 persons per year for a good part of this period (see tables in appendix 1), but Fr. Lenihan faced added problems.

The Downside of Mission

Four elements seem to have contributed to the difficulties Lenihan and Queen of Angels faced from 1945 to 1957. First, funding dried up because the grant from the Conservation of the Faith that Bishop Walsh made available to the colored missions was no longer forthcoming, although it is not certain when it was stopped or why. At one point, Lenihan borrowed several thousand dollars from St. Teresa's, an affluent suburban parish where his brother, Msgr. John P. Lenihan, was pastor.[3]

The second, and possibly equally damaging reason, was that the channel of motivated leadership from the grass roots to the episcopal level was seriously impaired. In this regard, it is important to keep in mind the devastation that Ahern felt at Duffy's departure, and to recall the insight of Fr. John LaFarge that those who worked in African American missions "languished" as much from "general apathy" as from overt hostility, and that, essentially, the work engendered "little or no appeal to the average American Catholic's sympathy or understanding."[4]

Lenihan did not have a person on the episcopal level who supported him in the manner that Duffy supported Ahern, and the Trinitarian sisters, whose work was all-encompassing, had been reduced to two by the 1950s, and at times none at all. The circumstances that existed in 1930 with the initiation of Queen of Angels simply was never duplicated, and probably could never be duplicated. The chain of energy, motivation, and cooperation that existed then did not surface in quite that way ever again in the church's history. The Clergy Conference on Negro Welfare wanted to make people "colored conscious" at every level of the church, but they made little headway in that regard.

The third nagging predicament that plagued the enterprise at Queen of Angels was mission status itself. The critics of separate missions for the "colored," "Negroes," or "blacks" (from each of the eras that those labels designate) realized that disadvantage. Self-separation was preferred to alienation by founders like Ethel Wright, but when the church created a separate colored church, it, in effect, sanctioned their separation. Was it a "no-win" situation? Acquiescing to that choice represented the failure on the part of Catholic Church leadership to change the hearts and minds of the person in the pew to accept African Americans fully and without reservation. If that had been accomplished in 1930, indeed, if it *could* have been accomplished, there would have been no reason for Queen of Angels.

Fourth, and compounding all of these developments, even though Lenihan had a desire to do great things, he appeared to lack the personal resources to accomplish them. First of all, he did not have Ahern's charisma or gregarious nature. And, second, he left a lasting impression with his parishioners that he did not listen to them. At times he even seemed to act against himself. For example, he asked Walter Brown to leave Queen of Angels when Brown insisted on offering his viewpoint on things to be done at Queen of Angels. Accustomed to independent thinking, he and his very active family often questioned Lenihan's decisions, wreaking havoc with the priest's authoritarian administrative style. "[Lenihan] didn't like anybody questioning what he was going to do . . . He expected me to help him, but every time he wanted to do something, he had to buck me and (my relatives) the O'Laughlin's. So that's when he said that the Church can do very well without me, and . . . I went up to Holy Spirit [Church]."[5] But on the other hand, many years later, Brown discovered that Lenihan had secretly paid for his tuition to Seton Hall Prep.[6]

Some parishioners appreciated Lenihan's complexity, Brown among them; they abided and worked with him for a number of years. Two of the people I interviewed that genuinely liked him, Ruby Jones and Nathaniel Potts, are also well known in the community as forceful and direct people.[7] Perhaps the measure of autonomy that the people enjoyed under Ahern, and would later obtain under Fr. Thomas Carey, contributed to the more pleasant legacies they left behind. And perhaps Lenihan's contribution is even greater, considering his liabilities.

But regardless of the style of the person who administered Queen of Angels, St. Peter Claver, and Holy Spirit, the job was monumental, stress producing, and exhausting. The reality always entailed doing too much with too little. The social needs were great, and as Ahern discovered, spiritual and financial support from fellow priests and the diocese was tested and often found wanting. With Duffy and McLaughlin gone, the mission seems to have lost its episcopal advocate. And in 1952, Archbishop Walsh died, and with him the final hierarchical connection to the foundational years at Queen of Angels.[8] His successor, Thomas Boland, appointed in 1952 and installed in 1953, had, at times, a strained and even volatile relationship with Queen of Angels during his years as archbishop.

A Struggle for Survival

For many years the parish had no school or rectory. During all of Ahern's time, the priests lived either on Tenth Street or Court Street, several blocks from the church. In 1942, Lenihan made the decision to purchase a Presbyterian church and rectory in Orange for Holy Spirit Parish and made it the center of operations for all the churches.[9] From 1942 until 1948 the priests commuted between Holy Spirit in Orange to Queen of Angels in Newark and to St. Peter Claver in Montclair. The Trinitarians eventually moved their cenacle to Orange near Holy Spirit Church and commuted to their assigned territories from there. Lenihan closed the St. Thomas Mission in the Third Ward in 1944, the Mother Boniface Mission in Elizabeth in 1947, and sold the property for the St. John's Mission in the Ironbound Section on October 31, 1949.[10] One wonders what could have happened to the experience of Queen of Angels if he would not have found it necessary to close these missions and terminate the access they provided in those areas.

Also, a bizarre reversal of roles occurred with this change of residence. In the Official Catholic Directory, Queen of Angels, the mother church for almost twenty years was attended by Holy Spirit Church. The mother church became the daughter for seven years. The effect of this situation on Queen of Angels and St. Peter Claver is difficult to measure, but it must have been disheartening to both priests and parishioners to observe other Catholic parishes with rectories and schools while they were without. With no clergy close at hand to attend to the constant needs of the parishioners, they would have felt even more abandoned. "The move seems to have created a gap between the clergy and their flock in Newark. However, the efforts of the Trinitarians sisters tended to bridge the gap to a great extent."[11] Finally in 1948, Lenihan purchased a rectory across the street from the church at 230 Academy Street. Fr. Paul Hayes joined Lenihan as his assistant from 1949 to 1951. This was the same Paul Hayes who built the darkroom for the Trinitarian sisters when he was a high school student in order to develop pictures for publication in the local newspapers.[12]

During the 1950s many of Queen of Angels' original programs and activities fell by the wayside. The number of ministerial staff remained about the same, but Holy Spirit and St. Peter Claver were full parishes now, requiring the presence of priests to celebrate Mass, and to triple the programs on the various premises.[13] Somehow, the momentum of those original years could not be sustained.

A small but noteworthy handwritten letter has survived, dated July 13, 1955, illustrating the number of parish functions and personnel that had been eliminated. The letter was signed by George J. Marshall, the president of the Holy Name Society, and Winifred Van Doren, the president of the Rosary Society, on behalf of their organizations and the Little Flower Guild.

It presented eight "suggestions to Monsignor Lenihan, our Pastor: (1) A Youth Program (2) Boy Scout Troop (3) Have Social Affairs (4) We need more than one sister (5) We would like the Summer School continued (6) We need a Sexton (7) Playground equipment (8) Children's Choir at 9:00 A.M. Mass."[14] Every item on the list had been part of the parish from the beginning, and now the people were forced to band together to petition for them, hoping that the pastor would restore what they had had under Ahern's tenure. At Lenihan's request, Ruby Jones started a Girl Scout troop and helped with the catechism classes. She and other laypeople did the best they could under difficult circumstances, but with a feeling of little support from the diocese.[15]

In the 1950s, even though it was not official diocesan policy, Lenihan began treating Queen of Angels as if it were a territorial parish rather than the mission that it was. He insisted that parishioners who lived within the boundaries of another parish receive their sacraments there.[16] It is difficult to know what his motivation was. Maybe he felt as many others did that a separate church for African Americans simply would not do. But his policy presented his parishioners with a dilemma, because they were not or did not feel welcome in many white neighborhood churches. Consequently, Lenihan's stand on the issue created a sense of anxiety rather than acceptance.

To complicate matters even more, Queen of Angels did not have a school and they were reduced to only one Trinitarian sister for catechism classes. Parishioners who wished a Catholic parochial education for their children had to send them to another parish. In addition, the standard parish mandate demanded that families attend the church where their children went to school. Therefore, parents had to attend both churches if they wanted to remain faithful to Queen of Angels.

And some did just that. Elma Thornton Bateman, who had been baptized at Queen of Angels as a child, lived with her three children in Blessed Sacrament parish. She did not want to have to choose between her children's Catholic education and her affiliation to her lifelong faith community. Consequently, during the time that her three children attended Blessed Sacrament school, she took them to 8:00 Mass there and then traveled to Queen of Angels for the 10:00 Mass. Not all parishioners could make the sacrifice, and they left Queen of Angels for their children's school parish.[17]

At the end of 1956 Lenihan left the parish for an extended vacation to Ireland, and when he returned he was sent to St. Joseph's Parish.[18] Fr. Patrick Trainor, an assistant at St. Patrick's parish, was assigned to Queen of Angels pro tempore on March 1, 1957, but the situation was not as simple as that piece of recorded detail implies.[19]

After Lenihan left, Queen of Angels had to request a priest on a regular basis to celebrate Sunday Mass and hear confessions. Not believing that the chancery would comply with a woman's request, Ruby Jones asked one of the men from the Holy Names Society to make the call. This state of affairs gave her the feeling that the closing of Queen of Angels was imminent. At this juncture in Queen of Angels' history, when Lenihan was gone and no priest replaced him permanently, the community had a feeling of abandonment, a recurring experience in the history of the parish.[20] Just as they were able to organize and function before they acquired their parish, they carried on without a pastor—at least for a while. Their tenacity demonstrated a confidence in their identity and a refusal to relinquish their piece of the Catholic landscape.

A Mecca for Civil Rights

The story of Queen of Angels in the next fifteen years is the kind that is difficult to envision in the cynical, self-conscious, and scandal-obsessed twenty-first century. The actions and responses of the players seem almost naive to us now. It is a story—as is possibly the entire history of Queen of Angels—that seems more legend or tale than reality. It is doubtful that what occurred in the 1960s and early 1970s could be reproduced today, with its newness and sense of adventure into the unknown. And at times it is not certain if we are much better for its playing out. With few exceptions, we seem disconnected from the fervor, boldness, and passion of those days when respected people risked reputations and went to jail for their convictions. They were days that, for good or ill, may never be seen again.

Fr. Thomas Carey arrived at Queen of Angels at 237 Academy Street in Newark on September 26, 1957, to assume the position of administrator.[21] Although he found the church "very simple, but very pretty," other conditions of the property betrayed a sense of desolation to the newly arrived priest. The rectory that Lenihan had purchased in 1947 contained almost no furniture; a large cardboard box functioned as a kitchen table. "There was nothing there, except the people," Carey said. "The people stayed. Amazingly."[22] Later, after he presided at the two Sunday Masses, he looked at the fifty-four-dollar collection and wondered how he would be able to run a parish on such a paltry sum. The task must have seemed particularly daunting considering the population was numbered at 300 families—800 adults and 250 children.[23]

The Fire

Initially, Carey was kept busy maintaining the activities of the parish, including the Novena to St. Jude every Thursday, and getting to know his parishioners and the community. He and his first assistant, Fr. Wilfrid C. Yeo, began to devise many ways to both improve the educational and social condition of the people and to bring in public and private funding to do so. On July 10, 1958, less than a year after Carey transferred to Queen of Angels, something happened that added further hardship to the beleaguered parish. The pretty little church burned to the ground, leaving the struggling parish in the reverse position of having a rectory but no church. The parish had fire insurance with approximately $150,000, but the archdiocese called in a loan for $60,000 that was dispersed to Queen of Angels from the Conservation of the Faith to establish the initial missions.[24]

The rectory across the street from the church occupied the middle building of a three-building complex. The parish improvised a chapel in one of the buildings next to the rectory where the parish met for Mass for the next four years. A local church donated some pews, but because of the small size of the room, people often had to stand in the hall and sometimes out on the sidewalk. An inconvenient predicament, to say the least, but Ruby Jones remembered the parishioners enduring the adversity with stoicism. "What else was there to do?"[25]

At this juncture, the concept of mission status again surfaced. After the fire destroyed Queen of Angels church, Carey wrote a letter to Archbishop Thomas A. Boland offering his views on what to do with the mission of Queen of Angels "in light of the present nationwide interest in the problem of integrating Negroes into full participation of American and Catholic life."[26] Carey suggested that it would be a mistake to rebuild Queen of Angels church and perpetuate the mission to Negroes. For one thing, the wide disbursement of Negroes throughout the city made it impossible for the priests of one church to "render proper spiritual care." Carey found himself traveling for hours to visit a sick parishioner in Union County, and the parishioners had to travel great distances as well. But in addition to these circumstances, he argued that

> [s]egregation is an outmoded social and moral principle. It impedes the conversion of the Negro to Catholicism, especially among the young, thinking Negro. Therefore, to rebuild Queen of Angels Church would merely continue patterns which perhaps a generation ago might have been accepted but today would be construed as

> perpetuating the inequalities which accompany segregation. There should be no segregation among Catholics where no reason for segregation exists. Moreover, a segregated church can be an excuse for some pastors to be delinquent in their obligation to the souls of colored in their own parish.[27]

Carey echoed the objections that had been voiced by others in Newark and elsewhere for years, but the archbishop never responded to Carey's letter, and from this Carey assumed that the idea of closing Queen of Angels was never seriously entertained.[28] Eventually the poor communication on these issues would lead to one of the most controversial events in the history of the archdiocese of Newark. Left on his own, Carey filed away his copy of the letter, along with his opinions on the topic, and continued at Queen of Angels.

A New Church and School, Finally

In 1954 Newark had redrawn its wards from numbered designations to directional wards of North, South, East, West, and Central. The Central Ward included the old Third Ward that Ahern wanted to avoid as a location for the church in the 1930s. It also included areas that white flight transformed to more solid blocks of African Americans as Newark's white residents moved to the suburbs.

In the middle of the Central Ward, surrounded by high-rise apartment projects populated mostly by African Americans, stood a German Church called St. Peter's. By 1959, the community had lost most of its parishioners to either the perimeter of the city or to surrounding suburbs. St. Peter's German parishioners moved mainly to Irvington and worshipped at St. Peter's Chapel and Orphanage. That year, St. Peter's parish in Newark asked the churchless Queen of Angels to share their church with them each Sunday. Two Masses were offered for Queen of Angel's parishioners and one for St. Peter's.

On July 1, 1962, the German parish vacated their nineteenth-century complex of buildings and gave them to Queen of Angels permanently, and the German parishioners moved to Irvington.[29] Suddenly, Queen of Angels was in possession of a church, school, convent, rectory, and activities building.

Using the remainder of the money from Queen of Angels' fire insurance, the men of the parish made extensive renovations to the school building, including a new electrical system and lights, new plumbing, two new bathrooms, and new flooring. In addition, all of the buildings received a new white weatherproof brick facing, which gave them the distinctive look that remains today.[30]

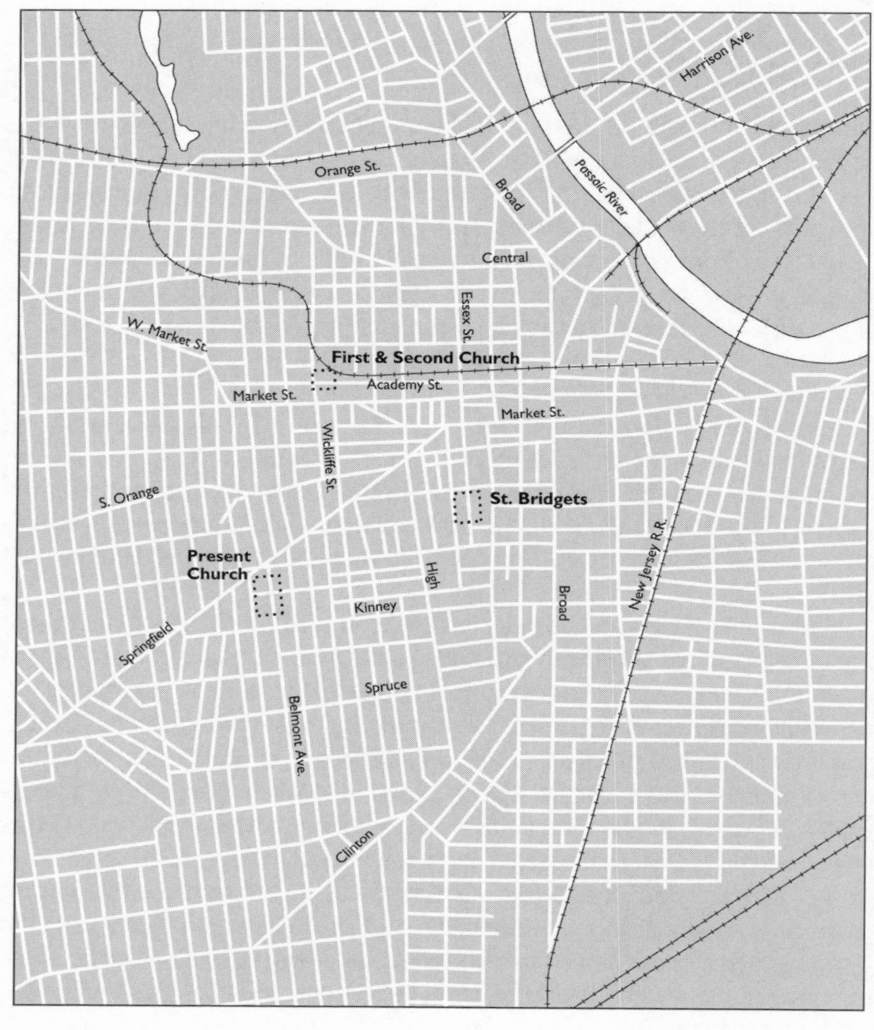

Newark, 1912. A. St. Bridget's on Plane Street. B. First Church Building, Wicliffe and Market Streets. C. Second Church Building, 24 E. Academy Street. D. Present Church, 44 Belmont Avenue, now Irvine Turner Blvd. Newark Public Library.

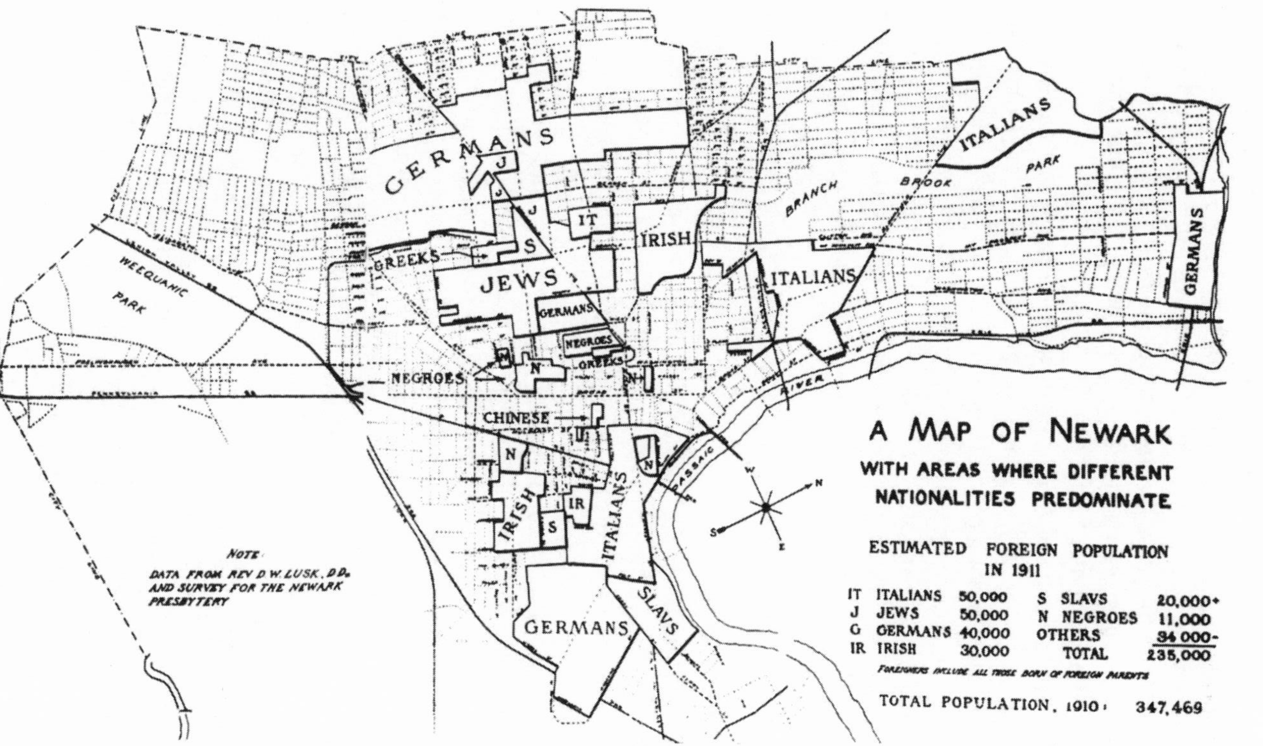

Directory of Social Agencies, *issued 1912, mapped areas of foreign born.*

Minority population distribution in Newark, 1911. Compiled by A. W. MacDougal and published through the Initiative of the Bureau of Associated Charities, with the cooperation of the other private charitable organizations of the city.

With a school building at their disposal, Queen of Angels opened its first elementary school in its thirty-three-year history. The first year, Carey acted as administrator of the school and hired lay teachers. In 1963, the Oblate Sisters of Providence, an African American religious order, agreed to staff the school. Carey established a tuition-free policy and required that the families pay only for their children's uniforms.[31]

The school placed Queen of Angels on a par with most other parishes in the archdiocese, and it opened a venue to the black community that had diminished with the shrinking of Trinitarian educational involvement in the 1930s when they provided various programs from prekindergarten to adult.

In 1968, Lewis Roland became the first black, non-Catholic layman to head a parochial school in New Jersey when he was hired as the principal of Queen of Angels.[32] Another black teacher, George Curetan, who was later selected as New Jersey Teacher of the Year in 1970, developed a unique reading program for the school.[33]

To Bother Consciences

By 1968 Queen of Angels had five priests: Thomas Carey, Joseph A. Stulb, Thomas J. Comerford, William J. Linder, and John J. Maloney. The priests who came to Queen of Angels in the 1960s were those who were drawn by its reputation as an innovative parish.

Fr. Thomas Comerford's experience is probably representative of many other priests at Queen of Angels and other black inner-city parishes of the time. He had been placed as a curate (assistant to the pastor) in a large, middle-class Irish parish near Seton Hall University. It was a comfortable position for a priest of the archdiocese, and in the context of the 1960s, it was an establishment position. With the Civil Rights movement intruding on the complacency of many, and the Second Vatican Council blowing winds of spiritual revolution through the church, Comerford began rethinking his role as a priest. The Second Vatican Council (1962–65), a gathering in Rome of Catholic bishops, theologians, and Catholic and non-Catholic observers from all over the world opened the church to cataclysmic changes that reverberated with incredible power. No Catholic was unaffected by the council.

In addition to the larger context of the 1960s and Vatican Council II, a seemingly small incident occurred that was a turning point for Comerford. Possibly to discourage any ideas his young cleric might have, the pastor directed him never to use the word *Negro* from the pulpit. But rather than squelch revolutionary views, the pastor's mandate had the opposite effect for Comerford. In the summer of 1966, he traveled to California to study with moral theologian Bernard Häring. Delving into the new theology that arose from Vatican II, Comerford felt changed and charged with a new approach to his ministry. When he returned to Newark, he resolved to find an opportunity to concretize his new ideas. For one thing, he wanted to speak and work openly for social justice. And that meant Queen of Angels. After interviewing with both Fr. William Linder, who had been his classmate in the seminary, and Carey, Comerford requested a transfer.

In 1968, a few months after the Newark riots, Comerford took a bus ride from the affluent suburbs where he grew up and worked as a priest. He watched the landscape turn from lovely to poor, neglected, and sad. He was not sure what to expect from the new path he had chosen for himself.

Things were different at Queen of Angels, and not simply the landscape. From the very first day he noticed an uncommon administrative style from Tom Carey. He "didn't claim he knew everything, but was willing to try anything that you felt was going to help the people." He was supportive of his assistant priests, willing to delegate responsibility to others, and encouraged innovative methods. Compared to the middle-class affluence of the parish he left, Queen of Angels was "a real step down, but in terms of spirit and a happy way of living, it was much better at Queen of Angels." In a real sense, Comerford finally felt that the purpose for his ordination was being fulfilled.[34]

The innovations the clergy introduced to the parish pushed the baptismal numbers back to the peak years of Ahern and Lenihan. Parishioner Joyce Smith Carter remembered: "We had at that point about five very, very young, energetic priests. We had, of course, Tom Carey, Bill Linder, Jack Maloney, Tom Comerford and another priest named Jim McManus [1969]. Each of them was gifted in their own way, but each of them had a strong commitment to social justice and so they began to speak to what they saw as the needs in terms of housing and education."[35]

In a sense, the parishioners of Queen of Angels and the people of the surrounding community contributed to and lived out concretely what Martin Luther King Jr. called the emergence of a "new Negro . . . with a new sense of dignity and identity."[36] Queen of Angels began a process of emergence from a mission church, a receiving church and a place of refuge, to a giving and deciding church—a Mecca, as some have called it, and formation center for civil rights and community activist leaders.[37]

Praxis and the People of God

Why did Queen of Angels take the shape it did? One of the central reasons can be found in the ethos of the parish that both fed into and absorbed the spirit of the 1960s. It was distinctively open to change, challenged established authority, and was a leader in civil rights and social justice issues. The mission model that proved effective but covert in the 1930s was absorbed into a larger cultural revolution where it seemed that everyone was on a mission. And with the roots of civil rights that were planted in the black church, African American leaders like Martin Luther King defined the high moral ground, challenging other religious institutions to follow. Queen of Angels wanted to and worked to meet the challenge.

From the beginning of its preecclesial history, strong laypeople led Queen of Angels, but once it was formed as an official church, its pastor established its boundaries. In a sense, Carey led the parish beyond boundaries. As a pastor, he anticipated the Second Vatican Council's document called *Gaudium et Spes*, which asked that the people of God "listen to and distinguish the many voices of our times" and "interpret them in the light of the divine word, in order that the revealed truth may be more deeply penetrated, better understood, and more suitably presented."[38]

Carey spurred the people to prophetic action that challenged the status quo when it defended or ignored injustice. In this very different era from the 1930s, the social programs initiated at Queen of Angels were not informed as much by an evangelistic agenda as they were by liberation theology's preferential option for the poor. Priestly concern for personal salvation, specifically of the exclusivistic and triumphalist variety, was subordinated to the gospel call of praxis: to not merely believe as Christians, but to put into practice what one has heard by helping the poor and oppressed. Accommodation to societal marginalization was rejected and replaced by the goal of helping the marginalized to "become the agents of their own destiny."[39] Carey's maxim was, "If it's good for the people, you can do it."[40]

In addition to anticipating Vatican II and liberation theology, Queen of Angels concretized Martin Luther King's philosophy of nonviolent activism, which he developed during his time at Morehouse College and Brown University. He applied it when he led the first test case against bus segregation in the South, when, in Montgomery, Alabama, the now famous and revered Mrs. Rosa Parks became the center of the 381-day bus boycott that lasted from December 1955 to December 1956.

These events reverberated to Queen of Angels as it did all over the world. Carey and his ministerial team of clergy and women religious heard King's vision articulated at the March on Washington on August 28, 1963. Carey, Linder, Comerford, and busloads of people from Queen of Angels were among the 250,000 blacks and whites in the crowd when King gave his "I Have a Dream" speech. They heard him declare that the destiny of whites was tied up with the destiny of blacks. King spoke about "equal opportunity, [and] the equitable distribution of privileges and property." He wanted to do something to bring about "a time when gifts and resources are publicly shared, the dignity and worth of all persons are affirmed, [and] where decision-making responsibilities are publicly shared." King longed for the "beloved community," shaped in "concrete social, political, and economic terms."[41]

In a paper called "The Spirit of Non-Violence and the Spirit of Freedom: What It Is and Why We Support It," Carey articulated his complete adherence to King's nonviolent crusade. He recognized the moral high ground that the movement established for society. He summarized his thoughts this way:

> Therefore, we recognize as morally justified, the legitimate aspirations of Negroes in the South to enjoy an unsegregated existence and to exercise the full rights of American citizenship.
>
> We hold, therefore, that those who have taken part in nonviolent demonstrations, whether as "sit-ins" or freedom riders, not only have been justified in taking these steps, but also have given the nation and the world an outstanding example of Christian forbearance in their refusal either to hate or to answer violence with violence.[42]

In due course, Carey quickly learned that the greatest resource of Queen of Angels was its steadfast and dedicated parishioners, and that African Americans would trust a priest and give him confidence more quickly than they would other whites. However, a priest could not maintain that position of trust and confidence if he did not take sides. He had to demonstrate that he was with them in a world that took sides against them continually. And if a priest was concerned about offending white sensibilities, the inner city was no place for him; in fact, "to bother consciences" was his purpose.[43] As difficult as it was to live and work in the inner city, he encountered the beauty of it in the people he met. He expressed his observations in 1966 when he said: "To most people the inner city is a cold, hard place. I live in the heart of the inner city, and while it is true it is cold and hard, the people there are also the most wonderful. Never before in my experience have I seen such spontaneous assistance for people in need as in the Central Ward of Newark."[44]

The people wanted to be involved, and had future plans, hope, and needs. "If we [the church] get out into the community and help the people with their plans, they will come to church and help us with ours. The worst thing is for a church to flee from the city and escape to the suburbs where the poor people won't benefit from it."[45]

Speaking for the voiceless, defending them, and aligning "himself with his people against power, money, influence, [and] evil" was an integral part of his role as priest. But the immediate and extremely important caveat was that although he spoke for them he always had to listen to them, "with ear and heart."[46] More than twenty years later, African American Archbishop James Lyke of Atlanta would use the same criteria when he said that the church must appoint pastors who "enter the Black community as listeners and learners in order to be good pastors and teachers in the faith."[47]

The ethos of the 1960s was tumultuous; people tore down the old and demanded change in every aspect of society. This contrasted with the 1930s, when Father Ahern's more paternalistic advocacy was accepted and the black establishment worked within the system to effect change rather than using overt protest. Ahern, as a white religious leader and advocate, drew his black parishioners into a paternalistic embrace. He saw himself as protecting them, advocating for them, wielding whatever influence he had in a white world to get what they needed. Ahern fashioned his rectory to be the "Father's house" where his people could go when the world cast them aside.[48]

By contrast, during Carey's era at Queen of Angels, African Americans began to expect whites to take a back seat in the struggle for justice. Like Ahern, Carey provided a space for the people to feel welcome, but perhaps more importantly, he created the width and breadth for them to think big and to accomplish things for themselves.[49] Ahern and Carey were very similar in the passion they brought to the work, and had Ahern lived in the 1960s, at least one parishioner felt that he would have been very "Carey-like" in his approach.[50]

In his paper "What Can Be Done by the Church for the Problems of the Inner City?" Carey stated that the first step toward helping the black community was for the church to change its paternalistic attitude. He stated, "The paternalistic approach is false. It creates an atmosphere where leadership cannot grow."[51] He specifically addressed the history of the clergy's attitude toward the use of authority: "Often as clerics, we feel we know what is best for the people, and so there might well develop a growing tendency to direct everything. We become self-appointed experts in almost all fields, and slowly but surely we refuse to trust anyone else with important decisions. Our long identification with the exertion of authority makes us almost incapable of recognizing the inherent right of all persons, acting either individually or collectively, to determine their own destiny."[52]

Essentially, Carey felt that his task was "to enable priests and people to dare good and great things for the spiritual and social well being of [their] community," because the church's role must be supportive rather than directive.[53] His posture toward his parishioners was that they could be themselves, and that the parish was theirs. He created a climate in which the church could grow.[54] This is not to say that a black parish did not require pastoral leadership; parishioners take their cue from their pastor. His power is formidable to encourage empowerment or to discourage it. As the pastor goes, so goes the parish.

Civil Rights Activities at Queen of Angels

From 1929 Queen of Angels had joined forces with many civil rights organizations. In the early preecclesial years, the Urban League worked with Monsignor Duffy, Sr. Peter Claver, and the first group of women—and later with Ahern. That tradition continued with Carey. The parish connected with several civil rights organizations: Carey was a board member of Newark's chapter of the National Association for the Advancement of Colored People (NAACP), and in the late 1960s Queen of Angels became Newark's headquarters for Martin Luther King's Southern Christian Leadership Conference (SCLC) and later his Poor People's Campaign.

Queen of Angels was at least one of the places where César Chávez stayed when he visited the New York area. Chávez started the National Farm Workers Association in 1962, and it merged with Dolores Huerta's Agricultural Workers Organizing Committee to form the United Farm Workers Organizing Committee, AFL-CIO (UFWOC), later known as the United Farm Workers.[55]

Queen of Angels' involvement with Martin Luther King's organizations demonstrated the radical posture of the parish. This is true particularly in regard to the Poor People's Campaign, which was quite unpopular even with those close to King.[56] Around 1964 Queen of Angels became the SCLC headquarters in Newark by default. The parish was not SCLC's first choice for its home base, but it settled on Queen of Angels after the organization found no black churches willing to accept the role.[57] Similarly, when King was setting up his advance teams for the Poor People's Campaign, Herman Jenkins, SCLC's organizational person, asked for assistance from several black churches first. When they turned him down, Queen of Angels became the Poor People's Campaign's East Coast Caravan for New Jersey with Fr. William Linder as its director.[58]

On the whole, many black church leaders in Newark and around the country kept their distance from King. As in the South, King had to overcome the reticence of black leaders "who felt they were being pulled into something that they had not helped to organize."[59] He was viewed as a troublemaker and an interloper, especially in the North. After years of engendering the goodwill of white civic leaders, black leaders did not want to be marginalized even further by overtly affiliating with King. Many black ministers in Newark offered their churches for meetings, but they would seldom go beyond that in their involvement.[60] Possibly, as James Scott suggested, the priests at Queen of Angels had less to lose because they had the power of the Catholic Church behind them, while African American churches were alone and at the mercy of a white city government backed up by a white police force.[61]

Under Fr. William Linder, high school and college students belonging to the Christian Worker Movement and the Christian Student Movement staffed a room with sixteen telephones, where they provided organizational and civil rights work for the parish and the Newark community, especially civil rights strategy and legal groundwork. They performed clerical activities, did research, and took statements from people who came to Queen of Angels looking for legal redress when they were discriminated against.[62]

In the fall of 1967, two of these young people, Joyce Smith and Dora Barnes, were assigned as the advance team for the Poor People's Campaign. They were to raise funds, recruit volunteers, orchestrate events in Newark, and set up way stations in several churches for the volunteers on their way to Washington, D.C. On March 28, 1968, a week before King was murdered in Memphis, Tennessee, he paid a visit to Newark, stopping at Queen of Angels to make contact with Poor People's Campaign volunteers. One moment that Smith remembers vividly occurred on the staircase at Mount Pleasant Baptist Church on Hawthorne Avenue in Newark. As King descended the stairs he stopped for a moment to gaze at the stained glass window dominating the stairwell, and his eyes fell on the two young women following behind him. The moment of silence between them confirmed Smith's future life's work with youth at Quest-Essex Catholic Youth Organization in Newark's South Ward.[63]

Insulated by Color and Collar

Not to be counted among those white clergymen that King admonished for their "pious irrelevancies and sanctimonious trivialities," Carey uncharacteristically placed himself in the limelight when he rejected a Brotherhood Award from the New Jersey region of the National Conference of Christians and Jews in February 1966.[64] Carey refused the award because it was also offered to Charles W. Engelhard, chairman and president of Engelhard Industries, a company with large mining interests in the Union of South Africa. The NAACP and the American Committee on Africa had organized a protest against honoring Engelhard to bring to the fore the involvement of American corporations with that oppressive and apartheid government.

At the time Carey was a member of the board of directors of the Newark chapter of the NAACP, which set up a picket line outside the Robert Treat Hotel during the award's dinner. Other organizations that demonstrated were the Congress of Racial Equality (CORE), Students for a Democratic Society (SDS), the Newark Community Union Project (Tom Hayden's organization), the National Federation of Catholic Colleges, and the W. E. B. DuBois Clubs. Students came in busloads from Columbia, City College of New York, Queens College, Manhattan College, and the New School to join the Newark demonstrators led by Robert Curvin, the regional director of CORE.

By way of explanation, Carey said in an interview with the Newark archdiocesan newspaper, *The Advocate*, that "it would be very strange for me to cross picket lines by people protesting the deprivation of basic human rights."[65] When in his acceptance speech Engelhard defended himself by saying that, as a businessman, he was obligated to stay out of a country's internal politics, Carey said that he was even happier that he had not crossed the picket line.[66]

Carey's action thrust him into the public eye and caught the attention of black activists like Robert Curvin and Kenneth Gibson. Queen of Angels had evolved into a parish that was ahead of its time, a place of activism, and a resource for other activists that provided moral leadership in the Central Ward.[67] Carey associated with other ministers sympathetic to civil rights activities: the Reverend James Scott of Bethany Baptist; the Reverend Homer J. Tucker of Mount Zion Baptist Church; the Reverend John Collier of Israel Memorial African-Methodist Episcopal Church; and the Reverend Horace H. Hunt of First Baptist Peddie Memorial Church.[68]

James Scott's observation was that the Newark community considered Carey "a trumpet blower" and an "advocate for equality and justice." His sense of "identity with the black community was almost total, as was their identification with him."[69] This is not to say that he could or wanted to replace black leadership in the city. He did what he could as a white priest, but his self-perception included a keen awareness of the "limitations on any white leader in a Negro area." He conceded, "I'm insulated by my color and my collar."[70] Starting with the Engelhard protest, Carey directed Queen of Angels into a prophetic posture vis-à-vis the Catholic Church that continued to harden, and culminated in the explosive and controversial Newark Twenty confrontation with Archbishop Boland in January 1969.

Meeting Needs and Desires

Although Queen of Angels was always and remains a struggling parish, the maxim of "whatever is good for the people" launched many educational, medical, and artistic programs. In a letter to Cardinal Cushing of Boston, Carey said that going into debt seemed to be the only way to accomplish all of the "charitable, spiritual, educational and missionary" goals that the people Queen of Angels had for themselves and the surrounding community.[71]

Carey was pressured by the diocese to make good on the parish's obligation of $2,500 per year to the Retirement Plan of Diocesan Priests of Newark established by Archbishop Boland in December 1968. He responded to Msgr. Edward P. Looney why he could not pay Queen of Angels' contribution: "The fact is that five priests here are present because of missionary need of the area not the number of members in the congregation. Our Sunday collection runs in the neighborhood of $400 to 500.00 per Sunday. I doubt we could pay our bills and lose five weeks income plus four more if we count the diocesan assessments."[72] On paper, five priests for Queen of Angels appeared to be a generous amount. But because of the mission status of Queen of Angels, Carey (and Ahern in the past) was obligated to serve all blacks in the archdiocese. In the 1960s, within only the ten-block area surrounding Queen of Angels, was a population of approximately 80,000 African Americans. The number of priests assigned to the parish was based on that number and not the membership of the parish.

The Medical Clinic Re-Opens

The medical facilities available to the poor in the inner city of Newark had not improved a great deal from the depression years of the 1930s when Fr. Ahern opened a medical clinic that closed in the 1950s. African Americans dreaded being admitted to Martland Medical Center, the city hospital of Newark, because of its long waits, poor standards of health care, and lack of sensitivity to patients. Carey was struck by the people's dislike for the hospital when giving a lesson on Christ being born in a stable. He said to the class, "None of us can say we were born in a stable." One woman raised her hand and said she was born in a worse place. When asked where that was she said, "Martland."[73] The thought of the hospital struck fear in the hearts of those whose last recourse was to enter a place from which so many of their family and friends never returned.

Malnutrition was high among the inner-city children in Newark. The cold-water, kerosene-heated flats that still in existed in 1968 were breeding grounds for tuberculosis and other respiratory illnesses and were generally unfit for human habitation.[74] In addition, the poor were unable to afford ongoing medical care, which led to their crisis care pattern. According to a statement by inner-city priests in 1969, Catholic hospitals had begun turning away "the poor sick in great numbers," and clinical services were reduced to a minimum. The priests declared in stark language, "blue cross rather than the cross of Christ admits a patient in many instances."[75] Something needed to be done to address these problems.

To that end, Carey and Dr. Leon G. Smith, the director of medical education at St. Michael's Hospital, set up a medical clinic at Queen of Angels. Three times a week, Dr. Smith and two other staff specialists from St. Michael's, Dr. Thomas Scully and Dr. Virginia Malfitan, donated their services to the clinic.[76] On Monday and Tuesday nights and Saturday afternoons those with minor ailments came for treatment to the clinic. If the patients needed more extensive care, they were directed to the appropriate hospital. The church also operated a clinic for the aging at the Hayes Housing projects near Queen of Angels. Carey believed that the medical facilities were the most successful way to reach the people.[77]

Education

In 1964 a "Higher Achievement Program: A Year Round of Community Service" was developed in a collaborative effort between Queen of Angels and St. Peter's, the Jesuit college in Jersey City. It was based upon the perception that a large number of students from the inner city who were potential leaders capable of academic success were having difficulty "breaking the vicious cycle of poor education, poor employment, and poor family life."[78] Even if they had sufficient academic potential to go to college, they failed to do so "because of insufficient motivation, inadequate counselling and deficiency in verbal skills."[79] Even with the desire to go to college, it was felt that without special assistance they would be "unlikely to meet the single standard, [and] intense competition involved in entering college and doing well there."[80]

The program was for the summer with a year-round follow-up for boys going into the eleventh and twelfth grades. The goals were to (1) increase academic skills in reading, oral expression, and math; (2) increase educational motivation by an atmosphere of high expectations, small classes, and individual attention; (3) provide trips to colleges and universities; (4) cooperate with, encourage, advise, and learn from the parents of the students by visiting their homes and by a special program for the parents; and (5) create a peer group of inner-city students who would be positively orientated and share similar aspirations for higher education.[81] The goals were "animated by this spirit of self-activity," and "any sort of patronizing attitude [was] shunned," with "understanding, respect, acceptance and high expectations" informing the program.[82]

Also in 1965 a Summer Reading Improvement Program was offered by a joint effort of Queen of Angels and Seton Hall University. The program was funded by government antipoverty agencies and the Victoria Foundation, Inc., an organization in Montclair, New Jersey, that provides grants for education, neighborhood development, and urban activities for youth and families in Newark's inner city. The Summer Reading Improvement Program offered 177 elementary students several weeks of remedial reading instruction and was administered by Fr. William Linder of Queen of Angels and supervised by Joseph Zubko from the Department of Special Education of Seton Hall University.[83] Mrs. Mary Smith of the United Community Corporation assisted with the project as well. Smith would later emerge as the head of the very successful Babyland Nurseries.

Performing Arts

Elma Bateman was representative of many in the parish who came from a family tradition of appreciating poetry, music, and drama. After voicing a desire for such activity at Queen of Angels, Carey told her to think big, and as a result, in 1960 Queen of Angels initiated an annual theatrical event staging large-scale productions of Broadway shows and musical reviews. The Queen of Angels Players, as they called themselves, utilized professional directors and choreographers to stage their productions and drew on the parish and the local community to cast the shows. The parishioners had a dream of establishing a permanent performing arts center that did not materialize, but for ten years their efforts were a yearly event in Newark and the surrounding community.[84]

Queen of Angels Credit Union

To offer some solution to the economic difficulties of its parishioners, Queen of Angels established a credit union in 1959. Poor blacks were the victims of high interest credit plans to rent and purchase items, keeping them continually in debt. The credit union gave members the opportunity to save money and borrow at a reasonable rate, and to become educated in principles of money management. Carey contacted the Essex–West Hudson chapter of the New Jersey League of the Credit Union of North America (CUNA) for assistance in establishing a chapter at Queen of Angels. The lay parishioners were the officers and directors of the credit union, receiving the public relations support of the clergy.[85] The parish credit union continued at Queen of Angels until September 1993, when it merged with New Community Corporation's credit union.

The Predictable Insurrection

In 1938 the Newark Housing Authority (NHA) was established to meet the need for low-rent housing projects and to execute an urban renewal program for the city with the dual objective of slum clearance and the prevention of "further slum and blight through rehabilitation and conservation."[86] Of the 13,681 public housing units in the twenty-two cities of Essex and Union Counties, 10,769 units were in Newark. Sixty-five percent of Newark's housing projects were nonwhite. By 1970 Newark held a number of dubious records. It had the highest incidence of fires in the nation, the highest number of new tuberculosis cases of any city, and an aggregate death rate 35 percent above the national norm. One-third of the housing was substandard, and "the number of blacks employed above the janitorial-stock room level in Newark's chief industry—insurance—[had] scarcely progressed beyond tokenism."[87] One is reminded of the admonition in the Queen of Angels 1940 anniversary brochure demanding that Prudential and other Newark insurance companies hire black men, "or else." The "or else" they may have been warning about materialized in the 1960s.

The housing and economic problems of the inner city of Newark were building to a climax some felt coming. On June 30, 1966, the New Jersey

State Advisory Committee to the U.S. Commission on Civil Rights held an open meeting to gather information on the state of public housing in Newark. Among those who appeared to speak were both Msgr. Thomas Carey and CORE's Robert Curvin. Carey was troubled about Newark, describing the city as a boiling "pot on the stove," and was filled with apprehension "about things that might happen."[88]

Early in 1967, the Newark Priests' Group, an organization made up of inner-city priests, appointed a committee to "provide the background perspective required for decisions as to the involvement of the priests and Catholic institutions in contributing to the solutions of the problems facing the people."[89] Their report, *The Needs of the People of Newark and the Resources of the Archdiocese,* conveyed a sense of urgency regarding the city's housing, educational, employment, antipoverty, recreational, and health needs. The report suggested that the church in Newark "exercise its moral force," especially with people who would be inclined to invest financially in the city's future, and sponsor the funding of governmental monies to the city for housing and other areas.[90] No response to their appeal for action was forthcoming from the archdiocese as conditions worsened and frustrations mounted to the breaking point. Carey's uneasiness was, unfortunately, well founded.

On July 13, 1967, around the corner from Queen of Angels Church, Newark erupted in mayhem and violence. It was rumored that a cab driver, John Smith, had been beaten and then killed by police at the Fourth Precinct, which was in the shadow of the tall Hayes Housing Projects, one and one-half blocks from Queen of Angels. Robert Curvin; Kenneth Gibson; Timothy Still, president of United Community Corporation; John E. Porter Jr., of the NAACP; Philip Hutchings, field coordinator of the Student Nonviolent Coordinating Committee (SNCC); and James Threatt of the Newark Human Rights Commission all attempted to bring calm to the angry crowd that gathered outside of the police station. They gave up after they were threatened, pushed around, and heckled. Though he was the victim of some harassment, Curvin said, "It is an expression of long-felt pressures of powerlessness in the city . . . The people are fantastically aggrieved."[91]

What began as an angry crowd outside police headquarters turned into widespread destruction and the death of twenty-six people. Gov. Richard J. Hughes, police, and white activist Anthony Imperiale viewed the riots as an insurrection against the established governmental authorities, while blacks and those sympathetic to them preferred the term *rebellion* to indicate the oppressive circumstances contributing to the troubles.[92] Tellingly, *Life Magazine* called it "The Predictable Insurrection," a point of view shared by many, before and after the riots.[93] The Commission on Civil Disorder, appointed by Gov. Richard J. Hughes to study the causes of the July 1967 disturbances, rejected "any notion of a conspiracy"; instead it cited "many deep-rooted sources of unrest." The main cause was the fact that "city officials failed to see the dynamite on their doorstep."[94] Dynamite or Carey's boiling "pot on the stove," Newark ignored the warnings.[95]

Gov. Richard J. Hughes called a state of emergency and brought in the National Guard the next day to quell the disturbances, creating a state of siege in the city and contributing to greater polarization between police and citizens. For five days the front pages of Newark's newspapers counted battles, deaths, and wounded in Vietnam on one side of the page and in Newark on the other.

The National Guard conducted house-to-house searches, innocent people were beaten in retaliation for the riots, and looters were shot in the back with shotguns.[96] The rumor of snipers spread paranoia among people and guardsmen alike. State Troopers and National Guardsmen firing at snipers killed several innocent people who had hoped they were safe in their apartments. Some stores owned by African Americans were shot up in "a pattern of police action for which there [was] no possible justification."[97] Since most stores closed or were looted during the days when the state of emergency existed, the many residents of Newark were not able to obtain food. Suburban and inner-city energy was galvanized to bring staples through to the residents. Carey remembered how

> [a]ll the stores were burnt down and we were on the curfew, not only curfew, but we were surrounded by the National Guard. So people had no way of getting food. So we got truckloads of potatoes, Spam, milk, bread. And the poor people, we delivered the stuff to their door. Most of the kids did it, interestingly enough. And then Our Lady of the Lake in Verona . . . [the pastor] had kids go through the neighborhood collecting canned goods. They would leave them on the corner, and their fathers came around with trucks and picked them up and brought them to us . . . Lines were down the street and they would snake into the hall, and we would give them a basket full of food to take home; thousands of people in three days. And again, the kids did that. Our young people, the young teenagers. They were terrific, really.[98]

Queen of Angels and St. Bridget's parish acted as distribution centers for the $20,000 worth of donated food staples.[99]

Finally, Sunday night a community meeting was called at the Robert Treat Hotel attended by 600 people. They appointed a committee of six community leaders, of which Carey was one, to meet with the governor. The committee drafted a statement to present to the governor asking that the National Guard and the state troopers be removed. They called the governor to ask him to meet with them; he agreed to the meeting and instructed the committee to wait at the armory for him. The governor arrived at three o'clock in the morning, approved of the letter with a few minor alterations, and that same morning the guard and the state troopers were removed.[100]

In an editorial for *The Advocate,* July 20, 1967, Carey observed that the rioting made it obvious that "the Church had made very little headway in the Negro community." He called for priests to be placed in the seven parishes in the heart of the Negro community who had the desire and the ability to work there. He proposed that suburban parishes assist in the support of city parishes, that studies on urban development be conducted, and that the church assist in capturing the federal money that was slipping away because of the lack of programs to utilize them.[101]

On the same page of *The Advocate* as the above editorial was an article announcing a meeting of a group of priests who called themselves the "Priests of Riot-Torn Newark." Boland was asked to attend the meeting at Queen of Angels' rectory and he toured the area around the church.

In a six-page document addressed to Boland, the priests outlined the problems and some solutions. They suggested that a Department of Community Affairs and a Committee for Urban Planning be organized under the auspices of a Human Relations Committee and the Department of Urban Studies of Seton Hall University. These organizations could assess the needs of the inner cities of the archdiocese as a first step toward the practical goals they had outlined.[102]

The most salient aspect of this document was the priests' willingness at this point to name parishes guilty of neglect. They had become less and less diplomatic as the Newark environment disintegrated. In strong language they named the inner-city national parishes they felt demonstrated a lack of concern and icy indifference to the Negro community. Father Ahern's former parish, the traditionally Irish St. Columba's, "offered nothing in any manner, beyond an example of grave scandal and callous neglect of its own [black] people."[103] St. Antoninus, Good Counsel, St. Ann's, St. Rocco's, St. Stanislaus, and St. Stephen's were all accused of being "unfriendly sepulchres" to the Negro community that encircled them. The parishes', and that meant their pastors', actions and "condescending and casual interest" toward Negroes fostered the "obvious conclusion that if any interest in them [was] to come from the Catholic Church, it [was] to be sporadic and territorially spotted according to the zeal of the local priest, with no general supervision or authority in evidence."[104]

This was the essence of their complaint. They were well aware of which priests were friendly to the black community and which priests were not. And they watched as the indifferent pastors remained in their parishes, refusing to address racial issues and to educate their white parishioners in how to deal with the demographic and cultural changes in Newark. The city had become more and more black, but their presence was resented and feared by whites. The Priests of Riot-Torn Newark wanted something good to come out of the riots, but they were afraid the situation would only worsen unless the church stepped in and implemented the changes they felt needed to be made.

6

Moving beyond Pious Irrelevancies

This attitude of paternalistic tokenism, and at times even total indifference, have become stumbling blocks to our people.

—Declaration of Brotherhood to Our People, the Newark Twenty

The Evolution of Operation Understanding

There are those who say that nothing positive came out of the Newark riots of July 1967. Others contend that it was the beginning of real change in the city. Msgr. William Linder believes that New Community Corporation, the highly successful nonprofit housing organization of which he is director, evolved because of the heightened interest of whites generated by the riots.[1] Some believe it was a wakeup call, a sign to whites that they had to do something or Newark would go down. But even with the positive events that occurred after the riots, they produced such traumatic aftereffects that Newark became known as the county's most unlivable city. This perception has been slow to change, in spite of the clear improvements in Newark's recent past.[2]

Whether positive or negative, the reaction of whites was intense. They flooded real estate agents with calls wishing to sell their homes as soon as possible. Insurance companies canceled the policies of white shop owners who may have stayed in Newark even after being looted of thousands of dollars in merchandise, forcing them to exit the city. Hundreds of whites tried to purchase guns, and some residents policed their neighborhoods with shotguns. One self-described militiaman summed up his attitude toward

African Americans with: "We don't want them—they're dangerous. They have no feeling of love or what it's like to have a family."[3]

Negative attitudes toward blacks were reinforced by the actions of the few who acted out their anger in those July days. As Msgr. Richard M. McGuinness of St. Bridget's told *The Advocate:* "Only 5% of Newark's Negroes rioted, . . . [n]ow the biggest job will be to get the people in the suburbs to avoid blaming everybody, not to hold grudges, to love the Negro people and work with them."[4]

The North Ward Citizen Committee, a quasi-vigilante group headed by its president, Anthony Imperiale, did not seem inclined to fulfill McGuinness's wish. One of their answers to urban unrest was the adoption of a police canine corps. But recalling the images of dogs released on nonviolent civil rights marchers in southern cities, the concept did not sit well with Newark blacks or white advocates like Fr. Thomas Comerford at Queen of Angels.

A city council meeting was held to discuss the corps' implementation; Comerford and some Queen of Angels' parishioners went there to try to stop it. The meeting was attended mostly by white North Ward residents and Imperiale's North Ward Citizen Committee. It was a noisy affair filled with a hostile crowd. As Comerford made his way to the podium to give his point of view, he was assailed by blatant verbal hostility from Catholics who ordinarily would have been respectful toward a priest. He was shaken by it, but he spoke to the crowd. He wanted them to know why dogs were not only unnecessary but also ultimately would be instruments of more violence and degradation.

After the meeting he attempted to leave the premises but was surrounded by an irate crowd. For a moment he was not sure he would be allowed to leave unharmed. But Imperiale, watching from the sidelines, finally told the group to leave him alone. Thoroughly shaken by that time, Comerford drove to Queen of Angels' parking lot. At ten or eleven o'clock at night it was dark and empty, except for one parishioner who also was just returning from the meeting. It was Joe Chaneyfield, a black community leader who had over the years been Comerford's mentor, teaching him about the inner city and the black community. Chaneyfield walked up to the priest, looked at him, and in a quiet voice said, "Thanks, Father, for what you did for my people tonight."[5] Comerford was beginning to learn that Queen of Angels' parishioners did not expect that kind of public support from white folks. The experience moved Comerford closer to the people, and pushed him to engage in more public action on behalf of the black community.[6]

But not all reactions from whites were angry and negative. And here we have a very important mechanism that existed at Queen of Angels. An ethos of respect and dialogue between white ministry and black community encouraged a level of communication between African Americans and European Americans that extended out to the surrounding community. For years Monsignor Carey had encouraged the parishioners "to dare good and great things for the spiritual and social well-being of [their] community." And in so doing, they became a highly visible parish. Therefore, it was logical for white suburbanites to make contact with Queen of Angels in order to understand the problems in Newark. And they did so in great numbers. Calls from concerned white suburbanites flooded the Queen of Angels' telephone lines asking questions and offering assistance.[7] They wanted to know why the riots happened and what they could do to change things.

One of the organizations at Queen of Angels that was able to respond effectively was the Christian Family Movement under Comerford's direction. They decided to invite whites, often other Christian Family Movement members, to come to the parish to "discuss the causes of the Newark Rebellion and racial polarization."[8] To offer a clear and credible articulation of these issues, they asked Willie Wright, president of the United Afro-American Association and a Queen of Angels convert, to speak to the interracial meeting about Newark's inner city.[9]

Willie Wright was an African American activist who for years had publicly and persistently directed the attention of the white establishment to such problems as housing and unemployment in the inner city. He was the catalyst that led to Operation Understanding and the events that followed. In so doing, Wright was criticized from both sides. He was branded a subversive and watched by the police because of his public criticism of white treatment of blacks. But as a result of his involvement with the interracial Operation Understanding, black militants disavowed him as an ineffectual dupe of the white establishment.[10]

In Wright's speech to the group at Queen of Angels, he stated that if they were really interested in finding out what it was like to live in the ghetto, they should see it for themselves. He offered to take them on a tour of the area most affected by the civil disturbances. A group of about thirty people arrived for Wright's tour. Afterward, in response to his challenge to do more, a special committee was formed, co-chaired by African American George Marshall and white suburbanite Dave Foley. Eager to get beyond words, the committee planned a study day to discuss the problems and generate solutions. They extended invitations to suburban parishes to come to Queen of Angels on February 25, 1968.

The committee expected approximately 200 or 300 people, but the Day of Understanding, as it was called, attracted nearly 800 people seeking "personal involvement in the problems of the ghetto."[11] One hundred of them stood around the perimeter of the hall for the daylong event of speeches, discussions, and worship ending with a meal and socializing. Comerford recalled the excitement of the day: "We had all these people jammed into the hall and . . . Willie [Wright] gets up on the stage in front of all these people. Ken Gibson was there, before he became mayor, the Payne brothers, Donald who is a black congressman now, and his brother Bill Payne were there. Everybody was there. Willie says, 'If you really want to find out what it's like, come down here again and I'll take you on a tour.'"[12] Wright told the assembled crowd that they had to demonstrate their concern in some visible way to avert what he believed would be an inevitable armed confrontation between the races. For the second time, he offered to conduct whites on a goodwill tour of the ghetto, an action that "could be one of the best ways to prove our communities can get together."[13] After Wright spoke, David Foley suggested that the group march on Palm Sunday, April 7, 1968. He reasoned that if they could walk peacefully and in solidarity through the ghetto, they would achieve both educational and symbolic goals. The idea was greeted with an enthusiastic response.

Carey challenged the visitors to join Queen of Angels' parishioners in trying to solve the city's problems in a unified manner.[14] Volunteers handed out questionnaires to the attendees to determine their skills and interests and to match them with areas of need. At that meeting, Operation Understanding, an interracial group dedicated to improving conditions in Newark, was officially formed, and plans for the walk were set in motion.

The Walk for Understanding

Operation Understanding distributed press releases to the local newspapers to publicize the coming Palm Sunday Walk. Soon the American Jewish Committee endorsed the walk along with the Anti-defamation League of B'nai B'rith. In light of this development, and in a spirit of ecumenism, Operation Understanding changed the name from "Palm Sunday Walk" to the "Walk for Understanding." The United Community Corporation (the city's antipoverty agency headed by African American leader Timothy Still), the New Jersey Association of Laymen, and the Protestant State Council of Churches also endorsed the walk. Invitations were sent to Archbishop Boland, Auxiliary Bishops Joseph Costello and John J. Dougherty, Archbishop Terrence Cooke of the New York Archdiocese, Rabbi Joachim Prinz of Newark, Episcopal Bishop Leland Stark of Newark, and others. Operation Understanding, made up of active Catholics, had a readymade public relations network through their pulpits and church bulletins. The following announcement, read from the pulpit of every Catholic Church in the archdiocese ended with the following: "It is also hoped that through meeting person to person [and] the interpersonal relationships established during this walk, many people will feel a commitment to help relieve the situation in Newark through mutual assistance and most importantly, under black leadership. Do not bring banners, placards or signs of any kind—your presence is enough."[15] According to the organization, the purpose of the walk was not to protest the conditions, but to sensitize whites to their nature and to form a bond between black urbanites and white suburbanites in order to bridge the chasm that laid between them.

While these events were taking place in Newark, Martin Luther King Jr. had returned to Memphis from his tour of the New York area in order to lend his support to an energetic but besieged sanitation workers' strike. On the evening of Thursday, April 4, 1968, King was preparing to go to dinner with Ralph Abernathy, Jesse Jackson, John Lewis, and other civil rights workers. As he stood on the balcony of the Lorraine Motel, King was murdered by a sniper's bullet.

In reaction to the tragedy, many cities across the country met with bloody and devastating riots, but Newark encountered only minor disturbances. The night of King's murder, Police Director Dominick A. Spina brought militant white and black leaders together. Anthony Imperiale; poet, writer, and activist LeRoi Jones (later known as Amiri Baraka); Robert Curvin; and several others attended the meeting and, according to the *Star-Ledger,* achieved some kind of real dialogue.[16] Although some sporadic looting took place, Newark remained calm, an achievement that Governor Hughes accurately attributed to "the dedicated actions of community leaders, elected officials and private citizens."[17]

But many civic leaders, black and white, felt that the Walk for Understanding was ill-timed, inviting the violence that so far they had avoided. Mayor Addonizio called Carey and said, "I want you to cancel that march." Carey told him that he would think about it. After a while he called him back and said, "We're not canceling, we're going on with it."[18] At an emergency meeting at Queen of Angels, members of the community also spoke of their fears if the march took place. But African American leader Willie Wright stood behind Carey's decision, plans for the march went forward, and, politically, Mayor Addonizio would be forced to participate.[19]

A movement arose to extend the walk to honor King. The Greater Newark Chamber of Commerce awakened store managers at 3:00 A.M. on Friday morning to obtain black bunting to drape the photograph of King that would be carried in the walk. The chamber also provided 10,000 black-and-white "I Care" buttons to distribute to the interfaith marchers.[20] In preparation for an even greater number, they finally manufactured 10,000 more.[21]

On April 7, 1968, thousands of suburbanites streamed into Newark on chartered buses, in cars, on foot, and by public transportation. What began as a group of several hundred swelled to 25,000 people, approximately 40 percent black and 60 percent white. Led by Grand Marshall Joe Chaneyfield, thousands walked thirty blocks through the streets of Newark to the Essex County Court House on Market Street. Mayor Addonizio accompanied Willie Wright; in the absence of Archbishop Boland, Bishop John J. Dougherty represented the archdiocese.[22] Lay suburbanites Pat and David Foley, who were active in Operation Understanding, created the leading banner, on which was written: "Walk for Understanding / People Care." Two of their sons helped carry the banner. And not one violent or negative incident marred the day's proceedings.

At the podium in front of the courthouse Willie Wright said, "This is the most beautiful sight anywhere in the country."[23] Carey declared that Martin Luther King Jr. "was a Prophet, that is, one who speaks for God, a man who delivers God's messages to erring mankind about how God wants the wrongs corrected; men's lives adjusted. A prophet is a man who bothers people because when people are wrong they do not like to hear it."[24]

After the walk, the information Operation Understanding had gathered was used to identify volunteers and to develop programs to address issues such as illiteracy, voter registration, remedial education, and employment assistance. To continue the education of whites in the suburbs to the problems of the ghetto, a panel was organized consisting of Newarkers and suburbanites who traveled to several suburban parishes. They showed slides of the housing projects and discussed the conditions in Newark's inner city. Their aim was to start a dialogue between white suburbanites and inner-city blacks, and to spark an active interest in real solutions.

Approximately thirty-five members of Operation Understanding led the panel discussions in dozens of parishes and church organizations, Catholic, Protestant, and Jewish. Among the those who led the panels were Deacon

Al Bradsher, Bennie Fields, Richard Welch, Mary Smith, Gloria Guess, John Welch, Sarah Oliver, Eugene Johnson, George Marshall, Sr. M. Antonia, Frances Bowen and Tom McCudden. Members of St. Philomena's of Livingston, Little Flower Church of Berkeley Heights, St. Joseph Church in Oradell, Lutheran Church of the Savior in Paramus, Our Lady of Sorrows of South Orange, and dozens of other parishes and non-Catholic religious organizations participated in the panels, formed working groups, and worked with drug and employment programs in Newark. As of June 1969, approximately 4,000 people had attended the panel discussions. The fervor of their participation, as Monsignor Linder has indicated, lent a reality to the suburbanites' commitment that in great part led to the formation of New Community Corporation and Babyland Nurseries, and other programs.

Deacon Albert Bradsher from Queen of Angels and Daniel O'Connor from the suburbs co-chaired one of the panel discussions. A lifelong member of the Baptist Church, Bradsher, a World War II veteran who worked in auto repair until his retirement, was a convert to Catholicism in his adult years through the influence of Fr. Jack Maloney, a priest of Queen of Angels Parish. The concern that the parish showed him in difficult times drew him to the parish and to Catholicism, echoing the reasons for the success of Queen of Angels in the 1930s. With Fr. William Linder's encouragement, Bradsher eventually became one of the first black lay deacons to be ordained in the archdiocese of Newark. His work on the panel was some of the most important and satisfying of his life because of its impact on the city of Newark and its relationship with white suburbanites.[25]

In addition to the panel discussions, Operation Understanding began a "Vacation in the Suburbs" program to increase positive contact between blacks and whites on a personal level. In 1968, nearly eighty urban children spent a week or two in the summer with a suburban host family.[26]

The volunteers of Operation Understanding helped lead voter registration drives and successfully campaigned for the election of the first black mayor, Kenneth Gibson. In addition to tutoring students in various subjects and job training, several organizations pressured retail establishments and the major corporations of Newark to change their hiring practices. In affiliation with Rev. Jesse Jackson's Operation Bread Basket in Chicago, Newark's Social Progress and Developing Economy (SPADE) negotiated with the A&P food chain to hire black store managers, sell black products, use black contractors and lawyers, and transfer bank accounts to those sensitive to the community. Not long after the riots, all major supermarkets moved out of the Central Ward.[27]

Comunidades de Base: *A Concept for Newark*

In the summer of 1968, Fr. Tom Carey paid a visit to San Miguelito, an experimental community in Panama in Latin America. The Reverend Leon Mahon from the Chicago archdiocese organized *comunidades de base* (base communities) meant to empower lay leadership in small local groups.[28] Mahon's perception was that the church's mission was not just to save its members in the hereafter, but to help them realize the reality of being God's people in the here and now. To accomplish this, the local church was organized in small, manageable communities rather than in parishes of hundreds or thousands. "For community means knowing one another and sharing. It can happen only in face to face encounter. If dialogue on the gospel is essential in order that it reveals to us the meaning of our lives, we must encounter it in a relatively intimate setting. We can deepen our commitment only in the personalizing atmosphere of real community."[29] In that context, they could be a saved people rather than a savior people, who could bring the gospel to the world on spiritual and material levels.[30] Carey was so struck by Mahon's work and theology that he decided to attempt something similar in Newark. He sent the priests and sisters of Queen of Angels to San Miguelito for an eleven-week course of gospel-centered dialogue designed to form Christian leaders, especially among men. According to Tom Comerford, who was a trainee:

> [T]hey . . . met in the homes, they gathered people around and they talked. They divided themselves up into teams of a priest, a sister and then looked for lay deacons. They thought it was very important to focus on the male because if you didn't get the male in, you [would have] a church of women in Panama. So the priests primarily worked with the men and the sisters with the women . . . But the idea was in these little meetings in the homes, the people would talk about what was in their hearts, and that was really their expression of faith. And they weren't there to build buildings, but they were to build the church among the people. And they would have the central parish, but each team would have a district.[31]

Carey then asked each person from Queen of Angels who was trained in the base community approach to bring the knowledge back to Newark and utilize it somehow in the ministry of their choice. For example, Comerford chose housing; Linder chose the youth group and civil rights activities such as King's Southern Christian Leadership Conference and the Poor People's Campaign.

The Newark Twenty: Taking Sides

From 1968 to 1971, Newark and Queen of Angels were on fire. The city had its agitators like Tom Hayden of Students for a Democratic Society who organized in the ghetto and started the Newark Community Union Project, and LeRoi Jones and others. And although the Newark priests were not considered radical enough by some, a group called the Newark Twenty created the closest thing to a revolution that the Newark archdiocese ever experienced.[32]

For the Newark Twenty, revolution meant change, fearless risk-taking, antiestablishment thinking, and deviance from authority at the service of accomplishing what was seen as the greater immediate good. Any priest from the archdiocese who lived when the Newark Twenty events occurred feels strongly about what happened. Many, maybe most, think it was a mistake.

The twenty priests were caught up in the ethos of the 1960s zeal and Vatican II, and they were suffering from battle fatigue. After years of work, with small victories in a history littered with casualties, Carey and several other inner-city priests were tired. The tenor of their documents and letters are reminiscent of Ahern's before he left the work. Their determination to persevere had the hollow ring of those unsure of the measure of their endurance. Like Ahern, they looked to the episcopate for what they thought were the answers, but they did not get the answers they wanted. Unlike Ahern, the caution, obedience, and restraint of the 1930s was replaced with the protest, boldness, and blunt accusations of the 1960s.

By the end of 1968, the priests were beginning to help establish many programs, apparently sanctioned by the church but peripheral to it. They felt the archbishop was not doing enough to implement the needed changes in the Catholic community toward blacks or in the black community itself. They observed that Catholic inner-city schools, like St. Benedict's Prep, served "bussed-in whites" and "premier" blacks who could pay the tuition. And they saw that Catholic churches were still segregated, with blacks forced to "take busses for Mass on Sunday to come to parishes where they know they are accepted, bypassing 'normal' churches."[33] The church ignored the "deterioration of public and private housing," the "poor management of necessary federal monies," and made "minimal attempts at cooperating with the civic community in bringing such needed monies to the city."[34]

The inner-city priests believed that the diocese ignored their proposals and resented its reports on the conditions in Newark.[35] Archbishop Boland's "encouraging words of understanding" to the "long lines of Black Catholics" were not backed up with "implementation."[36] To use the words of Martin

Luther King that Carey was familiar with, they agonized over the "pious irrelevancies and sanctimonious trivialities" of their own white clergy, and Carey and his fellow priests vowed not to be lulled into what they considered to be Boland's lack of action.

Approximately sixty-four priests established the Newark Archdiocesan Association of Priests to consider and develop approaches to the problems of parish ministry, particularly in the cities, and to communicate these problems to the archbishop's office.[37] In December 1968, the Association of Priests drew up a list of demands concerning inner-city parishes and sent this along with a telegram to Archbishop Thomas Boland requesting that he meet with their representatives to discuss the demands. Probably reluctant to acquiesce to the "demands" of his priests in a growing power struggle, he did not do so.

Subsequently, twenty of the original sixty-four priests formed another group called Inner City Priests United for Christian Action.[38] They notified Boland in writing that they would go to the press with their demands if he did not agree to meet with them. After receiving no satisfactory response from the archbishop, they called a press conference at the Military Park Hotel in Newark on January 9, 1969. At the press conference they presented a thirteen-page letter to Archbishop Boland to over two hundred newspaper and television reporters. The next day the headlines spoke of racism in the church. The priests brought to public view what they perceived as episcopal authority blind and deaf to their calls for leadership and support. Carey and nineteen other priests from the inner city moved the discourse previously carried on in letters, memoranda, reports, and anonymous editorials to the media and signed their names to the declaration.[39]

The letter outlined the priests' view of what the "Official Church is saying" to their black brothers and sisters by its apathy, indifference, and lack of social involvement. "The Church is evolving," it said. "But the evolution, once a promising hope of revitalizing the Church, has slowed to a placid pace of promises and platitudes but little social involvement."[40]

To encapsulate some of those thirteen pages, they drew up a "Declaration of Brotherhood to Our People," in which they stated that they wanted to be independent "of the present attitude of the Archdiocese, since this attitude of paternalistic tokenism, and at times even total indifference, have become stumbling blocks to our people."[41] Some of the seven demands outlined were reiterations of written proposals in previous written communiqués to the archbishop. The following are those seven demands in abbreviated form:

1. The formation of a committee of experienced inner-city priests to work with an action council of black lay leaders. The two groups would meet weekly with the archbishop "until the present urgency is relieved."
2. The committee would prescreen all priests assigned to inner-city parishes to determine if they possessed the psychological attitudes for the work and the stamina to "tolerate the endless frustrations."
3. Instant transfer of all pastors proved by their actions to be ill-suited for work with black and Spanish people.
4. Abandon, pro tem, the parochial role, and "permit co-equal parish management to the team of priests assigned to the work."
5. Make all church property in black or near-black areas available to the people, including bowling alleys and playgrounds.
6. Recognize the need for experimentation in living the Christian life. "Know and approve their need to 'fight City Hall' on an individual personal basis—but—dignify their work with your approval."
7. Dissolve the Human Relations office in the diocese since it is a "Madison Avenue gimmick" explaining "why we do nothing in the inner city."[42]

They ended the letter with a defiant declaration of independence: "In closing, Archbishop Boland, it must be said that we anticipate your resentment of our public stance. We need you as our Brother in Christ, we respect you and your personal spiritual life, we honor you with our continued invitation to understand our compulsion to work actively, today, NOW, for the black community—*but we don't fear you.*"[43]

Although the twenty priests insisted that their public announcement was not a personal attack on the bishop, this final statement symbolized the power struggle between them and the authority over them.

Item 6 spoke to the recurring theme of working in an isolated context without support from the episcopal level. "Know and approve their need to 'fight city hall,' but dignify their work with your approval," states in clear terms what Ahern, LaFarge, and the Clergy Conference on Negro Welfare struggled with and spoke of so often. Those priests of the 1930s believed that bishops feared the response of white parishioners, and so they failed to challenge them. But rather than diplomatically assist and convert bishops to their cause as the earlier group suggested, the Newark Twenty used a direct and public approach. They demanded sanction for their innovations and craved that their work be given dignity by the bishop's open and unequivocal approval. They had little chance of winning this struggle. But they apparently felt they had nothing to lose.

The Newark Twenty were, in fact, attempting to call attention to what they felt was *institutional racism* inherent in the Catholic Church, which, without direct action, would not change on its own. The priests were concerned with passive racism even more than active racism because it was more "cancerous and difficult to detect."[44] As Harold Baron defined it in his essay "The Web of Urban Racism," institutionalized racism is not so much the result of "specific discriminatory decisions and acts" by individuals as the following of rules and procedures that were put in place long before.[45] Under such circumstances, "the individual only has to conform to the operating norms of the organization, and the institution will do the discriminating for him."[46]

But these nuances were lost on the archbishop and his supporters. From Boland's point of view, he backed the priests by not interfering with their plans and strategies. He gave Queen of Angels five priests and he believed that every priest in the inner city wanted to be there. In a letter released to the press January 9, 1969, Boland protested that if he "issued directives," he was considered "authoritarian," and if he did not, he "lacked leadership." If he "urged and exhorted," he was not acting strongly enough; if he gave orders, he was "not acting democratically." In light of his dilemma, he felt that all he could do was follow his conscience.[47]

Boland laid out some of the programs that the archdiocese had put into place or was planning. He ended by reminding the priests that "they cannot operate legitimately within the Church independently of the authority of the Ordinary [bishop] to whom they have promised reverence and obedience at their ordination."[48]

The United Black Catholics countered with a press release indicating that the bishop's response only confirmed "what was charged—an aloofness and lack of understanding of the Community."[49] In addition, they listed specific data challenging the bishop's examples of diocesan programs for not having been "developed through community involvement and direction."[50]

Commendations and Condemnations

The twenty priests had their supporters and detractors. As indicated above, many fellow priests stood behind the archbishop. Laypeople were divided also; some defended the Newark Twenty and felt that they had been courageous in their actions, while others, mainly white, condemned them.

Msgr. Thomas M. Reardon, the pastor of Sacred Heart Parish of Bloomfield, who utilized priests from Queen of Angels for weekend liturgies, sent Carey a letter stating that their services were no longer needed. He told the press that he dismissed them because the charges against Archbishop Boland were "unfounded and prejudicial—and I don't believe they can substantiate them."[51]

Msgr. John Hourihan from the Mount Carmel Guild wrote to Carey that he was sickened and saddened by the actions of the Newark Twenty. Hourihan was one of the Newark Priests' Group who crafted the report on Newark in 1967 that systematically demonstrated the plight of Newark's inner city (see appendix 3). In a letter (with an attached check for $150 from the Mount Carmel Guild to offset the loss from Reardon's dismissal), he told Carey that the statement of the twenty priests was irresponsible and that the priests' emotions were "bordering on hysteria." He believed that such statements would "harm the cause in which we all have a stake."[52]

Contrary to the opinion of some priests who remember the Newark Twenty incident, Carey, Comerford, and Linder all stated that if they had a chance to do it over, they would repeat their actions of 1969. Msgr. Bill Linder stated in 1998 that if he were younger, he would send the same letter again, because conditions have not really changed that much.[53] Carey did not regret the stand he took, but he did regret that the action did not prove fruitful. The relationship of the twenty priests and the archbishop was strained, and nothing of consequence seemed to arise from the declaration in terms of policy.

The leadership of Queen of Angels was behind the Newark Twenty. The Little Flower Guild and the Rosary Society composed a letter signed by Mouselle Shelton and Dorothy Murphy voicing an unqualified vote of approval. "We feel very proud of you, the 20 priests, who decided to speak out for social and spiritual equality. We pray that this is the beginning of a new day when our lives as Catholics will be more meaningful as servants of the God of all nations."[54]

The priests' supporters held rallies and protests in front of the chancery and Queen of Angels' Church. And although some parishioners were disconcerted by the public nature of the priests' confrontation with the archbishop, none left Queen of Angels because of it. In contemplating the possibility of such an occurrence, one parishioner asked the question, "Where would they go?" When white priests (and one black priest) risked their reputations and careers for them, would black parishioners go to white parishes that were at best indifferent to them? Or would they leave the Catholic Church when the priests aligned themselves with them publicly? After all, what the priests were protesting were real inequities that needed to be righted, and the parishioners knew who was on their side.[55]

Carey's most enduring memory surrounding those events was when parishioners were invited to give their opinion at Mass regarding the actions of the twenty priests. Many said that though they loved their parish and their priests, they never thought they would see the day when white priests would publicly take a stand for them in the way the Newark Twenty had done.[56] And this response seemed to be the only one that mattered to Carey.

Stella Wright Housing Project

The Newark Twenty incident did not seem to slow the efforts of the inner-city priests, at least not in the early 1970s. To fulfill the mandate from Carey to utilize what he learned at San Miguelito, Tom Comerford chose to go into the projects to develop base communities there. He worked in the Stella Wright Housing Project, which was a twelve-story high-rise with 1,200 families, or about 5,000 tenants, in a two-square-block area. Sr. Maureen McDonough, a Sister of Charity who lived at St. Vincent Academy, worked full time with Comerford, knocking on doors, visiting people, and gathering groups together: "We went around and we had meetings in the different apartments and we would begin the meetings by talking about the problems because people just had to get that out . . . After about an hour or so, someone would say, "What can we do about these [problems]." And that's when we developed some action steps. And then we always had a bread and wine service."[57] Two things became evident to Comerford from the discussions that ensued. First, he saw that the people lived in fear. "They would come into the building and go right into their apartment because they were afraid."[58] Second, by hiding away in their apartments, a lack of communication developed among the residents of the projects. The meetings gave people the opportunity to meet their neighbors and plan strategies to experience some control over their environment.

Father Comerford and Sister McDonough led the meetings in the beginning, but eventually two African Americans led the regular monthly meetings in about eight of the twelve buildings. One of these men, Ed Satterfield, was not religious but showed a great interest in religious questions. He ultimately became a Baptist minister and recently was named pastor of his church in Jersey City, where he has served as assistant for many years.[59] "We are striving to live Christianity as the early Christians did," expressed Satterfield in an interview with *The Advocate*.[60] The objective of the Stella Wright activity was not to convert people to the Catholic faith, but to foster lay leaders who would follow their own religious and spiritual path and play an active role in their own community. Other lay leaders were Mrs. Louise Brummell, who was Baptist, and James Lewis and Mozetta Moon, who were members of Queen of Angels.[61]

In December 1969, Tom Comerford made the decision to move into the Stella Wright Apartments. He wanted to close the gap between the reality of his life and those of the people in the community. Subsequently, when he found the apartments unlivable he was even more motivated to take some kind of overt action regarding the conditions in the projects.[62] The groups that had been meeting for some time at Stella Wright decided to form a tenants' association (the Stella Wright Tenants' Association), as did many other Newark Housing Authority projects in the city. On April 1, 1970, in the face of deteriorating conditions and a proposed increase in rent, the various tenant associations initiated a citywide rent strike. During the first year, they made no progress in their negotiations with the Newark Housing Authority (NHA) or the federal Department of Housing and Urban Development (HUD).

Carey Resigns

On June 30, 1970, Carey resigned from Queen of Angels for medical reasons and at his own request. His health had suffered during the ensuing years at Queen of Angels, the Newark Twenty incident possibly taking its greatest toll.[63] He felt he was "not by nature a rebel" and took to heart the criticism of his fellow priests. After his decision, the parishioners voted to refuse admittance to any priest "if they were not allowed to participate in his selection."[64]

Their spokesperson, parishioner Joyce Smith Carter, explained that their actions were based on the new teachings of Vatican II and the "growing sense of black awareness and self-determination that Monsignor Carey encouraged throughout his tenure."[65] Under Carey's leadership, "[t]he parish not only was of the community, it was the community, but without the traditional kinds of relationships existing between the church administration and the people."[66]

Their position signaled a new juncture in the parish's history, where the social, cultural, and theological context began to redefine Queen of Angels' relationship to church. The clergy had modeled this new way of being for the parishioners, but they were all acting out the influences that had affected them, namely, the Civil Rights movement and Martin Luther King Jr., the Second Vatican Council, liberation theology, and the Black Power movement.[67] The impact of the latter did not cause as much upheaval at Queen of Angels as it could have because of the activism integral to the parish's life.

In a gradual process, the parishioners were affected by the "growing sense of black awareness and self determination" encouraged in the parish and the strong identification of the parish with the community; for Queen of Angels the revolution had already happened.[68]

Newark's Tenants' Strike

When Carey resigned from Queen of Angels in 1970, Thomas Comerford became temporary administrator of the parish with William Linder and John Maloney as assistants. Comerford maintained his residence at Stella Wright Homes and continued his preoccupation with the tenants' strike. The parish and much of the Catholic community, black and white, supported the tenants' strike strongly and publicly.

On March 28, 1971, Operation Understanding joined with Stella Wright Tenant Association (SWTA) to sponsor a Day of Judgment to garner the support of the larger community. According to a report in the Legal Service's publication, *Clearinghouse Review:* "Stella Wright had emerged as the primary force in the Newark rent strike. The Stella Wright Tenant's Association was highly organized and its leadership was capable and committed. The Association developed support from Operation Understanding, a suburban based group, and later from Concerned Citizens for Stella Wright, a group of prominent citizens headed by Monsignor Thomas G. Fahy, President of Seton Hall University."[69] Stella Wright tenants negotiated with NHA, reaching an agreement to "depopulate" the project and improve security, but HUD, after long delays, rejected the agreement.[70]

The courts and both NHA and HUD began to focus on the escrow funds withheld by the tenants of Stella Wright. The superior court judge ordered a report on the funds the tenants supplied in March 1972, disclosing that they had collected $94,460. Subsequently, the judge ordered SWTA to show cause on November 17, 1972, why the court should not order the funds paid to NHA.

The SWTA held a meeting on November 14, 1972, to discuss a course of action, and it was decided, considering the refusals of the NHA to meet any of their demands to make repairs and improve conditions, that the monies would be returned to the people. Without informing their lawyers, Tom Comerford and Toby Henry, the president of the SWTA, and Edward Satterfield, withdrew the money from the bank and returned it all to the tenants at a public meeting. The tenant association said to the NHA, "Not one penny has been lost, but if you want the $95,000 you must get it from the individuals who have to walk up 10 and 12 flights of stairs every day, and breathe in the fumes from the incinerators, and have their children play in the filth of the stairways."[71]

On November 17, the court was informed of the action. The prosecutor, Mr. William Brach, asked the judge to "order the three leaders to be arrested and held in contempt of court. He also demanded that the three lawyers representing them, Gerry Clark, Michael Callan, and Harris David, be held in contempt."[72] The charges were dropped against Satterfield, but Judge Irwin I. Kimmelman ordered Comerford and Henry to serve forty-five days at the Essex County Corrections Center in Caldwell, New Jersey. Comerford was going to be placed in a protected area in the infirmary and Henry in with the general population; when Comerford refused this arrangement, both were placed in the infirmary.[73] They served thirty-two days of their sentence. The Catholic community of Newark, white and black, rallied around the two men in prison and the Stella Wright rent strikers under the ad hoc leadership of Thomas Fahy of Seton Hall and Operation Understanding.

NHA had threatened to close down Stella Wright and move several people to other housing projects. Those who could move on their own did, rather than facing closure and forced eviction. Unfortunately, the people who were left were those on welfare, the elderly, and the unemployed. But in November 1973, the tide turned for Stella Wright when it won a historic and far-reaching legal victory in the case of *Housing Authority of the City of Newark* v. *Aikens*. The court found that "living conditions at Stella Wright evidenced such pervasive uninhabitability that the tenant defendants were entitled to an unprecedented 80% abatement of their past and future rentals."[74]

Eventually, the large housing projects were abandoned in fact and as a model for low-income housing. They remained empty for years, and smaller two-floor and two-family dwellings are gradually replacing them. In the last years of the 1990s, Stella Wright, Hayes Homes, and other projects surrounding Queen of Angels, reminders of a tumultuous and heady era, have been and continue to be demolished one by one.

New Community Corporation

Within the climate created by the Day of Understanding, Operation Understanding, and the Walk for Understanding, a concrete cohesive organization evolved with black Newarkers and white suburbanites. According to Msgr. Bill Linder, discussions with militant blacks at Queen of Angels concerning the conditions of African Americans in Newark led to a commitment to build housing for low- and moderate-income residents. Using the principles and strategies outlined in the 1967 priests' report, "The Needs of the People of Newark and the Resources of the Archdiocese," they designed development programs to improve the residents' quality of life and to keep revenues and employment in the inner city.[75]

The initial goal was to raise the $50,000 needed to purchase the first piece of land. Linder's friend and fellow classmate from the seminary, Fr. Kevin Ashe, who was located at Little Flower Church in the affluent suburb of Berkeley Heights, agreed to work in his community to make contacts with those who could assist in their objective. They knew they would have a greater chance of attracting larger contributors as a foundation rather than as individuals. Consequently, in 1969 Little Flower parishioners John Turney and Warren Roche, and Herman Haenisch, a Methodist and a member of the New Providence–Berkeley Heights Junior Chamber of Commerce founded the nonprofit New Community Foundation. They asked Thomas Button, David Kirkwood, Charles Stonehill, Robert Schacter, John Connors, Julius Foster, James Varner, and Fr. Kevin Ashe to join their board.[76]

Appealing to the desire of suburbanites who wanted to do something for the inner city, the foundation asked them to invest in a housing development company called New Community Corporation (NCC) and were given symbolic shares as evidence of their participation.[77]

The vision took shape as a city within a city on a forty-six-acre tract, or fourteen blocks, of abandoned and dilapidated buildings in the Central Ward, where affordable housing would be built and made available to the local community that most needed it. To maintain a community-based organization, a nine-member board of directors was formed with Willie Wright as the president of the board; black activist Timothy Still as vice president (in memoriam); Elma Bateman as secretary; and Thomas Carey, as treasurer. The board members were Kenneth A. Gibson, Robert Curvin, Arthur J. Bray, Joseph Chaneyfield, and William Linder.[78]

After raising the needed $50,000, the foundation discovered that the corporation that owned the property wanted much more for it than New Community felt it was worth. Because the foundation had become part of a network of people who were or would later become politically powerful, they were able to elicit the support of Gov. Richard Hughes, who called the president of the company to discover why they would not sell at the asking price. It came to light that since the company had listed the property's worth at the greater amount, they could not sell it for less without the appearance of a loss on their books. The problem was solved when the company donated the difference in price to New Community Corporation, who in turn was able to purchase the property at the listed cost. Through his involvement with this process, Ashe and the foundation learned the efficacy of making contacts with those whose reach extended as far as the corporate board room and the governor's mansion.[79]

By August 1970, after two and one-half years of effort, the nonprofit NCC had received more than $200,000 from private sources, including $70,000 raised by the New Community Foundation and a second interest-free loan from the state totaling $273,000.[80] The money was to be used to buy land and options in the project area bounded by South Orange and Fifteenth Avenues and Jones and Bergen Streets.[81] It was not until 1973 that construction of the first building was begun, and in 1975, 120 low-income-housing units consisting of six five-story buildings were completed. After that, critical mass was reached, and the nonprofit corporation grew rapidly.[82]

Babyland Nursery

Babyland Nursery emanated directly from Operation Understanding and its spin-off group, Operation Housewives. Newark resident Mary Smith, a social worker and director of the Memorial Senior Center in the Memorial West United Presbyterian Church of Newark, was part of a panel visiting suburban parishes. After her presentation one evening in the summer of 1968, a group of white women asked her if they could meet with her to share their stories and to take some kind of action. They organized a thrift shop to offer used clothing and small household items at minimal cost, the proceeds of which would be used to send children to camp or for other needs.

Mary Smith was president of an organization called the Central West Service League that opened a storefront at 302 South Orange Avenue in Newark in August 1968. The Maplewood group of supporters was led by Mrs. Beverly Holleran of the Prospect Presbyterian Church, which was linked through ministerial programs to Smith's church, Memorial West United Presbyterian.[83]

Smith started a day care center for infants in an apartment in the Scudder Homes projects. Since no governmental guidelines existed for infant day care at that time, such an establishment could be opened but could not receive public or private foundation funding. The women pressured the state senate to draw up guidelines, which it ultimately did, with the help of the women. Once the guidelines were in place, they received foundation money to buy two storefronts on South Orange Avenue near the Vailsburg section.

Subsequently, they were able to receive public money as well. Babyland #1 was open for about five years, at which time NCC built Babyland #2 in their new housing complex on South Orange Avenue across from the new University Medical and Dental Hospital. Babyland is now incorporated under NCC and operates on seven sites throughout the Newark area.[84]

Today, almost thirty years later, New Community Corporation and Babyland Nursery remain Queen of Angels' most visible and powerful legacy. NCC is the largest redevelopment corporation in the country. Recently, NCC was responsible for building a new Pathmark store, the first supermarket in the Central Ward in twenty-five years. Its work extends to employment, training, and workforce development, a leadership development service, and a long list of others. It consists of thirty legal entities, including six for-profit operations worth $80 million per year. NCC, still a grassroots organization, generates revenues obtained from real estate, health care, and retail that are put back into the community in the form of training, jobs, services, and housing—including transitional housing for the homeless.[85]

Laypeople, women religious, and priests outside of an official church venue accomplished the efforts and tangible work just described. But the seeds of their extra-ecclesial accomplishments were planted in ground nourished in an explicit church environment. Some claim that *doing* theology is both a process and a product. That is, the people of a faith community discourse with the contemporary culture and experience, and the result of that discourse hopefully leads to a transformation in the faith community and the larger culture. Using this form of analysis, New Community Corporation and Babyland may be seen as products of the theological process that began with African American laywomen in the 1920s and 1930s, developed in the Queen of Angels' missions and sprouted again in the community in the 1960s and 1970s. And those products continue to transform Newark today as it proceeds toward renaissance.

7

The Mission Is Accomplished

Church is Church.

—Mrs. Roberta Thornton

Black Power

Martin Luther King's nonviolent activism and emphasis on integration as a goal and a methodology, to a great extent, died with him on April 4, 1968. In the last few years of his life, King's influence politically waned, due to public positions that alienated conservative blacks and whites, namely, his stance against the Vietnam War and for the inclusion of Communist China in the United Nations. His apparent failure to galvanize power against Mayor Richard Daley's political machine in Chicago, and the white vitriolic opposition to his nonviolent tactics in that city, weakened King's reputation among militant blacks and borderline whites.[1]

He was viewed as out of touch and out of date by the rising Black Power movement, with its leading proponents, H. Rap Brown and Stokely Carmichael of SNCC.[2] And, finally, his Poor People's Campaign, with which he attempted to unite people beyond racial categories, was seen by the powerful (including President Lyndon Johnson) as an attack on the corporate establishment and the federal government, and by many blacks as too little, too late.

The separatist slogan "Black Power," coined by Stokely Carmichael in 1966 and promoted by Willie Rink, became the byword for militant blacks, much to King's consternation.[3] Arguably, black power became the most significant factor in the continuing history of African Americans. King's nonviolent strategies that included whites were rejected. Tired of years of effort to extract concessions from whites for voter rights and equality of treatment in housing and public facilities, some blacks spurned the goal of integration and to varying degrees advocated separation as the most viable response to white institutional and individual racism. Brother Joseph M. Davis, S.M., vice-chairman of the Black Catholic Clergy Conference explained that in the past the gains made by blacks were "viewed as so many hand-outs to half-human beings granted for their power to buy more time for a society built on the notion of white superiority. In 1969 the prospect of integration in the United States appears as remote as it was in 1865. There has yet to be a manifestation of a sincere attempt on the part of white America to eliminate the obstacles to complete integration."[4] Therefore, the goal of Black Power was "to enable black people to establish control over their own lives and map out their own destinies" with solidarity among themselves and with no direct role of whites.[5]

On July 21, 1967, at about the same time that Queen of Angels was reaching out to white suburbanites, a four-day conference on Black Power was held in Newark, summoned by Dr. Nathan Wright Jr., executive director of the Department of Urban Work of the Episcopal Diocese of Newark. About 400 persons representing forty-five civil rights groups in thirty-six cities attended, including H. Rap Brown of SNNC and Jesse Jackson of the Southern Christian Leadership Conference. Notably absent were Roy Wilkins of the NAACP, Whitney Young Jr. of the National Urban League, and Martin Luther King Jr. According to Nathan Wright, the emphasis of the conference was on black empowerment rather than on the "deficiencies of the white community."[6]

Black Power's influence extended to all of black society, including African American Catholics who, in an unvarnished manner, began to address the official church publicly regarding past inequities. In Detroit, on April 16, 1965, prior to the annual meeting of the Catholic Clergy Conference on the Interracial Apostolate, a group of black priests met for a caucus. Cyprian Davis calls this event the "turning point for Catholic involvement in the Civil Rights Movement."[7] The priests developed a militant statement listing the grievances and demands of black Catholics in the United States. They then formed the National Black Catholic Clergy Caucus, becoming a voice and a "catalyst for change on behalf of the Black Catholic community."[8] The National Black Sisters Conference was organized that same year, and in 1971 the National Office of Black Catholics was established in Washington, D.C.[9]

The emergence of eleven black bishops and two black archbishops between 1973 to 1988 finally positioned African Americans in the highest ranks of the church, where they focused the church's attention on the theological and sociohistorical implications of African Americans in their midst. One of those bishops was Joseph A. Francis of Newark, who was a voice for African Americans in the archdiocese until his death in 1997.

It was no accident that the twenty priests' confrontation with the archbishop in 1969 possessed the tone it did, considering the influence of the Black Power movement on the inner city and civil rights activism. The twenty priests (nineteen white and one black) demonstrated their awareness and acceptance of the right of African Americans to lead their own efforts to achieve power.

And although some Queen of Angels' parishioners were uncomfortable with clergy or laypeople openly questioning church authority, it would be difficult for them to disagree with Brother Joseph Davis's statement:

> When in the Church's own institutions racism, prejudice and occasional discrimination still obtain, why should they not be questioned? It is overwhelmingly apparent that segments of the Church are still ready to rush into black communities with unskilled, untrained, unprepared clerics and religious as saviors, waving sociological solutions in their hands, but these segments shy away from confronting the problems of white racism in the White Community. The latter problem is too tricky for them to tackle.[10]

The Newark Twenty tackled it, albeit with ambiguous results. Many of Davis's objections echoed the priests' published statement six months earlier in regard to the inappropriate placement of pastors in the inner city and the problems of white racism within the church. The church would not admit to racism, and the controversy became a matter of political infighting. Could this have been a signal that the time had come for African Americans to take up the gauntlet on their own? Many blacks thought so and insisted that that be the case.

Administrative Transitions

By 1972 both Tom Carey and Tom Comerford had left Queen of Angels parish. At that point, William Linder became temporary administrator. While functioning in that capacity, he continued as the director of New Community Corporation. Linder remained outspoken in his approach to social improvements, and with the organization's trajectory gaining speed and influence apart from the archdiocese, he was gathering a circle of parish, civic, and corporate leaders around him. When he left the parish in 1974 to become the pastor of St. Rose of Lima Parish, most of the parishioners from Queen of Angels who had worked with him on NCC followed.[11] This development stripped the parish of many of its core lay leaders (leaving only New Community Corporation board member Elma Bateman) and divested it of its connection to a historic prophetic tradition.

In 1977, Fr. William C. Reed became the first African American pastor of Queen of Angels.[12] But he remained there only until 1980, when he decided to resign in order to enter hospital chaplaincy work. At that point Newark's Archbishop Peter Gerety invited the Society for African Missions to administer the parish.[13] Thus, for the first time in its then fifty-year history, Queen of Angels came under the auspices of a missionary order rather than its own diocesan priests. Its ties to the diocese, through its priests, were severed. Only the Little Flower Guild, originally started by Ethel Wright in 1929, exists to this day as a reminder of the parish's beginnings.

Since then Queen of Angels has functioned in a more priestly or spiritual mode rather than a prophetic one. Over the past ten years, social programs have emerged either as parish programs or affiliations with nonparish programs that utilize the parish facilities. The Newark Family Resource Network, an emergency family program for the prevention of parental abuse, has operated out of Queen of Angels for the last fourteen years and is being used by the State of New Jersey as a model for similar programs. The parish conducts an adult literacy program with parish volunteers. The Mbasie Society was formed to minister to a growing but fluctuating membership of African nationals, most of whom now attend St. Mary's Abbey a few blocks away.

Since 1994, Queen of Angels has seen a development of new groups with names more distinctive of the Black Church tradition. The Men of Victory (formerly the Holy Names Society), Women of Wisdom, Women's Bible Study, and the Pillars of Peace Youth Program have all been organized with the gradual recovery of membership that had been eroding since the 1980s.

Queen of Angels' parish school demonstrates a surprising capacity to thrive when most Catholic schools are having difficulty keeping their doors open. The school recently expanded its program to include a kindergarten in a newly renovated building on the premises. And since the Marist Brothers left in 1999, laypeople now run the school with Mrs. Everlyn Hay as principal and Mrs. Sharon Massey as assistant principal. Mrs. Hay and Mrs. Massey were both teachers at Queen of Angels School for several years before they became administrators.

Younger black Catholics at Queen of Angels are not familiar with the history of the church. Although it is recognized by the city to be the historic black mother church, it is no longer on the cutting edge of missionary innovation or in the forefront of political and societal progress. In a sense, it has been absorbed into the fabric of Newark's African American life, which is highly represented in city and state government as well as the traditional venue of the Black Church. Queen of Angels has become one of several black Catholic churches in Newark. But unlike Queen of Angels, churches like St. Rose of Lima, St. Mary's, and Blessed Sacrament have become predominantly black because of demographic shifts that began in the 1940s.[14] It appears that Queen of Angels' purpose as a mission church is past, and at least for the time being, its focus is of a more priestly or spiritual nature.

Functioning Outside Parish Boundaries

Just as New Community Corporation and Babyland function outside of the boundaries of the church, another Queen of Angels' program does the same. Queen of Angels provided a dynamic Catholic Youth Organization that served youth from the larger black community for many years. When that ceased to exist in the 1970s, Joyce Smith Carter started a specialized youth program in the archdiocese of Newark called QUEST/Inner City Catholic Youth Organization. She leased the former St. Charles Borromeo School building and still operates independent of any parish, but within the Catholic archdiocese. QUEST's goal was and continues to be support of the spiritual, educational, social, and career needs of inner-city youth. Although constantly struggling, it does so while maintaining a prophetic stance toward the church to ensure that a distinctively African American youth organization continues to be available in the inner city.[15]

Church Is Church

Women (Not Men) in the Early Movement

Women were the central leaders of the preecclesial efforts of Newark's black Catholic community. Men, and their role in these organizations, appear almost nonexistent. They are not mentioned in Ethel Wright's history and only one male name is listed in the Theresa Lane Council's minutes.[16] It is possible that they acted behind the scenes, but we have no evidence to confirm this. It was only after Queen of Angels became part of the official church that men emerged in leadership roles and filled the ranks of the various lay societies of the parish.

Without more substantial documentary evidence, the reasons for this are not immediately apparent. One can only speculate. Over the centuries women historically have performed untold amounts of work behind the scenes with no promise of formal recognition in the shape of official leadership roles. The women who formed the early movement prior to the establishment of Queen of Angels had nothing to lose in acting either autonomously or anonymously, and in so doing were merely continuing a centuries-old tradition. Their reward was the process of the work itself, a sense of accomplishment, and the benefit of close interaction with others toward a common goal.[17]

Conversely, since before the Civil War the role of minister in the black Protestant church was the most powerful open to black men (not women) in American society. But in the Roman Catholic Church the only leadership role for men of any ethnic group in the 1920s and 1930s was that of the celibate priesthood. We have touched briefly on the various complex historical and cultural reasons why African American men were not ordained in any significant numbers until the 1960s. Daniel Rudd and Thomas Wyatt Turner organized lay Catholics to promote the role of blacks in the church and to encourage non-Catholic blacks to embrace what they considered to be the universal church. But those movements were fraught with controversy and ended after only a few years. With so few Catholic priests, the role of the black Protestant minister was the most visible in African American society. Until the permanent diaconate was restored to the Catholic Church, nothing comparable was within the reach of the black man at that time in the American Catholic Church.

But the early movement in Newark tells us more about women than it does about the men who were not involved, and that is where our focus should be. The facts are that the women did not expect or ask for permission to organize and press for what they desired. They did not wait for someone else to lead them; they did not stand by passively relying on others, namely men, in the case of the Catholic Church, to offer them a church or a priest. They brainstormed; they worked; they networked; they wrote letters; and they approached the bishop. How was it that they perceived themselves as doers? What empowered them?

For one thing, they believed and latched on to the official teaching of the Catholic Church regarding the equality of all in Christ. For another, African American women had developed a habit of self-reliance that helped them survive as slaves and freed people in a hostile environment. Finally, the history of the black church—whether Protestant or Catholic, African American or West Indian—reveals that women were leaders and doers in their communities, providing a paradigm for the role of women in church. These were the resources of the women of the Theresa Lane Council and the Little Flower Guild as they made their way in the urban wilderness of Newark.[18]

Worship

A nineteenth-century liturgical movement that originated in Europe—particularly Belgium, Germany, and France, and specifically within the Benedictine Order—influenced the American Catholic Church. But while most of the East Coast of the United States did not feel the impact of the Liturgical Movement until the 1950s, Queen of Angels, with the help of Fr. Benedict Bradley, O.S.B., of St. Mary's Abbey, was on the cutting edge from as early as the 1930s. Permission to translate the missal into the vernacular was not given until the turn of the twentieth century, and by the 1930s, the very limited use of the recently printed missals was controversial.[19] In a desire to make the liturgy more accessible to the parishioners, Father Ahern instituted the dialogue Mass, or missa recitata, in 1932, using a pamphlet of an English translation by Father Bradley.[20]

In the dialogue Mass at Queen of Angels, a designated man of the parish read the English translation of the Mass aloud and then led the parishioners in the English responses. This version of the dialogue Mass was similar to the ideal described in Keith F. Peckler's recent work on the liturgical movement in the United States. In different parts of the country other versions of the dialogue Mass were experimented with, but even in 1954 it "was either infrequent or non-existent in most American parishes."[21] The dialogue Mass at Queen of Angels continued until the 1960s when the Second Vatican Council instituted the new vernacular liturgy. At that point, in the midst of the revolutionary ethos of the council, African Americans began to insist that the liturgy become something of their own.

The best word to describe African American Catholic worship as it has evolved today is *holistic*. It is a complex of the contemplative, the exuberantly emotional, and, with its emphasis on community, contains strong elements of welcoming, inclusivity, and warmth. It may consist of quiet prayerfulness between God and the individual as well as emotive shouting, spontaneous singing, and even ecstatic dance. Traditionally, historical black church members have come to expect their ministers to have a strong command of Scripture and to artfully apply their interpretations to every facet of their lives.[22]

The qualities of the African American Catholic liturgy were appropriated from the American black Protestant church. The gospel Mass of Queen of Angels and other African American Catholic parishes is not African, but African American; it is layered with centuries of Christian worship that is at once Jewish, Greek, European, and African American. It is a testament both to the fluidity and constancy of Catholic liturgical tradition, its ability to remain the same and yet, with time, allow diversity.

Music

The hundreds of converts to Queen of Angels during its pre–Vatican II days did not find the Latin Mass an insurmountable deterrent to their conversion to Catholicism. On the contrary, the Latin Mass and its traditional European classical or chant music became yet another facet of the people's spiritual and cultural lives. In the 1940s, the circumstances of two teenage sisters provide a striking example of how this occurred. The Thornton sisters (now Elma Bateman and Bennie Fields) walked to Queen of Angels on Sunday morning, passing their neighbors' homes and apartments along the way, where radios were tuned to popular Sunday religious programs. Through the windows, the sounds of spirituals performed by such groups as The Wings Over Jordan, the Southernaires, and the Coleman Brothers Quartet would envelop the girls as they passed. The music created a spiritual atmosphere for them as they walked. In their words, they "experienced church all the way." When they arrived at Queen of Angels, they were prepared to sing the Latin Mass that they loved just as well.[23]

After Mass they would often join their friends around the piano in their mother's living room, singing popular songs or listening to jazz records. Their appetite for church and music still not satisfied, their mother allowed them to attend the storefront sanctified or holiness churches on Sunday night to listen to more music and watch with fascination as the congregation became "caught up in the Spirit." Mrs. Thornton did not mind, since, after all, "church is church," she would say, demonstrating a respectful attitude toward religious diversity not uncommon in African American culture.[24] The sisters' experience served to solidify their Catholic faith rather than pull them away.

In the 1970s, the appropriation of African American Protestant cultural styles of worship entered Queen of Angels in a bold and pervasive way. In this process the parish had access to someone unique to assist them. The famous jazz musician Mary Lou Williams began performing at Queen of Angels. During her long career, she played, composed, and arranged for Louis Armstrong, Cab Calloway, Tommy Dorsey, Duke Ellington, Benny Goodman, and many others. After converting to Catholicism in the 1950s, Williams took time off from secular music, turning her energies to compositions such as "The Mass for Peace," "Mass for the Lenten Season," and "Jazz Mass of St. Martin De Porres." These compositions were presented at Queen of Angels, to which the greater Newark community was invited. Williams's works gave full expression to a melding of the African American musical art form and Catholic liturgy. Drums, guitars, and bass were added to the accompaniment, and spirituals and gospel music were included in the Sunday liturgy.

This is not to say that all African American Catholics, or Protestants for that matter, are comfortable with all worship styles. African Americans are not monolithic in this respect or any other. Ollie Pierce, born in 1893, was raised Baptist in Macon, Georgia, and moved to Newark as a young woman. For several years she enjoyed attending various churches with friends: Baptist, African-Methodist Episcopal, Episcopal, and Presbyterian. When in 1949 she converted to Catholicism at Queen of Angels, she left the others behind. "You are what you are. Don't try to be two things at one time . . . If I wanted to belong to a 'holy roller' church, I would just go join it. I wouldn't try to mix the 'holy roller' and the Catholic, because I don't feel that."[25] Mrs. Pierce located her personal religious faith within a "felt" contemplative liturgical experience that seemed right to her, and she never liked the gospel Mass—a major difference among those who are black and Catholic; but, then again, as a man from Georgia said, there "ain't no special religion called Black Catholicism."[26]

Starting in the 1950s, Mrs. Beatrice Gordon from Savannah, Georgia, stood, raised her hands, and shouted "Amen," "Alleluia," or other words of affirmation during the sermon or when she felt inspired at any time in Queen of Angels' liturgy. Her actions enthralled other "born" Catholics like Cecilia Moses Faulks, who had only been exposed to a strictly "respectful" and quiet form of worship from the sisters of her Catholic childhood training in Lakeland, Georgia. Mrs. Gordon inspired her to embrace, at least tentatively, a submerged African-rooted spiritual sensibility. "It took me years and years before I [could] express openly what I may have been feeling inside, to say it out. I used to watch Mrs. Gordon, before anyone else in that church ever expressed themselves, whether they were feeling anything or not, she was always very open. She would answer the priest."[27]

Another woman would lift her hands when she received the Eucharist, apparently caught in a moment of ecstasy. "I always remember Miss Bartholomew, she felt her religion so that when she would go up to communion, . . . and before she would receive, she would just [*she demonstrates by clapping her hands and quickly lifting them high*], [I always felt that] she must feel so good. I always would watch her . . . I felt that she was enjoying a very special relationship."[28] These are movements "created by the Spirit," in silent or spoken prayer, that become prayers of "praise and self-commitment."[29] These spontaneous emotional displays of inner spiritual movement began to expand the definition of Catholic worship at Queen of Angels even before a more publicly articulated black consciousness movement exerted its influence on the parish's worship practices much later.

Thoughts on Conversion

As a local ethnographic study with anecdotal data from oral histories we can find indications of why African Americans converted to Catholicism. From his case study on St. Augustine's Church in Washington, D.C., John Muffler concluded the following:

> While there is no direct evidence, one may conjecture that the people of St. Augustine's reasoned that if they could distance themselves from other "lesser" Black Americans, particularly those whose religious roots were in pentecostal and holiness traditions, and gain a meaningful foothold in a large white religious institution, their entree into proper Washington society and participation in the American dream would be enhanced . . . Thus was their perceived route to the American mainstream, and respectability.[30]

Were the majority of Queen of Angels' converts attempting to distance themselves from "lesser" African Americans through their alliance with the Catholic Church? We have seen that Father Ahern was greatly concerned that the church gain membership from the professional and middle class to ensure its viability. Did that lead the people of Queen of Angels into an entrenched stratification based on class or skin color? From oral histories of Queen of Angels, it seems that was not the case.

It might be helpful to compare Queen of Angels to another church in Newark. Bethany Baptist was perceived by many as restricted to upper-class and light-skinned African Americans. The former apprehension was to a great extent true, but the second, probably not. A longtime Queen of Angels' parishioner remembered congregating with her teenage friends at a local soda fountain and sensing the boundaries between Bethany and Queen of Angels' teens. It seemed that Bethany's class status was a marker differentiating its young people from those of Queen of Angels.

When speaking of Newark churches in the 1930s and 1940s, another woman I interviewed had the impression that, unlike Queen of Angels, Bethany Baptist members were both upper class and light skinned. But, as Gary McDonogh posits in *Black and Catholic in Savannah, Georgia*, "Identification as an elite, . . . tends to inform suspicion of color: any upper-class church is likely to be accused of being 'light-skinned' by outsiders regardless of the phenotypes of its members."[31]

There was one documented example of the color issue at Queen of Angels. In the 1930s, the very fair Mrs. Elizabeth Houston, grandmother of the popular singer Whitney Houston, encountered hostility from some darker-skinned parishioners who believed she was condescending to them because of their skin color. Houston blamed Father Ahern's attention to her status as an educator for fostering jealousy in others in addition to the difference in skin hue.[32] It is not clear what the prevalence of such occurrences were at Queen of Angels, and except for Houston's very reluctant admission, no one acknowledged any stratification along color lines. But even with an understandable hesitancy of African Americans to speak to this issue, the historical consistency of class mixture at Queen of Angels argues in support of their assertion that color or skin tone did not exclude membership.

Queen of Angels' parishioners were proud of their accomplished members, but the bulk of the parish population appears to have been a combination of the working class, the working poor, and those desperately in need of economic assistance, in addition to the middle or upper classes. Rather than distancing themselves, it appears that Queen of Angels parishioners were able to forge "a strong unification of church, class and education," a unification that sustained them and enabled them to participate on a level playing field within the parish culture and in the larger community.[33] This fact would have militated against even an appearance of stratification based on color. Of course, such a class mix almost assured that the church would never have a surplus of resources with which to work.

In *Conversion Theories—Converts, Dropouts, Returnees,* Dean R. Hoge develops three successive conditions for becoming a Catholic convert: (1) the convert must have a religious worldview; (2) he or she must have a felt need for spiritual life or church involvement or a change in that involvement; and (3) there must be an opportunity to develop affective bonds with a priest, religious, or church leader and with members of the parish.[34]

If these criteria are utilized to determine the conversion of Newark's African Americans to the Catholic Church, we find compelling reasons for its occurrence. I found that the religious worldview or sacred cosmos was already in place within the people. Also, the historical Black Church had instilled a "felt need for spiritual life or church involvement" by virtue of the prominent place it held in the lives of African Americans since the eighteenth century. It was evident that no one was unaffected by some childhood church experience, even if it had not always led to consistent church membership in adulthood. The final criterion is quite apparent in the intensive and systematic outreach programs sustained by Queen of Angels over the years. There was a major effort to ensure frequent opportunities to develop affective bonds with a priest, sister, or members of the parish, often all three.

One example of conversion from Queen of Angels' oral histories fulfills all of these criteria plus the added faith dimension of a moment of transformation at the early age of nine. In the 1940s, Lucille Turner lived in an area of the city that was mixed with Italian and Polish neighbors. She became familiar and fascinated with the feasts and processions of the Italians, their practice of wearing black, and hanging wreaths on their doors to honor the dead. Then she met Theresa Lane and was thrilled to be able to go inside a Catholic church. "It seemed like a new awakening," she said. "When I walked in the church and I saw all of this stained glass and all the candles lit and St. Jude and the Madonna, it was like a spiritual metamorphosis for me. I can't explain it. It was almost like I was being lifted up. Like something was happening in my life."[35] She immediately asked her mother if she could be baptized as a Catholic.

Lucille Turner was the only one of her family not a Baptist, but her mother said that all that mattered was that she belonged to a church. The operative norm at Queen of Angels seemed to be church affiliation based upon the honest, affective experience of the believer. In other words, if the faith was real and inspired you to attend church, it was sufficient. With the support from their mother, the Thornton sisters, who experienced church from their neighbors' radios, felt comfortable with a wide range of religious music evoked by both African American spirituals and the Roman Catholic Latin Mass.

By the same token, Ollie Pierce and Lucille Turner ceased to participate in their familial church traditions after they converted to Catholicism, but neither severed ties with the larger black community or were excluded from it because of their choice—one did not unseat the other. As the Rev. James Scott explained, the African American community does not "need homogeneity in terms of religious doctrine or ideology to keep the family in shape."[36]

Some African Americans I spoke to were drawn to the Catholic Church because of something as small as a childhood enchantment with nuns' habits that would lead to an adult conversion many years later.[37] Many said they became Catholics because of the quiet, dignified, and spiritual service. Another mentioned that it was her belief in the real presence of Christ in Holy Communion that caused her conversion, and others, the teachings of the church or its interpretation of the Bible and a belief that it is the "one, true church." Some mentioned the importance of the person rather than money or status, and the assistance given in time of need.

Black Catholics did hear opposition from their Protestant friends and relatives on occasion. Turner found it trying at times to hear Protestants object to Catholic devotions in regard to saints, or what they called "praying to statues." And the Sacrament of Reconciliation (confession of sins to a priest) was a practice that did not square with their theological worldview. Lucille Turner understood and accepted these Catholic beliefs and explained them as well as she could. But these differences did not mar her relationships with those who did not understand or accept them.[38]

Although Turner did not remember any criticism of the Catholic Church based on any racial criteria, another parishioner related that he at times "got a lot of flack from a lot of black people saying that I belonged to the white man's church."[39] He ignored it because being a Catholic was something he wanted. It was not a social decision, but a faith decision that informed his entire life. To draw the conclusion that African American Catholics at Queen of Angels relinquished their identity to a white man's church is to underestimate their power of self-determination and self-identity, and the honesty of their faith choices.

No matter how the debate ends on separate churches or conversion, the final analysis must bow to the mystery of the relationship between the person and God. We can chart and plan religious experience in its cultural and social context, but in the last analysis and in the words of historian Will

Herberg, it "takes on a dimension that relates it to the divine-human encounter to which it ultimately refers."[40] The reasons for conversion may only be the initial glint of light that attracts the eye, and then the stuff of faith floods the believer in the light of a deep relationship with God, a religious community, and a way of life. We must stop at some point in our attempt to explain it and simply say with Mrs. Thornton, "church is church."

Respect for Who You Are

Over the seventy years of the history of Queen of Angels, people did not always agree on how to live out their Catholic faith. Both blacks and whites continually debated over the wisdom of a separate church. But can we definitively say that the way in which they negotiated through the murky waters of faith, religion, and society was accommodation? Let us not fall into the trap that sociologist Max Weber warned against by trying to fit the complexity of history and humanity into a single typology.

Queen of Angels began in a time when the black churches in Newark were small and unable to address the great social and religious needs of the thousands of black immigrants from the South. In this context, Father Ahern seized the opportunity to prove to black people that the Catholic Church was a church that cared for them. To a great extent, he succeeded in doing that one thing, if he did no other.

Sr. Mary Mathew, a Trinitarian who visited people in the housing projects surrounding Queen of Angels in the 1960s, found that Queen of Angels Church became her calling card. "You were respected. All I had to say was, 'I'm from Queen of Angels,' and for the most part people opened up to you. Opened the door and opened up personally to you. I never felt any black or white issue at all—just a lot of respect for who you are and where you come from."[41] This was a testament to the forgiving nature of African Americans in the face of their achingly painful history in this nation, as well as to the respect that Queen of Angels earned over many decades.

The common denominator that runs throughout Queen of Angels' history is the respect the priests and sisters demonstrated toward the people they were evangelizing. We have seen the Trinitarians and priests living with the people and using the Corporal and Spiritual Works of Mercy as paradigms of Christian behavior. We find the same model in Rauschenbusch's *A Theology for the Social Gospel* with his "kingdom of God" theology, in Martin Luther King's "beloved community," and the praxis of the theology of liberation's preferential option for the poor, the marginalized, and the powerless.[42] We find it in Carey's taking sides and Queen of Angels' emphasis on empowerment, listening, and thinking big.

In her analysis of the black church and Community Development Corporations in "Bootstrap Ethics: Churches Helping Communities to Help Themselves," Melodie M. Toby indicates the importance of empowerment when black churches strive to address social inequities. Without an emphasis on empowerment, a selected few gain at the expense of "those who are most vulnerable."[43] Toby also focuses on the cooperative nature of any assistance enterprise from the church rather than on the individualistic, the melding of resources among churches including human resources, rather than isolated ventures that tend to place churches in competition instead of cooperation. I would argue that during the 1960s and early 1970s, Queen of Angels at least closely approximated the ideal that Toby upholds, and that New Community Corporation and Babyland Nursery continue to strive toward that ideal today, although outside an explicit ecclesial venue.[44] The history of Queen of Angels holds many lessons for today, in Newark and the country, as we struggle as a nation to unravel the problematic legacy of slavery and its attendant racism. When Mrs. Thornton said "church is church," I believe she also meant that people should be respected for who they are and what they believe, and that there is plenty good room for us all. Would that we could learn a lesson from her and the history of her little church in Newark.

Appendix 1

Tables on African American Populations

The following table illustrates the great geographical disparity in the black population between the Northeast (New England and Middle Atlantic States) and the South.

Table 1.
Geographical Location of Blacks in the United States, 1790–1860

	Northeast			South			
	Free Blacks	Slaves	Total	Free Blacks	Slaves	Total	% Total
1790	27,070	40,354	67,724	32,457	657,327	689,784	91.0%
1810	75,156	27,081	102,237	107,660	1,160,977	1,268,637	92.5%
1820	92,723	18,001	110,724	133,980	1,508,692	1,642,672	93.7%
1830	122,434	2,780	200,370	181,501	1,980,384	2,161,885	91.5%
1840	141,559	765	142,324	213,991	2,427,986	2,641,977	95.0%
1850	149,526	236[a]	149,762	235,569	3,116,629	3,352,198	95.7%
1860	155,983	18[a]	156,001	259,346	3,838,765	4,098,111	96.3%

Source: U.S. Census Reports, Statistical Abstract, 1949.

[a] The remaining slaves of 1850 and 1860 inhabited New Jersey. The last eighteen did not reside in Newark or Essex County. Giles R. Wright, Afro-Americans in New Jersey (Trenton: New Jersey Historical Commission, Dept. of State, 1988), 36.

Table 2.
Priests in the Negro Apostolate in 1929

Order	Number of Priests
African Mission Society	17
Benedictines	1
Capuchins	3
Divine Word, Society of the	16
Franciscans	3
Holy Ghost Fathers	38
Jesuits	4
St. Joseph, Society of	80
Vincentians	4
Subtotal	166
Secular Priests (Diocesan Clergy)	30[a]
Total	196

Source: John T. Gillard, S.S.J., *The Catholic Church and the American Negro; Being an Investigation of the Past and Present Activities of the Catholic Church* (Baltimore: St. Joseph's Society Press, 1929), 79.

[a]15.3% of the total number priests working with African Americans.

Table 3.
Priests in the Negro Apostolate in 1940

Order	Number of Priests
African Mission, Society of the (S.M.A.)	19
Atonement, Franciscan Friars, Fathers of the (S.A.)	3
Benedictine Fathers (O.S.B.)	9
Capuchin Fathers (O.M.Cap.)	5
Divine Word, Society of the (S.V.D.)	54
Dominican Fathers (O.P.)	5
Edmund, Society of St. (S.S.E.)	10
Franciscan Fathers (O.F.M.)	21
Franciscan Fathers (O.M.C.)	2
Holy Cross, Congregation of the (C.S.C.)	3
Holy Ghost, Fathers of the (C.S.Sp.)	62
Jesuit Fathers (S.J.)	16
Josephite Fathers (S.S.J.)	153
Oblates of Mary Immaculate (O.M.I.)	10
Oratorian Fathers (Cong. Orat.)	1
Passion, Congregation of the (C.P.)	7
Precious Blood, Society of the (C.P.P.S.)	6
Redemptorist Fathers (C.SS.R.)	16
Sacred Heart, Sons of the (F.S.C.)	2
Salvatorian Fathers (S.D.S.)	1
Vincentian Fathers (C.M.)	9
Subtotal	414
Secular Priests (Diocesan Clergy)	72[a]
Total	486

Source: John T. Gillard, S.S.J., *Colored Catholics in the United States: An Investigation of Catholic Activity in Behalf of the Negroes in the United States and a Survey of the Present Condition of the Colored Missions* (Baltimore: Josephite Press, 1941), 181.

[a]15% of the total number priests working with African Americans.

Table 4.
Ethel Wright's Students, 1916–1930

Catholic		Non-Catholic
Carl Brinson	Josephine Mitchell	Elizabeth Clark
Charles Brown	Maratina Neuman	Edith Corbin
Lulu Brown	Mary Joy Ridley	Venns Corbin
Nattie Brown	Mildred Ridley	Beatrice Finch
Virginia Brown	Ethel West	Junior Hahnes
Walter Brown	Katherine West	Frederick Lake
James Daniels	Albert West	Margaret Moore
Regina Gibson	Florence Williams	Whitney Parker
Leonard Hurd	Francis Williams	
Florence Lewis	Frances Williams	
Norman Lewis	Dorothy Yancy	
William Lewis		

SOURCE: Ethel Wright, "Ethel Wright's History: A Brief History of the Preecclesial Lay Organizations by the Founder of the Little Flower Guild (1928), a Satellite Group of the Theresa Lane Council" (Queen of Angels Parish Archives, n.d.).

Table 5.
Priests Who Signed Open Letter to Rev. Thomas A. Boland, January 8, 1969[a]

Priest	Congregation
Rev. James McManus	Queen of Angels, Newark
Rev. John Egan	Experimental Community, Jersey City
Very Rev. Msgr. Thomas Carey	Queen of Angels, Newark
Rev. Richard Iaquinto	St. Ann's, Newark
Rev. Joseph Woerner	St. Peter's, Newark
Rev. Robert McDonald, S.J.	Experimental Community, Jersey City
Rev. Thomas Comerford	Queen of Angels, Newark
Rev. Frank Testa	St. Bernard's, Plainfield
Rev. Francis Schiller	St. Patrick's, Jersey City
Rev. John Maloney	Queen of Angels, Newark
Rev. Robert Call	Experimental Community, Jersey City
Rev. Walter Kulzy	St. Patrick's, Jersey City
Rev. Joseph Ochs	St. Ann's, Newark
Rev. Donald McLaughlin	All Saints, Jersey City
Rev. William Linder	Queen of Angels, Newark
Rev. Edward Jocham	Christ the King, Jersey City
Rev. James O'Brien	Christ the King, Jersey City
Rev. William Gibbons	Blessed Sacrament, Newark
Rev. Frederick Quinn	Experimental Community, Jersey City
Rev. Frank Hurtz	Christ the King, Jersey City

SOURCE: Collection of the Archdiocese of Newark, Special Collections Center, Walsh Library, Seton Hall University, South Orange, N.J.

[a]Names are listed in the manner and order they appeared in the letter.

Appendix 2

Figures on Baptisms at Queen of Angels Church

Baptisms under Fr. Cornelius Ahern

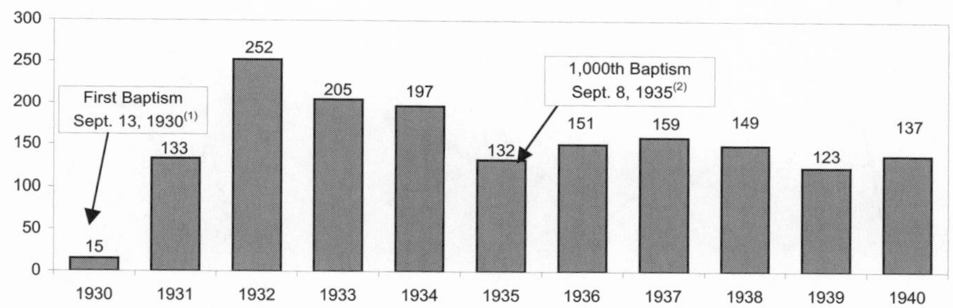

Baptisms under Fr. Joseph Lenihan

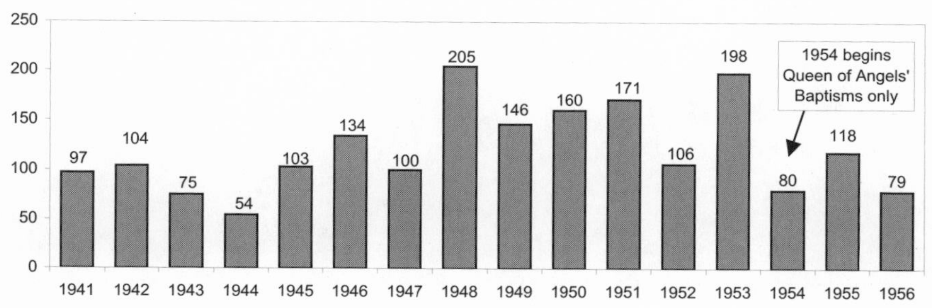

Baptisms under Fr. Thomas Carey

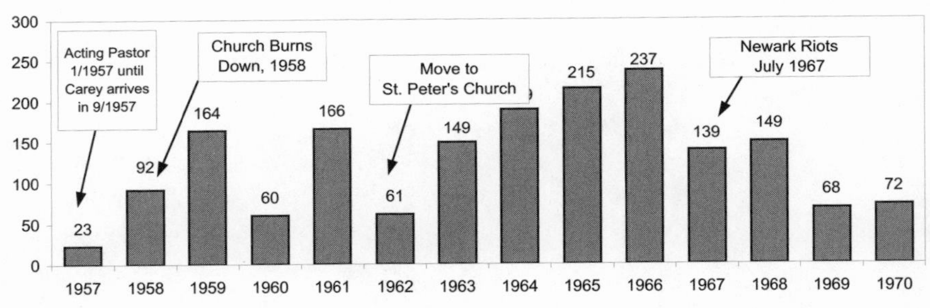

Baptisms at Queen of Angels, 1930–70

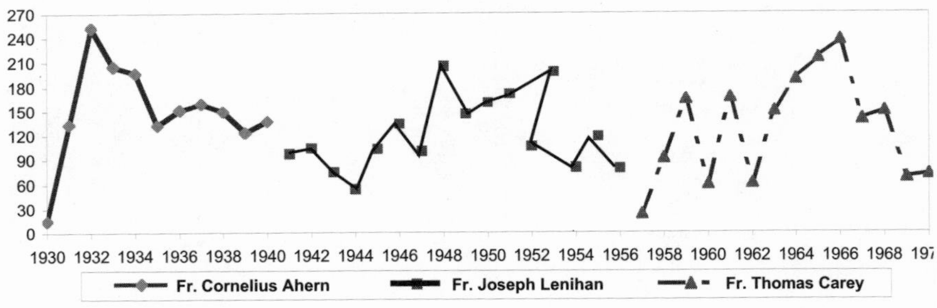

Baptisms at Queen of Angels, 1930–99

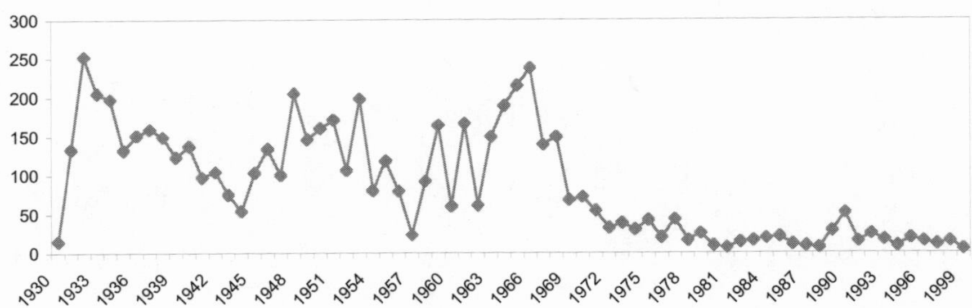

Percentages of Total Baptisms, 1930–99

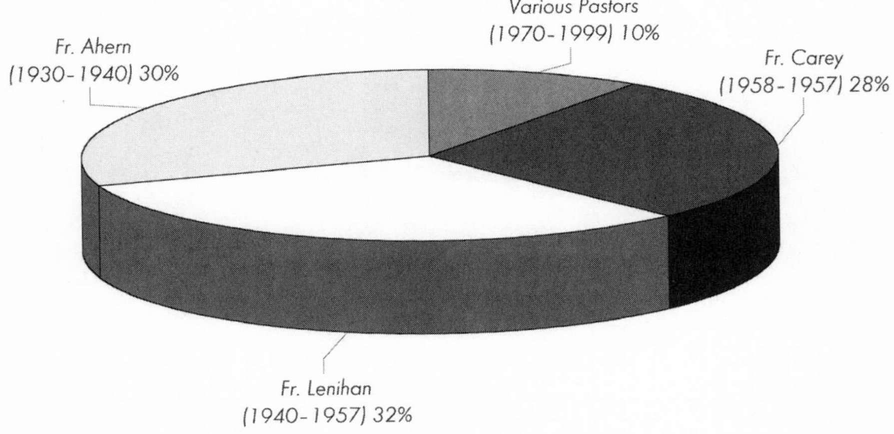

Appendix 3

Letter to Archbishop Thomas Boland from the Newark 20

JERSEY CITY, NEW JERSEY, 07305

The Most Reverend Thomas A. Boland, S.T.D., L.L.D.
Archbishop of Newark
31 Mulberry Street
Newark, New Jersey

Your Excellency:
Many men who seek the truth of Christ are confronted with a dilemma of conscience. We priests who are living and working in the inner city and are daily exposed to the shocking living conditions of our people, are particularly impelled by their dilemma to seek a solution. This dilemma cannot be ignored. It cannot be resolved with apathy or inaction. If we are to remain priests for our people then we must face the dilemma; and we must speak out.

The Church is evolving. But the evolution, once a promising hope of revitalizing the Church, has slowed to a placid pace of promises and platitudes but little social involvement. In the past we have diligently attempted to effect change but have been rebuffed. Having failed all else, no action short of this public expression remains open to us.

Dedicated Christians, lay and religious Catholic and non-Catholic plead in anguish to have the Church react to the inner-city social crisis. But we plead in a spiritual vacuum. The Official Church's concept of involvement is to change the liturgy from Latin to English. The poor are cold, hungry, housed in rat traps, largely ignored by the affluent society, denied employment opportunities, denied legal and moral rights, and the Official Church responds by changing the direction of the altar.

The blacks in our midst agonize in despair. They wither in spirit at the indignities and injustices of our Church's conspicuous contempt for their welfare. The Official Church reacts with the hypocrisy of a meaningless pastoral letter filled with promising rhetoric, but implemented with no action devices to relieve the suffering, no action to fortify the depressed spirit with hope for tomorrow.

Poverty funds decline while the police budgets escalate. Our society demands law and order, and city councils respond with discussions of police dogs and armed vigilante groups.

The hew and cry is for a law enforcement that will "keep *them* in their place," not the enforcement of the health laws, nor the sanitation laws, nor the housing codes.

The white dominated, apathetic establishment of the Catholic Archdiocese of Newark must be charged with the racism of indifference, the bigotry of indolence and the prejudice of apathy.

We, as Catholics, seem to be saying: "Pat the colored on the head, tell them to behave, assure them they are free. Ask them to go back to their cold shacks and let us enjoy the luxury of our country clubs, our winter cruises, our Llewelyn Park Mansions, our magnificent churches, and our pious preachments of love and brotherhood."

The Official Church is saying, "The church needs peace from 'their' complaints. We told 'them' they are free, what more do they want? What can the Official Church do if they won't behave?"

The Official Church is saying to our black brothers, "This is our church, our money, our buildings. It's ours; not yours. White men built these churches, not blacks."

The Official Church is saying, "We love you. Brothers and Sisters, but we'll love you better over there—out of our sight. We love you, but you make Catholics uncomfortable, you make us feel guilty. Certainly we love you. Didn't the Archbishop's pastoral letter tell you we love you?"

The Official Church is saying: "Suffering is ennobling. It's good for the soul. But suffering will be more noble, your soul more beautiful if you suffer lawfully, if you suffer in an orderly manner—like nice colored people should."

The Official Church is saying, "What are you blacks complaining about? Didn't Christ suffer for you? He accepted His suffering, why can't you? He didn't complain, why should you? Can't you see how the Official Church also suffers? We have to suffer through the endless meetings with the bankers, the architects, the professional fund raisers, the politicians, the travel cruise agencies. We have problems with our cooks, housekeepers, and gardeners, but you don't hear us complaining."

The Official Church is seeking isolation from the black—not involvement.

The Christian ideal calls for brotherhood of people. But the Official Church remains involved with things—buildings, investments, architects' plans, [and] property. The ideal of Jesus, which is love and brotherhood *is* contradicted by the practice of the Official Church which is indolence and apathy.

Thus our dilemmas: Can we, as priests, be good Catholics without first being good Christians? Or, expressed in loyalty terms, does not our obligation to Christ supercede our obligation to the Official Church? Perhaps the question is yours to answer, Archbishop Boland, and we herewith formally pose the question, and plead for your counsel. Can we serve the loving, merciful, compassionate Christ by being beholden to a cold, callous, calculating Official Church which responds to poverty with indifference, to injustice with indolence, to the need of the poor to be loved, with the hypocrisy of prejudice and racism?

Ultimately, you'll agree, the decision and commitment is internal, within the conscience of each of us as individuals endowed with free will. Therefore, and responding to our individual consciences which have been formed in meditative contemplation, it is decided, by the undersigned, that the Christian leadership needed to alleviate the suffering and indignities of the poor, especially the black and Spanish poor, is not present in the contemporary composition of the Official Church in the Newark Archdiocese. But the leadership is present in the Gospels of the Apostles. And the leadership is present in the Holy Spirit. The leadership is present in the integrity and orthodoxy of Jesus' concepts and commands of love and brotherhood. Why does the Official Church abandon its mandated, authoritative role of Christian leadership?

In the absence of the Christian leadership from the Official Church, it is necessary that we organize as a group whose main purpose is to respond, as priests, to the Holy Father's plea in Bogota, to work with the poor. Respond, too, to the command of the Lord who said, "that which you do to the least of these my brothers, you do also unto me." If we abandon the impoverished black in our Archdiocese, we also abandon Christ.

To this aim, we will immediately organize as a social force (we being only the seed core) and commit ourselves positively and publicly, for organization purposes, as the "Inner City Priests United for Christian Action." We will expand the organization by homogenizing lay and religious groups on a statewide basis (the Mercy of Christ cannot be fenced in with diocesan geographic boundaries) so the assets and contributions of concerned Christians in all areas of the state can be harnessed as a force focused to the turbulent inner cities.

We will operate laterally as Catholic priests—independent of, but not in defiance of, the Chancery Offices.

Lacking your leadership we don't want the zeal of our commitment to be diluted by the programmed apathy of the official Church nor the contrived inaction of your attitudes.

We seek positive Christian racial action, not popularity. We seek results—not approval. We seek justice for the black, not the rewards of obedient meek subservience to the politics of the Church establishment. Our reward is the relieving of the suffering of our people. This will be the joy of our work.

There is nothing to entice us from our mission to reduce the slum-life burden of our black brothers.

It is hoped that our action will be interpreted in the secular and religious press as a dramatic act of dissent from the racial and social indifference of many American Dioceses. We remain, you have our assurance, obedient to the inherent authority of your office; we accept it; we respect it; but when this authority is in direct conflict with our conscience, then the teachings of Jesus assumes primacy. If we are to be His priests, we must first be HIS.

We are confident that you'll be interested in the following social factors that motivate us.

Let us review: America denies equal opportunities—equal health facilities to our black brothers despite 10 years of aggressive, dramatic, justifiable pleas for equality.

The following figures tell a revolting, un-American, un-Christian story of America's continued neglect of our minority groups.

	Non-White	White
Still births per l,000 live births	27.2	13.9
Infant deaths under one year old (per 1,000)	40.3	21.5
Maternal deaths per 100,000 live births	83.7	21.0
Life expectancy at age one, males	62.9	68.3
Life expectancy at age, females	68.9	75.1

Meditate on these three conclusions Archbishop Boland, and you will comprehend, and we hope, share the depth of our anguish and witness the need of our actions:

1. Twice as many black children die stillborn than whites
2. Twice as many black babies in the hungry, unhealthy slums die as infants than whites
3. Four times as many black mothers die bearing God's children as do white mothers,

Now Archbishop Boland, help us examine our collective, diocesan condolence in the Newark Archdiocese.

Incident A: One priest in this diocese who is the Pastor of a large Church in a 65% black parish, constructed barbed wire fencing around his school playground to keep them black kids off his property and out of his gym. This callous isolation from social involvement, this denial of existing playground facilities and the use of the gymnasium to black youngsters, makes us share culpability for the "crimes" in the street. Such arrogant parochial actions inflict a 20th century thorn in the scalp of the crucified Christ.

Incident B: One pastor in your Diocese, who would identify himself as a Christian gentleman, does not have black altar boys serve when he celebrates Mass—and his parish is 95% black. Such acts of racial psychological cruelty serve as another nail in the body of Jesus our Redeemer.

Incident C: The Vicar General, Fr. Ansbro told one of the undersigned priests personally that the parish church does not belong [to] the Negroes because white people built it, and that Christ cannot possibly be living in the black community; they are just drunkards, carousers, and thieves.

Incident D: The Newark Public High Schools are certified by state authorities as being poorest in the state with concentration of black students ranging to 90%. And we, in our Catholic Diocesan schools, siphon off nearly 100% white students creating, in effect, the defacto segregation situation, in the public high schools. The Newark Diocesan Catholic High Schools is [*sic*] nothing less than the largest white racially segregated private school system in the State of New Jersey.

Incident E: During the last presidential election, the students at Essex Catholic High School, in a mock voting test, elected Wallace for president. That our Catholic high school students would "elect" the demagog Wallace for president does not speak well of the quality of the message of Christianity being receivers by these white Catholic students.

Incident F: A Hudson County parish, once all white, now mostly black, has on its premises four beautiful championship quality bowling alleys with spectator stands, which are in use one day a month. This parish also has a fully equipped, professional Broadway theatre seating 1200 people. The Pastor pays approximately $1000 annually in maintenance costs to keep the bowling alleys in tip-top shape—but he refuses to permit black people to use the bowling lanes. How many Catholic insults can we expect our black brothers to take—and remain unmilitant.

Incident G: A Pastor of a parish in a totally black area, and the secretary refer to black people as "niggers." This speaks for itself. It tells a multitude about the mentality of a man who would use such a degrading term for the people he should be serving.

Indeed, Archbishop Boland, the list is long, dreary, and unconscionable. The only relief of the sorrowful apathy in the Newark Diocese is the sadder fact that almost every other diocese in America is equally indolent, equally casual to the command of God to "Love your neighbor with your whole mind, your whole heart, your whole soul."

As the Official Church in the Newark Archdiocese, Archbishop Boland, you have prescribed a do nothing apathy for a social evil that is already pregnant with danger to the body and soul of the Christian Church. Your medication of look-the-other-way, is preventing the birth of a renewed Church with Christ-like involvement but it may produce the bastard of church corruption that will recreate the indolent, unconcerned evils of the pre-reformation period. Your vacuous abandonment of the 500,000 black souls in your diocese will do more world wide historical harm to Christ's Church than the Anti-Christs that have populated history.

You are aware, of course, that our group action is the only course remaining open to us. You have refused to be a leader in regard to the poor and suffering. Our ideas have been rejected by you for more than a decade.

We have heretofore fastidiously observed the traditional protocol procedures and you attempt to silence us with patronizing indifference and uncharitable aloofness. We have escalated our appeals to you through the stages of courteous requests, thence to urgent appeals, and finally to the frustrated drama of requirements.

But you have put us aside as disobedient little children who are not minding our own business. We remind you that we are mature citizens and Christians—convinced that the tension in inner cities is so frought [*sic*] with potential danger to the life and limb of black men, women, and children—and the frustrated policemen—that we can no longer approach you with ineffective courtesies.

You say you will not accept a mandate. We say our personal obligation to Christ as individual priests is so strong *that we will not be put aside* as children by the Official Church.

We resubmit our plan for Diocesan reform—hoping still it can be incorporated into a renewed Christian diocese.

It is not submitted in humility—but with pride and confidence in the Holy Spirit. We do not request, nor appeal, nor urge—we *demand* your attention and action. It is too late for Chancery niceties. It is time for the apathetic church to assume its historical militant role of Christian leadership as we are doing with these uncompromisable requirements.

The plan is simple. Priestly work in America's inner cities requires a precious empathy and experience with minority groups. Not all priests are suited for this peculiar missionary work. To be successful, the priest must want to work in the inner city. He must have the special talents of patience, of compassion, of aggressive love, a willingness to oppose officialdom, when necessary, cut red tape, and become righteously indignant at the built in bureaucracy of our structured politics. Above all, he must exhibit a tenacity which overcomes frustration. The successes are few, the road is rough, the problems are many.

But the promise of Christ is freedom in joy; the promise of America is freedom in the pursuit of happiness. One must love the journey of sacrifice and labor as well as the destination of peace, love and joy.

The validity of these seven suggestions which you have so ignominiously rejected, cannot be ignored.

1. From the priests in your diocese who are working for a year or more in inner city work, accept a committee as expert advisors to you. Provide them authority commensurate to the responsibility of the urgent social and spiritual needs of the 500,000 black and Spanish souls to whom they will minister. Accept too, black lay experienced leaders, who will serve with the priests as an action council. See them for one prescheduled hour each week until the present urgency is relieved—but see them, in the words paraphrased from the Gospel, with an open mind, with an open heart, and with an open soul.
2. This committee should prescreen all priests to be assigned to the inner city parishes having in mind that they must want to work with the black and Spanish and must possess psychological aptitudes for the work and evidence a stamina to tolerate the endless frustrations.

3. Instantly transfer all pastors in black areas who have not proven a predisposition for justice by their record of performance in their inner city churches.
4. In the inner city parishes, abandon, pro tem, the parochial role and permit co-equal parish management to the team of priests assigned to the work. One administrator will manage finances, but excepting this pragmatic chore, this will permit innovation of involvement of church facilities as indicated by the judgement and experience of this team.
5. Commit every pastor to instantly make available all church property in black or near black areas—remove the barbwire from playgrounds, open the bowling alleys and conceive of the Church as belonging to all people—all blacks and all whites.
6. In areas of high black density, recognize the need for experimentation in developing new ideas and approaches to living the Christian life. Know and approve their need to "fight City Hall" on an individual personal basis—but—dignify their work with your approval.
7. The establishment of the "Human Relations" office in the Diocese is ill-disguised nonsense. This office is nothing more than a cheap, deceptive Madison Avenue Public Relations trick to explain why we do nothing in the inner city. The principal contribution of this Madison Avenue gimmick is to explain why we fiddle while the soul of Christ burns in spiritual indignation at the indifferent, unconcerned attitude of the Official Church of the Newark Archdiocese. Dissolve it forthwith.

In closings Archbishop Boland, it must be said that we anticipate your resentment of our public stance. We need you as our Brother in Christ, we respect you and your personal spiritual life, we honor you with our continued invitation to understand our compulsion to work actively, today, NOW, for the black community—*but* we don't fear you.

Unless there can be forthcoming quickly some sincere evidence that you share our concern and share, too, our feeling of urgency, it is our intent to release—via *another* press conference a detailed record of diocesan indolence and relate the dismal record of performance to the unfulfilled promise of your November pastoral letter.

Our point of view, our analysis of the record shows a contradiction that will not evoke diocesan pride.

Obediently, in conscience, we assure you of our zest for a fulfilling Christian life with our impoverished black brothers.

Sincerely in Christ,

Rev. James McManus
Queen of Angels
44 Belmont Avenue
Newark

Rev. John Egan
Experimental Community
450 Grove Street
Jersey City

Very Rev. Msgr. Thomas Carey
Queen of Angels
44 Belmont Avenue
Newark

Rev. Richard Iaquinto
St. Ann's
16th Avenue & So. 7th Street
Newark

Rev. Joseph Woerner
St. Peter's
334 Lyons Avenue
Newark

Rev. Robert McDonald, S.J.
Experimental Community
460 Grove Street
Jersey City

Rev. Thomas Comerford
Queen of Angels
44 Belmont Avenue
Newark

Rev. Frank Testa
St. Bernard's
1235 George Street
Plainfield

Rev. Francis Schiller
St. Patrick's
492 Bramhall Avenue
Jersey City

Rev. John Maloney
Queen of Angels
44 Belmont Avenue
Newark

Rev. Robert Call
Experimental Community
460 Grove Street
Jersey City

Rev. Walter Kulzy
St. Patrick's
492 Bramhall Avenue
Jersey City

Rev. Joseph Ochs
St. Ann's
16th Avenue & So. 7th Street
Newark

Rev. Donald McLaughlin
All Saints
295 Pacific Avenue
Jersey City

Rev. William Linder
Queen of Angels
44 Belmont Avenue
Newark

Rev. Edward Jocham
Christ the King
766 Ocean Avenue
Jersey City

Rev. James O'Brien
Christ the King
766 Ocean Avenue
Jersey City

Rev. William Gibbons
Blessed Sacrament
Clinton Avenue & Van Ness Place
Newark

Rev. Frederick Quinn
Experimental Community
460 Grove Street
Jersey City

Rev. Frank Hurtz
Christ the King
766 Ocean Avenue
Jersey City

Notes

Works frequently cited have been identified by the following abbreviations:

AACN	Clement Price. The Afro-American Community of Newark: 1917–1947: A Social History. Ph.D. diss., Rutgers Univ., 1975.
ADN	Collection of the Archdiocese of Newark. Special Collections Center, Walsh Library, Seton Hall Univ., South Orange, N.J.
ADN: QAPP	Archdiocese of Newark. Special Collections Center, Queen of Parish Papers.
BCAAE	C. Eric Lincoln and Lawrence S. Mamiya. The Black Church in the African American Experience. Durham, N.C.: Duke Univ. Press, 1990.
CCAN	John T. Gillard, S.S.J. The Catholic Church and the American Negro; Being an Investigation of the Past and Present Activities of the Catholic Church. Baltimore: St. Joseph's Society Press, 1929.
CCIUS	John T. Gillard, S.S.J. Colored Catholics in the United States: An Investigation of Catholic Activity in Behalf of the Negroes in the United States and a Survey of the Present Condition of the Colored Missions. Baltimore: Josephite Press, 1941.
EWH	"Ethel Wright's History: A Brief History of the Preecclesial Lay Organizations by the Founder of the Little Flower Guild (1928), a Satellite Group of the Theresa Lane Council" (handwritten MS).
QAPA	Queen of Angels Parish Archives, 44 Irvine Turner Boulevard, Newark, N.J.
TLCM	Minutes of the Theresa Lane Council, the first lay group of African American Catholics, organized in January 1927.

Introduction

1. Norbert Brox, *A Concise History of the Early Church* (New York: Continuum Publishing Co., 1996), vii.
2. See chapter 6 of Albert J. Raboteau, *A Fire in the Bones: Reflections on African-American Religious History* (Boston: Beacon Press, 1995), 117–37.
3. Robert Anthony Orsi, *The Madonna of 115th Street: Faith and Community in Italian Harlem, 1880–1950* (New Haven: Yale Univ. Press, 1985).
4. The exhibit was sponsored by the Newark Archdiocesan Office of Black Catholics, director Lucille Forman, and mounted by the Special Collections Center of the Archdiocese of Newark under the direction of JoAnn Cotz.
5. Cyprian Davis, O.S.B., *The History of Black Catholics in the United States* (New York: Crossroad, 1990), vi.
6. Since then, through grants, the parish has been able to do some repairs, and the building has been declared a historic building.
7. An interesting related topic is the study of Mitochondrial DNA, (mtDNA) which suggests not only that race is not a biological category, but also that genetic markers indicate all human beings are descended from a common ancestor. A human phylogenetic tree based on vigilant data supports an African genesis hypothesis with long-term gene flow proceeding from an African woman and passed on through women donors alone. See Roy D'Andrade and Phillip A. Morin, "Chimpanzee and Human Mitochondrial DNA: Principal Components and Individual-by-Site Analysis" *American Anthropologist* 98, no. 2 (1996): 352–70.
8. Martin Luther King Jr., "Letter from a Birmingham Jail," reprinted in *Foundations of Theological Study: A Sourcebook,* Richard Viladesau and Mark Massa, eds. (New York: Paulist Press, 1991), 281.
9. Ibid.
10. See Mark S. Massa, S.J., Catholics and American Culture (New York: Crossroad Publishing Co., 1999), 180–82. Massa gives a clear explanation of the terms sister, nun, and women religious according to canon (church) law. Also, by way of a powerful

historical event, the reader obtains a snapshot of women religious in this country since the Second Vatican Council in 1965.

11. Raymond E. Brown, *The Churches the Apostles Left Behind* (Ramsey, N.J.: Paulist Press, 1984), 41.
12. See J. E. T. Eldridge, ed., *Max Weber: The Interpretation of Social Reality* (New York: Charles Scribner's Sons, 1971; reprint, New York: Schocken Books, 1971), page references are to reprint edition.
13. Carey told me several times that he most often would proceed without asking for permission, and he speculated that this was historically often the case. He felt that if he asked for permission, he would have been denied it; however, the archdiocese never seemed to notice anything untoward after the fact, either negatively or positively. Although he perceived the archdiocese's tacit permission as indifference, he was nonetheless grateful for the freedom it gave him.
14. Typologies are heuristic tools used to analyze sociological phenomena. See C. Eric Lincoln and Lawrence S. Mamiya in *The Black Church in the African American Experience* (Durham, N.C.: Duke Univ. Press, 1990), 10–16. They are derived from Max Weber's theories concerning ideal types. Evelyn Brooks Higginbotham characterizes the church "as a dialogic model rather than dialectical, recognizing "dynamic tension" in a multiplicity of protean and concurrent meanings and intentions more so than in a series of discrete polarities." Evelyn Brooks Higginbotham, *Righteous Discontent: The Women's Movement in the Black Baptist Church, 1880–1920* (Cambridge, Mass.: Harvard Univ. Press, 1993), 16. Her model may more accurately interpret the reality; however, Weber did express important cautions in the use of ideal types. He insisted that they be used in the service of the facts to uncover real causes and that they are beneficial in that regard only if the "ideal-typical developmental *constructs* and *history* are to be sharply distinguished from each other" (229). He warned against the danger of "doing violence to reality in order to prove the real validity of the construct" (230). The operative presupposition underlying this study is the dynamic rather than static, multileveled and multivalent character of human belief and behavior. These typologies are suggestive of reality rather than rigidly categorical.
15. Mechal Sobel, *Trablin' On: The Slave Journey to Afro-Baptist Faith,* 2d ed. (Princeton, N.J.: Princeton Univ. Press, 1988), xvii.
16. See also Melva Wilson Costen, *African American Christian Worship* (Nashville: Abingdon Press, 1993) for a comprehensive discussion of the African American Sacred Cosmos and its history and relationship to various worship styles within the community.
17. Interview with Cecilia Faulks, Aug. 18, 1993.

1. Errand into an Urban Wilderness

1. Although there were African slaves in Massachusetts, Connecticut, and Rhode Island before 1640, and New Jersey's first constitution of 1664, the "Concessions," offered seventy-five acres of land for every slave brought into the colony, there is no evidence that Africans were among the first band of Connecticut Puritans who set foot on the Passaic shore. "The first families had brought some servants from Connecticut, probably indentured young people with close spiritual or family ties to the founders." John Cunningham, *Newark,* 2d ed. (Trenton: New Jersey Historical Commission, 1988), 53.
2. "[W]hile the first aim [of John Winthrop's Massachusetts Bay Company] was indeed to realize in America the due form of government, both civil and ecclesiastical, the aim behind that aim was to vindicate the most rigorous ideal of the Reformation, so that ultimately all Europe would imitate New England." Perry Miller, *Errand into the Wilderness* (Cambridge, Mass.: Belknap Press of Harvard Univ. Press, 1956), 12.
3. Miller, *Errand into the Wilderness,* 4. William Bradford was the second governor of Plymouth Colony from 1622 to 1656. The motives for immigrating to what became the New England states were both for religious freedom and for personal monetary gain. There were those who entered into an explicit covenant with God, who sought the "very essence of organized Christianity" (5). The first Pilgrims to land in Newark were such as these. Among the many classic histories on early American Puritan history are Edmond S. Morgan, *The Puritan Dilemma: The Story of John Winthrop* (Boston: Little, Brown and Co., 1958); Sidney E. Mead, *The Lively Experiment: The Shaping of Christianity in America* (New York: Harper & Row, 1976); Robert T. Handy, *A Christian America: Protestant Hopes and Historical Realities,* 2d ed. (New York: Oxford Univ. Press, 1984); and Winthrop S. Hudson, *Religion in America,* 4th ed. (New York: Macmillan, 1987).
4. See Miller, *Errand into the Wilderness,* for the definitive explanation of this important aspect of the Puritan experience.
5. Jay P. Dolan, *The American Catholic Experience: A History from Colonial Times to the Present* (Garden City, N.Y.: Doubleday, 1985; reprint, Notre Dame: Univ. of Notre Dame Press, 1992), 71–76 (page number references are to the reprint edition). This is an excellent resource for an overview of Catholicism in North America from the arrival of Ponce de León in Florida in 1513.
6. Joseph M. Flynn, M.R., V.F., *The Catholic Church in New Jersey* (New York: Publisher's Printing Co., 1904), 12.
7. Wallace N. Jamison, *Religion in New Jersey: A Brief History* (Princeton, N.J.: D. Van Nostrand Co., 1964), 81.

8. Francis Newton Thorpe, ed., *The Federal and State Constitutions* (Washington, 1909), v, 2599.
9. Previous to that time, the majority of Irish who emigrated were Presbyterian or Anglican Ulsterites. The term *Scotch-Irish,* unknown in Ireland, was assumed by former Ulsterites to differentiate themselves from the hordes of poorer and Catholic immigrants to follow during the famine and after. See Noel Ignatiev, *How the Irish Became White* (New York: Routledge, 1995), 37–39.
10. U.S. Dept. of Commerce, Bureau of the Census, *Historical Statistics of the United States, 1789–1945* (Washington, D.C.: Government Printing Office, 1949). (Hereafter census data cited as *U.S. Census Report* and the appropriate year.)
11. Dolan, *The American Catholic Experience*, 202. Also see Joseph P. Chinnici, O.F.M., *Living Stones: The History and Structure of Catholic Spiritual Life in the United States* (New York: Macmillan, 1989), 95–96.
12. Carl D. Hinrichsen, "Winand Michael Wigger," in New Jersey Catholic Historical Records Commission, *Bishops of Newark, 1853–1978,* 15. Bayley was from a wealthy and prominent Episcopalian family of Connecticut and New York. He was related to the Roosevelts and was the nephew of Saint Elizabeth Ann Seton, who established the Sisters of Charity. He converted to Catholicism while an Episcopal priest, served on the faculty of St. John's College (now Fordham University), and, while acting as president of that college, obtained a charter from the state legislature to transfer the institution to the Jesuits.
13. Jamison, *Religion in New Jersey,* 111–15. See also Dolan, *The American Catholic Experience,* for more on the struggle between the democratically influenced trustee system of the laity and the hierarchy's success in bringing it to an end.
14. In 1881 New Jersey obtained two dioceses, Trenton and Newark, and Wigger was appointed to the Newark diocese.
15. Dolan, *The American Catholic Experience,* 297.
16. Flynn, *The Catholic Church in New Jersey,* 490–94.
17. Hinrichsen, "Winand Michael Wigger," 54.
18. *Official Catholic Directory* (New York: P. J. Kenedy & Sons, 1919).
19. Hinrichsen, "Winand Michael Wigger," 61–66.
20. Carol K. Coburn and Martha Smith, *Spirited Lives: How Nuns Shaped Catholic Culture and America, 1836–1920* (Chapel Hill: Univ. of North Carolina Press, 1999), 2.
21. Immigrants to the United States, mainly Irish and German, increased substantially from 1820 to 1870. The total number of immigrants to the United States from 1821 to 1850 was more than 2.4 million, and approximately 2.5 million in each successive decade until 1880. From 1880 to 1890, 5.2 million immigrants entered the

United States, dropping to 3.7 million from 1890 to 1900. From 1821 to 1850, the greatest number of Irish immigrants was almost 1.1 million, or 42.3 percent of the total; and in that same time German immigrants reached 593,841, or 24.2 percent, of the total. Irish immigration diminished from 35.2 percent of total immigration from 1851 to 1860 and to only 10.6 percent of the total in the decade from 1891 to 1900. German immigration remained fairly constant at 25.6 percent to 36.6 percent between 1851 and 1890, dropping to 13.7 percent in the decade between 1891 and 1900. The Italian population of New Jersey increased from 1,547 in 1880 to 32,487 in 1900. *U.S. Census Reports,* 1880 and 1900.

22. For an elucidation of the Catholic Irish and German story in America, see Jay P. Dolan, *Immigrant Church* (Baltimore: Johns Hopkins Univ. Press, 1977; reprint, Notre Dame: Univ. of Notre Dame Press, 1983). (Page references are to reprint edition.) Also see Ignatiev, *How the Irish Became White*; and Cahill, *How the Irish Saved Civilization,* for further reading on the history of the Irish in Ireland (especially with the penal codes imposed by the English) and their sojourn in America in the nineteenth century. See also Dolan, *The American Catholic Parish,* and Dolan, *The American Catholic Experience*.
23. John T. McGreevy, *Parish Boundaries: The Catholic Encounter with Race in the Twentieth-Century Urban North* (Chicago: Univ. of Chicago Press, 1996), 11.
24. Ibid., 33.
25. Dolan, *Immigrant Church*, 86.
26. See Ignatiev, *How the Irish Became White,* on the controversy that raged between the Irish and Irish Americans over slavery and labor issues. Ignatiev focuses on the Irish American effort to distance themselves from African Americans psychologically, socially, and pragmatically on the labor front.
27. Charles R. Morris, *American Catholic* (New York: Times Books, 1997), 76–78.
28. Based on lower figures credited by the federal government. *Record of Officers and Men of New Jersey in the Civil War, 1861 to 1865* (Adjutant General's Office; Adj. Gen. William Stryker, 1876).
29. Morris, *American Catholic,* 79.
30. Ibid., 78.
31. Dolan, *Immigrant Church*, 24.
32. Ibid.
33. Ibid. Dolan compares the position of blacks in the Catholic Church with that of "orphan" Italians of the nineteenth century, when resources were expended on the larger German and Irish immigrant populations. The children of blacks were refused entrance to parish schools, and of the estimated 1,500 black Catholics living in New York in 1865 not even 100 attended church.

34. Clement Price, *The Afro-American Community of Newark: 1917–1947: A Social History* (Ph.D. diss., Rutgers Univ., 1975), 16.
35. Walter P. Brown interview, December 5, 1992. Fr. Cornelius Ahern baptized Mr. Brown and many of his relatives in 1931 at St. Bridget's Hall. Brown made the point that when he returned from active duty in World War II, both his white and black neighbors remembered him and expressed pride in his service to the country.
36. Interview with former Mayor Kenneth Gibson, Nov. 1, 1997.
37. William J. Scott, *Passaic and Its Environs* (New York, 1922), 179.
38. Donald R. Wright, *African Americans in the Colonial Era: From African Origins through the American Revolution*, The American History Series, ed. John Hope Franklin and Abraham S. Eisenstadt (Arlington Heights, Ill.: Harlan Davidson, 1990), 74. For more on slavery in New Jersey see George Fishman, "The Struggle for Freedom and Equality: African-Americans in New Jersey, 1624–1849/50" (Ph.D. diss., Temple Univ., 1990), 31–39. Fishman details the presence of African slaves and free blacks brought to New Jersey by the Dutch and the Swedes before the English captured the colony. He points out that by 1664 settlements of blacks existed in areas now known as Hackensack, Jersey City, and Hoboken and were near the future settlement of Newark. See also Henry Scofield Cooley, *A Study of Slavery in New Jersey,* Johns Hopkins Univ. Studies in Historical and Political Science, ed. Herbert B. Adams, no. 14 (Baltimore: Johns Hopkins Press, 1896).
39. Ibid., 9. The Quakers, who were the first to organize opposition to slavery in 1724, used a strategy of buying slaves in order to either set them free or hold them in a virtually free state. They hired a young attorney, William Gaston, to defend their right to do so before the supreme court of North Carolina in 1827. John Hope Franklin, *Race and History: Selected Essays, 1938–1988* (Baton Rouge: Louisiana State Univ. Press, 1989), 80–85.
40. For more on this topic see Frances D. Pingeon, "Slavery in New Jersey on the Eve of Revolution," in *New Jersey in the American Revolution: Political and Social Conflict,* rev. ed., ed. William C. Wright (Trenton: New Jersey Historical Commission, 1974).
41. Marion T. Wright, "New Jersey Laws and the Negro," *Journal of Negro History* 27 (1943): 35. After 1800, when most northeastern states enacted laws of manumission or complete abolition, the slave population in those states dropped precipitously: 36,370 in 1800; 18,000 in 1820; 2,780 in 1830; 765 in 1840; 236 in 1850; and 18 in 1860. *U.S. Census Reports,* 1800–1860. See table 1, appendix 1.
42. For example, even though the 1840 U.S. census counted only 765 slaves in all of the northeastern states, in 1845 Alvan Stewart argued before the New Jersey Supreme Court that the state constitution of 1844 did not actually abolish slavery. He counted 4,000 slaves in New Jersey. He was referring to the life apprentices

whom he described as "property, in its base sense, slaves for years, [their] parents deprived of all jurisdiction of their offspring, all direction of their education, and paternal tenderness." Alvan Stewart, *A Legal Argument before the Supreme Court of New Jersey at the May Term, 1845, at Trenton for the Deliverance of 4,000 Persons from Bondage* (New York, 1845), 26.

43. Higginbotham, *Righteous Discontent,* 43.
44. Monroe Fordham, *Major Themes in Northern Black Religious Thought: 1800–1860* (Hicksville, N.Y.: Exposition Press, 1975), 34.
45. W. E. B. DuBois, *The Souls of Black Folk* (New York: Fawcett Publications, 1967), 42–54.
46. *BCAAE,* 8.
47. See Albert J. Raboteau, *Slave Religion: The "Invisible Institution" in the Antebellum South* (New York: Oxford Univ. Press, 1978), 99–108. For an in-depth analysis of the effects of the egalitarian nature of Evangelicalism on blacks and women in the South, see Donald G. Mathews, *Religion in the Old South* (Chicago: Univ. of Chicago Press, 1977).
48. Ibid.
49. See Sobel, *Trablin' On,* for her thesis regarding the "Sacred Cosmos" discussed in the introduction.
50. Methodist founders, Charles and John Wesley were not allowed to preach in churches and would hold meetings in fields for Bible instruction. Methodism was very attractive to the working class who felt the Church of England inaccessible because of its cold, intellectual approach.
51. Raboteau, *A Fire in the Bones,* 21–24.
52. *Newark Evening News,* May 28, 1966.
53. Ibid. Atkinson, *The History of Newark, New Jersey,* 162–63; Cunningham, *Newark,* 131; and Giles R. Wright, *Afro-Americans in New Jersey* (Trenton: New Jersey Historical Commission, Dept. of State, 1988), 30. Each of these sources gives a different name to this black church: Cunningham calls it the Fourth Presbyterian, which is most likely incorrect since there was a white Fourth Presbyterian in Newark pastored by Dr. Weeks at that time. Atkinson's history, written in 1878, identifies it as the African Presbyterian; Wright indicates the name was the Plane Street Presbyterian Church, which corresponds to a *Newark Evening News* article of May 28, 1966, citing Mrs. Mae Smith Williams, the church's historian. David E. Swift stated that when the Presbyterian minister and editor, the Reverend Samuel Cornish, took over the parish in 1840, it was called the Colored Presbyterian Church of Newark. David E. Swift, *Black Prophets of Justice: Activist Clergy before the Civil War* (Baton Rouge: Louisiana State Univ. Press, 1989), 2; *BCAAE,* 23–25.

54. *ACCN,* 78. For more on the Black Church and its relationship to the larger African American culture, see Clement Alexander Price, ed., *Freedom Not Far Distant: A Documentary History of Afro-Americans in New Jersey* (Newark: New Jersey Historical Society, 1980); Lerone Bennett Jr., *Before the Mayflower: A History of Black America*, 6th ed. (New York: Penguin Books, 1993).
55. Swift, *Black Prophets of Justice,* 2.
56. The movement to transplant freed African Americans to other countries began in 1816. A variety of motivations and agendas inspired the idea of African American colonization, but the overlying objective was the removal of freed slaves, who had economic and educational needs to be dealt with and who served as reminders to those still enslaved that the possibility of freedom existed. It was theorized that removing them entirely from the scene would eradicate this threat, as well as any competition to the rising immigrant population, who were often just as poor and uneducated and competed for the same housing and menial jobs. Prominent religious leaders of New Jersey advocated strongly for this solution to these problems, as did Francis Scott Key and President James Monroe. Theodore Frelinghuysen, a Newark lawyer who became the vice president of the American Colonization Society, helped collect funds for transportation, education, supplies, and housing for those relocated to Africa (Swift, *Black Prophets of Justice,* 24–25). Thomas Jefferson weighed in on the question by contending that the prejudices of whites and the resentment of blacks toward their ill treatment would prevent peaceful coexistence and lead to the extermination of one race by the other (Thomas Jefferson, *Notes on the State of Virginia,* ed. William Harwood Peden [Chapel Hill: University of North Carolina Press, 1995], 138). David Swift's *Black Prophets of Justice: Activist Clergy Before the Civil War* is an excellent reference for the history of colonization in the American-founded colony of Liberia, Africa, and the rise of African American leadership.
57. *U.S. Census Report,* 1870.
58. *AACN,* 78.
59. Some 64.2 percent of black men worked as unskilled laborers—servants, draymen, and living stable keepers; 88.3 percent of black women worked as laundresses and servants. *U.S. Census Report,* 1890.
60. See Walter F. Pitts, *Old Ship of Zion: The Afro-Baptist Ritual in the African Diaspora* (New York: Oxford Univ. Press, 1993), 28–29.
61. *AACN,* 75.
62. Giles Wright, *Afro-Americans in New Jersey,* 29–30.
63. John T. Gillard, S.S.J., *Colored Catholics in the United States: An Investigation of Catholic Activity in Behalf of the Negroes in the United States and a Survey of the*

Present Condition of the Colored Missions (Baltimore: Josephite Press, 1941), 76. Gillard's two books, *The Catholic Church and the American Negro* (1929) and *Colored Catholics in the United States* represented a considerable contribution to the African American Catholic historical record.

64. John T. Gillard, S.S.J., *The Catholic Church and the American Negro; Being an Investigation of the Past and Present Activities of the Catholic Church* (Baltimore: St. Joseph's Society Press, 1929), 13–14, 54–55.
65. *CCIUS,* 71.
66. With the lack of any hard data, Gillard estimated the figure at 100,000 (*CCIUS,* 95–99). Jay P. Dolan accepted this figure as generous, as did Randall Miller. See Jay P. Dolan, ed., *The American Catholic Parish,* vol. 1, *The Northeast, Southeast and South Central States* (New York: Paulist Press, 1987), 131; and Miller, "The Failed Mission," 164–70.
67. Dolan, *American Catholic Parish,* 13. For example, in 1890, 1,360,677 of 1,871,509, or 71.3 percent, of the Irish lived in the seven states of Massachusetts, Connecticut, New York, New Jersey, Pennsylvania, Ohio, and Illinois (*U.S. Census Reports,* 1850–1900). See table 1, appendix 1, for data on the geographical location of blacks in the United States.
68. Raboteau, *A Fire in the Bones,* 133. For a succinct and incisive history of African American Catholics, see Raboteau's essay, "A Minority within a Minority," contained in this work.
69. Diocesan priests are educated by and dedicated to a particular bishop and his diocese. They take vows of chastity and obedience to the bishop but do not take a vow of poverty. Religious orders are communities of men (priests or brothers) or women (called women religious, nuns, or sisters) who take vows of poverty, chastity, and obedience and live within a community such as the Society of Jesus (Jesuits), Franciscans, etc. A bishop may acquire the services of religious orders for schools, hospitals, and other institutions by a mutual arrangement with the community.
70. Davis, *Black Catholics*, 125.
71. *CCIUS,* 123.
72. Ibid., 124, and Dolan, *American Catholic Parish,* 184. See tables 2 and 3 in appendix 1 for data on priests ministering to blacks in 1929 and 1940.
73. *CCIUS,* 125.
74. In Ochs, *Desegregating the Altar,* 98–99, Ochs cites examples of bishops who either denied faculties to priests or gave them only temporarily to test them.
75. Davis, *Black Catholics,* 148. An indication of the different status accorded the Healy brothers by white clergy is the surprising fact that Gillard ignores their existence in his book *The Catholic Church and the American Negro* (1929), identifying Augustus

Tolton as the first African American priest. In his second book, *Colored Catholics in the United States* (1940), he mentions Tolton first and then follows with a description of the Healy brothers. At the end of the paragraph, he adds this cryptic caveat: "While it was generally known that the Healy brothers were colored, they were not known as Negro priests in the sense that the term is usually taken," 185.

76. Davis, *Black Catholics,* 145–62; also see Ochs, *Desegregating the Altar,* and Albert S. Foley, S.J., *God's Men of Color: The Colored Catholic Priests of the United States, 1854–1954* (New York: Farrar, Straus & Co., 1955).
77. For an excellent and thorough characterization of Slattery, see Jamie Theresa Phelps, "The Mission Ecclesiology of John R. Slattery: A Study of an African-American Mission of the Catholic Church in the Nineteenth Century" (Ph.D. diss., The Catholic Univ. of America, 1989); Ochs, *Desegregating the Altar,* also covers Slattery in his history of the struggles of black priests.
78. Davis, *Black Catholics*, 98–105.
79. Cyprian Davis, "Catholic African Americans," *Keep Your Hand on the Plow* (Washington, D.C., Committee on African American Catholics, National Conference of Catholic Bishops Office of Research, 1996), 16.
80. See also, Thaddeus J. Posey, O.F.M., C.A.P., "Praying in the Shadows," in *This Far by Faith,* ed. Judith Weisenfeld and Richard Newman (New York: Routledge, 1996).
81. Marilyn Wenzke Nickels, *Black Catholic Protest and the Federated Colored Catholics, 1917–1933* (New York: Garland Publishing, 1988), 2–3. Nickels records the federation's documentation of discriminatory practices in the Catholic Church, including lay organizations like the Knights of Columbus and the Holy Name Society.
82. Ochs, *Desegregating the Altar,* 230.
83. In addition to Ochs, *Desegregating the Altar,* 312, see Nickels, *Black Catholic Protest,* 61–135, 175–209, 266–285, 286–315, for the story of the Federated Colored Catholic's relationship with LaFarge and Markoe.
84. Ochs, *Desegregating the Altar*, 311.
85. Ibid., 312, 345–49.

2. A Priest of Our Own

1. Bennett, *Before the Mayflower: A History of Black America,* 344.
2. U.S. Dept. of Commerce, *The Social and Economic Status of the Black Population in the United States*.
3. *U.S. Census Reports,* 1920, 1930.
4. *AACN,* 103.
5. *CCAN,* 94–95.

6. Nicholas Lemann, *The Promised Land: The Great Black Migration and How It Changed America* (New York: Alfred A. Knopf, 1991), 6.
7. *AACN,* 118–19.
8. Ibid., 65.
9. This Methodist reform movement revived the Wesleyan tenet of sanctification or Christian perfection and proliferated across denominational and racial lines, culminating in the Azusa Street Revival in Los Angeles from 1906 to 1909 under the leadership of William J. Seymour, a Black holiness preacher (BCAAE, 76–79).
10. *AACN,* 121.
11. Cunningham, *Newark,* 101.
12. *AACN,* iii.
13. This organization was a branch office of the National Urban League and the consolidation of the National League for the Protection of Colored Women (NLPCW), the Committee for Improving the Industrial Condition of Negroes (CIICN), and the Committee on Urban Conditions. The founders, George Haynes, a black sociologist, and Ruth Standish Baldwin, a patrician white reformer, were more influenced by Booker T. Washington than W. E. B. DuBois, although the latter lent initial support. The league was backed by many white and black philanthropists and intellectuals, and through its volunteers addressed the problems of blacks in the northern city environment. See Nancy J. Weiss, *The National Urban League, 1910–1940* (New York: Oxford Univ. Press, 1974), 3–46.
14. *AACN,* 83.
15. The Newark diocese encompassed the following counties in 1919: Essex, Hudson, Passaic, Bergen, Union, Morris, and Sussex. *Official Catholic Directory* (New York: P. J. Kenedy & Sons, 1919).
16. Ibid.
17. Ahern letter to Duffy, Mar. 4 and Apr. 2, 1931, ADN: QAPP, Box 1. (Hereafter all Ahern's correspondence will be cited without ADN: QAPP, Box 1 reference). A great number of Cape Verdeans lived in the Boston area as well. (See William C. Leonard, "A Parish for the Black Catholics of Boston," *Catholic Historical Review* 83, no. 1 (Jan. 1997): 51.
18. *CCAN,* 125. Gillard erroneously stated that Bishop John O'Connor initiated the survey and that it was suspended when O'Connor died. But since O'Connor died on May 20, 1927, and the See of Newark was left vacant for ten months, Msgr. John A. Duffy would have been the one to initiate the survey.
19. See George Coll, *A Pioneer Church, Brief History of the Church of St. Benedict the Moor in the City of New York* (Elizabeth, N.J.: By the author, 1993), 35.
20. I have a certain hesitancy in using the phrase *black Catholics* because it may give the impression that they are in fact a separate kind of Catholic, which is not the

case. Urban anthropologist, Gary Wray McDonogh, makes a distinction between being black and Catholic. He referred to the position of one African American he interviewed who pointed out that there "ain't no special religion called *Black Catholicism,*" McDonogh concludes that "even if race was adduced as a socially powerful factor in their lives, such Catholics want to leave these divisions aside, symbolically, at the door of the church. Therefore, I have chosen the more neutral, if awkward, reference to *'black and Catholic'* throughout the text." McDonogh, *Black and Catholic in Savannah, Georgia,* 93.

21. The information referring to South Carolina and Georgia are from U.S. Census data, 1920. Sr. Peter Claver remembers Ethel Wright being from Maryland. Interview with Sr. Peter Claver, Oct. 11, 1992.
22. Parishioner Bennie Fields remembers the toughness and loyal Catholicism of Ethel Wright and her sister Marcella Thompson, who was the first housekeeper for the pastor, the Reverend Cornelius Ahern (telephone interview, June 2, 2000).
23. Interview with Walter P. Brown, Dec. 5, 1992.
24. For a list of her students, see table 4, appendix 1.
25. *Newark Star Eagle,* Oct. 15, 1933. Oral tradition holds that Theresa Lane was the oldest living black Catholic in Newark at the time. In this *Ledger* article on the history of Queen of Angels, which traced the beginning of the parish to Theresa Lane's conversion and Lucy Mulligan's efforts for a colored church, Ethel Wright was not mentioned. Of the three, Wright was the only living founder at the time of the article, but still she was not acknowledged for her work. In her defense, she wrote a brief written history in the back of the ledger book that contained the Theresa Lane Council's minutes. She described her efforts for a separate colored church and Mulligan's initial opposition to that goal.
26. *Newark Star Eagle,* Oct. 15, 1933.
27. "She knew how to run a group, and she was definitely in charge" (Interview with Sr. Peter Claver, Oct. 10, 1992).
28. Possibly the National League for the Protection of Colored Women influenced Mulligan. Founded in 1905 by white social worker Frances Kellor, the league helped women migrants obtain lodging and employment. Northern and southern churches networked with the NLPCW to identify the women, meet them when they arrived, and locate housing in lodging houses, churches, and working girls' homes (Higginbotham, *Righteous Discontent,* 180).
29. EWH, 89.
30. TLCM, 35. The experience of African Americans in Cleveland, Ohio, in 1922 mirrored Newark's to some extent in that they began as a social club, contacted other Catholics in the area, and took steps to obtain a parish of their own. See Dorothy

Ann Blatnica, V.S.C., *"At the Altar of Their God": African American Catholics in Cleveland, 1922–1961* (New York: Garland Publishing, 1995), 55.

31. The minutes, which end on May 13, 1928, indicate new members as they joined the council. Ethel Wright also listed the members in her history. See the list in the text preceding the next note number.
32. TLCM, 36; EWH, 93. The list comes from EWH, dated Jan. 8, 1927.
33. TLCM, 39.
34. See chapter 1 for a brief history of the Federated Colored Catholics.
35. Mrs. Wright advanced the six dollars necessary for the council to become a unit of the Federated Colored Catholics on September 5, 1927. In an entry entitled "Special Notes, September, 1927," Ethel Wright wrote and signed an account of the convention. TLCM, 54–55.
36. Nickels, *Black Catholic Protest,* 48, 57.
37. The actual quote from the article was in reference to oral histories and slave narratives collected by abolitionist recorders and is as follows: "Historians have come to realize that if you don't use this material, the history of slavery comes only from the owners." See Tony Horwitz, "Untrue Confessions: Is Most of What We Know about the Rebel Slave Nat Turner Wrong?" *New Yorker* 75, no. 38 (Dec. 13, 1999): 89.
38. Newspaper accounts of the time credit Bishop Walsh and the Mount Carmel Guild with the black work. See especially the *Hoboken Jersey Observer*'s article of April 7, 1938, and Newark's *Sunday Call of April 3, 1938,* Seton Hall Univ. Archives, Special Collections Center, Archdiocese of Newark, Walsh Papers. See also several newspaper articles on the beginning of Christ the King Parish that convey the same viewpoint, Seton Hall Univ. Archives, Special Collections Center, Archdiocese of Newark, Parish Files, No. 10, Christ the King. Hereafter all Newark archival material will be cited as ADN, with further designations such as Queen of Angels Files, Christ the King Files, Walsh Papers.
39. New Jersey Catholic Historical Records Commission, *The Bishops of Newark, 1853–1978* (South Orange, N.J.: Seton Hall Univ. Press, 1978), 108.
40. Ibid., 98.
41. TLCM, 86.
42. EWH, 94–95.
43. The Reverend Edward F. Kirk, "Survey of Negro Problem in Jersey City," n.d., one-page report; ADN, Christ the King Papers.
44. *Catholic News,* Saturday, July 29, 1932. ADN, Walsh Papers.
45. TLCM, 67.
46. Ibid., 75.
47. Ibid.

48. EWH, 99.
49. These Trinitarians should not be confused with the order of priests and brothers started by Fr. Thomas Judge, C.M. Called the Missionary Servants of the Most Holy Trinity, they received their approbation from Rome in 1929. See Sr. Joseph Miriam Blackwell, M.S.B.T., *Ecclesial People: A Study in the Life and Times of Thomas Augustine Judge, C.M.,* 2d ed. (Holy Trinity, Ala.: Missionary Cenacle Press, 1984), 169. The Trinitarian sisters (Missionary Servants of the Most Blessed Trinity) figured prominently in this history.
50. See *CCAN,* 86; Ochs, *Desegregating the Altar,* 290; and Foley, *God's Men of Color,* 111–14, for brief accounts of Father Derrick's life. Derricks received his opportunity to study for the priesthood because of his acquaintance with Fr. Anthony Giovannini, O.S.S.T, an Italian Trinitarian priest in Asbury Park, New Jersey. Father Giovannini's petition to Rome opened the door for Derricks to study at the seminary in Livorno in Tuscany. Derricks spoke Italian and four other languages and seemed to have been at home with his Italian parish in Bristol. He did go on speaking tours to various African American communities, which may be how Mrs. Wright learned of him. He was assigned to St. Ann's, an Italian parish in Bristol, Pennsylvania, after a year of advanced studies in Rome. He wanted to work among his people, but shortly after he received permission to do so, he died of complications from appendicitis on Oct. 22, 1929 (Foley, *God's Men of Color,* 112–13).
51. EWH, 99.
52. Ibid.
53. Sr. Peter Claver Fahy (born Hannah Elizabeth Fahy) was the daughter of a Jewish mother and Irish father from Rome, Georgia. Her mother converted to Catholicism when she was nineteen after hearing a lecture by a Redemptorist priest. The young Hannah was profoundly affected by her relationship with her African American nanny, the person she cites as responsible for her attraction to the black work.
54. The women's order, the Missionary Servants of the Most Blessed Trinity, received approbation from Rome in 1932 (Blackwell, *Ecclesial People,* 169).
55. Blackwell, *Ecclesial People,* 16.
56. Ibid., 69.
57. Unpublished writings of Fr. Thomas Judge, Archives-Missionary Servants of the Most Blessed Trinity, A-MSBT No. 00757, Jan. 15, 1923, Philadelphia. (Hereafter cited by A-MSBT number only.)
58. The Lay Apostolate stills exists under the auspices of the Missionary Servants of the Most Blessed and Holy Trinity.
59. Concurrently with Judge's work, Walter Rauschenbusch, a Baptist minister of German descent, developed his "Social Gospel" after working among poverty-stricken

German immigrants in New York City. See William M. Ramsay, *Four Modern Prophets* (Atlanta: John Knox Press, 1986), for a brief analysis of Rauschenbusch's social gospel; and Walter Rauschenbusch, *A Theology for the Social Gospel* (New York: Macmillan, 1917). Also see Dolan, "Toward a Social Gospel," in *The American Catholic Experience,* 321–46.

60. It is safe to say that Judge's characterization of the abandoned was distinctly analogous to the definition of the gospel poor, which included those economically deprived as well as those who were marginalized by a lack of education, ritual uncleanness through the neglect of religious laws or traditions, and inferior social status. See Albert Nolan, *Jesus before Christianity* (New York: Maryknoll Press, 1976), 22–24.
61. A-MSBT No. 003740, Oct. 31, 1922. John Gillard's ambiguous opinion was that it would be "almost impossible to raise . . . [the African American] to a high spiritual and moral level unless at the same time [they increased] . . . industrial efficiency," and contributed "to literature, science, art, and philosophy" (*CCAN,* 4). Also see Davis, *Black Catholics,* x, regarding Gillard's contribution and for Catholic lay and clerical negative attitudes toward African Americans (61–62, 133–34).
62. A-MSBT No. 003740, Oct. 31, 1922.
63. Ibid.
64. The fact that these two white women entered the home of a black person should not be taken lightly. Even now, in 1999, it is not a common occurrence (as has been remarked to me when I have visited African American friends in their homes). It must have had still more impact in 1928.
65. Interview with Sr. Peter Claver, Oct. 11, 1992.
66. Ibid.
67. Ibid.
68. Ibid.
69. Letter from William Kearns to John Duffy, Sept. 3, 1926 (ADN: QAPP).
70. Interview with Sr. Peter Claver, Oct. 11, 1992.
71. EWH, 97.
72. Ibid. Interview with Sr. Peter Claver, Oct. 11, 1992.
73. EWH, 99.
74. *Newark Star Eagle,* Oct. 15, 1933.
75. A letter to Msgr. Duffy from Anna Kerwin asked him for help in paying the mortgage on the house the Theresa Lane Council had purchased for their community center. It was dated August 23, 1930, and is the last document verifying the continued existence of the council.
76. Sr. Peter Claver remembered well the reconciliation that occurred among the women after they lost Mrs. Mulligan.
77. Interview with Sr. Peter Claver, Oct. 11, 1992.

78. Ibid.
79. Novena is derived from *novem,* the Latin word for nine.
80. Interview with Sr. Peter Claver, May 5, 1995.

3. A Mission with a Mission

1. The actual date of the first Mass is impossible to determine accurately. As mentioned above, Sr. Peter Claver remembered that the installation of Father Ahern as the director of the Negro Apostolate occurred on September 9, 1930, but Ahern's personnel card indicates that he became the head of the apostolate on September 13, 1930. To add to the confusion, Queen of Angels' tenth anniversary brochure states that the first Mass occurred on September 9, 1930. Ahern's installation would have to precede the first Mass, and therefore his appointment on September 9 would preclude the possibility of the Mass being on that date. The cause of the discrepancy is probably the tendency of the individual and corporate memory to create myth in order to heighten meaning. The most important truth here is the connection that all felt to the saint who devoted his life to the African people, and how the proximity to his feast day made their own endeavor more significant.
2. Sr. Peter Claver suggested the name Our Lady Queen of the Angels as a counterpart to Christ the King, the first black parish in Jersey City. That became its official name, but over the years popular usage has shortened it to Queen of Angels, which is what I use throughout. Over its history Queen of Angels has had four homes: (1) St. Bridget's Hall (from preecclesial beginnings in 1929 to Nov. 15, 1931); (2) the Sears and Roebuck building near Wickliffe at 242 Academy Street (Nov. 15, 1931 to May 12, 1935); (3) 237 Academy Street, across the street from the previous church (May 12, 1935, to July 10, 1958, when fire destroyed the church); and (4) the former St. Peter's Church (German) at 44 Belmont Avenue, which is now called Irvine Turner Boulevard (July 1, 1962, to the present).
3. Mr. Brown remembers women telling the children not to forget the altar made of egg boxes and the distances the people would walk to attend that first Mass at St. Bridget's Hall (telephone interview with Walter P. Brown, Jan. 6, 1998). Also, in his sermon at the funeral of Mrs. Roberta Thornton, Fr. Thomas Carey spoke of her memory of "walking long distances with baby carriage and children in tow down to St. Bridget's basement where Fr. Shovlin initially offered the 1st Q of A Mass, and then almost immediately the beloved Fr. Ahern" (Carey Papers).
4. Most Rev. Curtis J. Guillory, S.V.D., "Introduction," *Keep Your Hand on the Plow* (Washington, D.C.: Committee on African American Catholics, National Conference of Catholic Bishops Office of Research, 1996), xi.

5. John Gillard pointed out in 1940 that "[o]f the 296,998 colored Catholics in the United States, 189,423, or 63.7 per cent, claim membership in their own churches. The other 107,575 belong to 'white' or 'mixed' churches. This does not mean that colored Catholics claiming membership in their own churches do not attend other churches; as a matter of fact, Catholics, white or colored, may attend any Catholic Church anywhere in the world, as every Catholic understands and many do as a matter of convenience . . . Naturally the greater number of those attending colored churches live in the South where larger centers of Negro population make separate church units feasible and social circumstances make them advisable" (*CCIUS,* 138).
6. See *CCAN* for a history of missions to blacks in the United States. For an in-depth history of the American parish based on region, see also, Dolan, *The American Catholic Parish,* and for a popular historical overview of the Catholic experience, see Dolan, *The American Catholic Experience*.
7. If members of the ethnic group of a national parish were dispersed beyond the ethnic enclave, its parishioners had to travel to their church as well. But African Americans had little choice in their church, and Queen of Angels had to reach out for members over a wide geographic area to evangelize.
8. Everyone I interviewed who lived during the period of 1930 to at least 1960 either had the personal experience of being told to go to the black church or said that it was understood by all the Catholic parishes in Newark that black people were supposed to attend Queen of Angels or one of its mission churches.
9. Msgr. Eugene J. Reilly, a pastor of Christ the King in the 1960s, reminded the clergy that according to Canon Law a pastor is responsible for the spiritual welfare of every Catholic and non-Catholic in his parish. Missions "were never intended to remove the responsibility from the local pastor, or even to share the responsibility of the local pastor. It was an effort to make his work easier in a difficult period of adjustment, a concentration of effort on a small segment of his parish." Eugene J. Reilly, "The Apostolate to the Negro," in the Quarterly Conference of the Clergy in the Archdiocese of Newark, Sept. 19, 1962, 3, ADN: QAPP, Box 1. Also, McGreevy, in *Parish Boundaries,* describes the difficulties of Catholic resistance to the influx of blacks into northern urban neighborhoods and the stratification that occurred among them as a result of the issue of race and integration.
10. On August 19, 1933, Bishop Walsh received a letter from a distraught parishioner named Miss Jessie Thompson of St. Patrick's Church in Jersey City, begging him to force the Trinitarian sisters to move from their parish neighborhood because they would attract colored people to the area and depreciate the property. She praised the efforts of the pastor, Father Kelly, who "worked to keep the colored people away from [the] neighborhood," and urges the bishop to have the sisters move to the

"district of the colored people." On behalf of Bishop Walsh, Monsignor Duffy notified Father Shovlin of the letter and asked his opinion on the matter. The result was that the Trinitarians had to move four times before they were able to settle in a permanent home. Miss Jessie Thompson to Bishop Walsh, Aug. 19, 1933. Vicar General, Monsignor Duffy to Fr. Joseph A. Shovlin, Aug. 22, 1933. Anonymous draft of Christ the King History, Christ the King Files, ADN.

11. Carey told the story of a prominent Newark African American attorney whose parents many years ago were told by a priest to go to the Italian church instead of his own, using a derogatory term for Italians. That family left the Catholic Church for good.
12. Monsignor Reilly spoke to this problem from a position of hindsight when he observed, "One of the great difficulties brought about by the negro parishes, has been to give to priests of the Archdiocese the attitude that the negro is the responsibility of the negro parishes, e.g., Christ the King." If any black person came to them with any request including a "marriage problem," "problem with morals," or a "problem with instructions" they would tell the people to go to the black parish. Or sometimes the "priests would call and say, we have a negro family; may we baptize the children? We have a negro family; would it be all right to take them in our school?" "The Apostolate to the Negro," 3.
13. See Ochs, *Desegregating the Altar,* 318–19. The four priests in the United States in 1930 were Stephen Theobald, Charles Randolph Uncles, Norman Dukette, and Charles Logan. Theobald died on July 8, 1932, and Uncles died on July 21, 1933, leaving only two.
14. Monroe Fordham, *Major Themes in Northern Black Religious Thought, 1800–1860* (Hicksville, N.Y.: Exposition Press, 1977), 29.
15. Ibid., 23.
16. Ibid., 29.
17. Brown, *The Churches the Apostles Left Behind,* 41.
18. Ibid.
19. Ibid. Scholars generally agree that Paul was not the author of the pastoral Epistles, although they are ascribed to him—a common practice in antiquity. The evidence indicates that the pastorals were written several years after Paul's death.
20. Interview with Sr. Francis Damien, Sept. 30, 1994.
21. Interview with Sr. Theresa Ahern, July 26, 1992.
22. Interview with Nathaniel Potts, Aug. 22, 1993.
23. By mutual agreement between Ahern and the vicar-general, those mission reports ended in 1935, freeing Ahern of work and depriving history of a wonderfully detailed record.
24. Interview with Sr. Peter Claver, May 5, 1995.

25. Interview with Sr. Francis Damien, Sept. 30, 1994.
26. See Dolan, *Immigrant Church,* 64–65, for a description of the "hero priest" common in the late nineteenth century.
27. Sermon at the funeral of Father Remmele on Dec. 9, 1939, at St. Anne's Church in Newark, QAPA.
28. Ibid.
29. Ibid.
30. Sr. Mary Ruth Coffman, O.S.B., *Build Me a City: The Life of Reverend Harold Purcell, Founder of the City of St. Jude* (Montgomery, Ala.: Pioneer Press, 1984), 119, 175. According to Coffman, Purcell, Dorothy Day of the *Catholic Worker,* Father Ahern and Sr. Peter Claver Fahy became good friends when they met in Purcell's *Sign* office in New York City in 1933 (Coffman, *Build Me a City,* 105). The City of St. Jude contributed its grounds and facilities to the 1965 Selma-to-Montgomery civil rights marchers and many other marches after that. E. D. Nixon, an African American activist who helped launch the Montgomery bus boycott in 1954, gives Purcell some credit for making the Civil Rights movement happen because of his courageous and public defense on behalf of blacks (Coffman, *Build Me a City,* 3).
31. Fr. Harold Purcell, the founder of *Sign* magazine, lived at St. Michael's Passionist Monastery in Union City, a town adjacent to Newark. He served as a mentor and supporter until Ahern's death in 1945.
32. Father Ahern's sermon at the dedication of the Fr. Harold Purcell's City of St. Jude in Mobile, Alabama, Oct. 27, 1938 (QAPA). The City of St. Jude still operates today with educational and medical facilities for African Americans.
33. Although children at the time, Elma Bateman and Bennie Fields remember the power of Father Ahern's sermons and how much the parishioners appreciated them (interview with Elma Bateman and Bennie Fields, Apr. 27, 1994). See Raboteau, *A Fire in the Bones*, 141–51, for a description of the chanted sermon. Again, for something more comprehensive on the history of African American religion, see Raboteau's classic, *Slave Religion*.
34. See *How the Irish Became White* for a biography and analysis of Daniel O'Connell and his relationship to Irish Americans, the abolitionists, and slaveholders of the United States. See *The Life and Times of Frederick Douglass*, 223–25, for Douglass's tribute to O'Connell as a man, an orator and a warrior for freedom. See also, Davis, *Black Catholics,* and the author's description of O'Connell as a man with a deep sense of justice and an exemplar of an Irish Catholic empathic to the plight of the African slave, 62–63. Also see Thomas Bokenkotter, *Church and Revolution: Catholics in the Struggle for Democracy and Social Justice* (New York: Doubleday, 1998), 82–110.

35. Ahern lists O'Connell and his work with other major events in European history in a sermon to the Society of the Little Sisters of the Poor on the occasion of the 100th anniversary of their order in 1939. Since O'Connell's name was vilified in the Irish Catholic press of his day, it is striking that Ahern would remember him only for his fight against bigotry (QAPA).
36. Ahern to Duffy, Oct. 3, 1930.
37. Report to Bishop Thomas Walsh, Oct. 3, 1930.
38. Ahern also insisted that the Trinitarians have a chauffeur-driven car until the sisters convinced him that they should drive their own. The sisters persuaded him that Queen of Angels could hire another Trinitarian sister for the price of a chauffeur, which made him change his mind and allow them to drive the car themselves (interview with Sr. Peter Claver and Sr. Francis Damien, May 6, 1995).
39. Two years before this, Police Commissioner Fohs had white men picked up by the police if they were found in the Third Ward after midnight. They were charged with loitering and fined ten dollars. It was reasoned that they entered the Third Ward to patronize the illicit activities there (*The Newark News,* July 15, 1928). Price argues that most whites "were probably afraid to travel through the area at night. We should not assume that the fears of whites or the crime which the police unsuccessfully tried to stamp out during the period were accurate reflections of life in the Hill" (*AACN,* 63).
40. *AACN,* 63.
41. Ibid.
42. See *AACN,* 140–43, for a discussion of segregation practices of Newark, and 86–87 for the prevalence and importance of Newark's storefronts, sects, and cults in the Third Ward.
43. Interview with Sr. Peter Claver, May 6, 1995. With only ten cents allotted her for transportation, Sr. Peter Claver walked from the cenacle to her destination and used the money for the streetcar home.
44. Interview with Sr. Peter Claver and Sr. Francis Damien, May 6, 1995.
45. Ahern to Duffy, Oct. 3, 1930.
46. Dr. McCarroll actually lived on Hillside Place on the edge of the Third Ward, one of five black physicians (out of twenty-four) who lived in that Ward. See Interracial Committee of the New Jersey Conference of Social Work and the State Dept. of Institutions and Agencies, *The Negro in New Jersey, Community Study XIX* (Newark: Dept. of Institutions and Agencies, 1932), 32. Dr. Carroll joined the staff of City Hospital in 1946 (*AACN,* 144).
47. A division of five social classes consists of the underclass with no permanent connection to the workforce; the working poor whose wages do not bring them above

the poverty line; the working nonpoor who are blue-collar workers earning above the poverty line; the middle class, consisting of white-collar workers and professionals; and the upper class, with high incomes and an affluent lifestyle. (Taken from Committee on African American Catholics, National Conference of Catholic Bishops, *Keep Your Hand on the Plow* [Washington, D.C.: Office of Research, 1996], 67.) It must be pointed out that class stratification for African Americans was more complex at this particular time. Blacks who were educated and professional were often not able to obtain employment commensurate to their education and ability. Service workers with stable incomes and longstanding placement in the community were often considered middle class.

48. Interviews with the Reverend James Scott, the former pastor of Bethany Baptist Church in Newark (Dec. 12, 1994, and July 6, 1995).
49. Ibid.
50. Ibid.
51. ADN: QAPP, Box 1, Ahern to Duffy, Oct. 3, 1930. White Protestant churches in Newark posed little threat to Queen of Angels, as their congregations fled to the suburbs. See Moses Deleney, "The Interaction between Protestant Churches and Their Social Environment in the Inner City" (Ph.D. diss., Drew Univ., 1959). Deleney describes the "white flight" of white Protestant churches from downtown Newark to the surrounding townships. This left the inner city to the Catholic and Episcopal Churches, which had territorially based rather than congregationally based parishes.
52. Ahern to Duffy, Mar. 1, 1933.
53. As noted in Ahern's letter to Duffy, Jan. 3, 1931, "The figures [of our relief work] seem almost incredible, but they are real facts and we have forwarded them to the Colored newspapers. Our fame is spreading and we have been asked to give an address at the Urban League on Monday Evening, Jan. 12th, 1931, and I do think our Christmas efforts have given us a footing with the 'Non Sectarians' as they call themselves."
54. *AACN,* 65.
55. Ahern letter to Duffy, Dec. 12, 1930. In a talk at a clergy conference on "The Negro and the Catholic Church" in Chicago in September 1960, an African American priest, Rev. Rollins Lambert, confirmed Ahern's intuition when he said that lower-class blacks viewed the Catholic Church as the "Church of Charity." Lambert makes a distinction between middle- and upper-class attitudes, saying that the middle class was satisfied with Catholic parishes, but the wealthy African Americans were still not convinced. William A. Osborne, *The Segregated Covenant: Race Relations and American Catholics* (New York: Herder and Herder, 1967), 123–24.

4. Why Go to China?

1. Economic class did not protect even the leading black professionals from exclusion from the whites-only clubs and restaurants of Newark at that time. Clement Price referred to Newark as a "Jim Crow city" because of its blatant and pervasive segregation in public space, including theaters, city pools, and other recreational facilities supported by public funds (*AACN,* 140–41, 143).
2. Interview with Sr. Francis Damien, Sept. 30, 1994.
3. Evelyn Higginbotham confirms this point in *Righteous Discontent* when she says, "In time the black church—open to both secular and religious groups in the community—came to signify public space," 7.
4. Interview with Sr. Francis Damien, Sept. 30, 1994.
5. Ibid.
6. Ahern to Duffy, July 31, 1931.
7. Ibid., Aug. 31, 1932.
8. Ahern to McLaughlin, Sept. 3, 1934.
9. Ahern to Duffy, July 29, 1932.
10. For more on the Novena to St. Jude, see Robert Anthony Orsi, *Thank You, St. Jude: Women's Devotion to the Patron Saint of Hopeless Causes* (New Haven, Conn.: Yale Univ. Press), 1996.
11. Ahern to McLaughlin, Oct. 1, 1934.
12. Ahern to Duffy, May 2, 1932.
13. Ahern to McLaughlin, Nov. 3, 1934. Half of the 11,826 attendees at the novena over a two-year period were white.
14. Those I have interviewed who remember the early years indicated that Queen of Angels always welcomed nonblacks. There is little written documentation of this, but Ahern did mention the great number of whites who attended the novenas on a regular basis, and the nine-week instructions given to six young Italian men "who had strayed from the faith." They received their First Holy Communion in July 1933, and Ahern fully expected them to be around to "do some good work for us in the section of the City in which we find ourselves." Ahern to McLaughlin, Aug. 1, 1933.
15. Interview with Ollie Pierce, Nov. 14, 1994.
16. Thaddeus J. Posey, O.F.M., C.A.P., "Praying in the Shadows" in *This Far by Faith,* ed. Judith Weisenfeld and Richard Newman (New York: Routledge, 1996), 75.
17. Interview with Sr. Francis Damien, May 6, 1995.
18. Ibid.
19. Ibid.
20. Interview with Sr. Peter Claver, May 6, 1995.

21. Letter to Duffy, July 31, 1931.
22. After more than a year working alone between the church in Newark and the five missions, Ahern asked Duffy for a cleric to assist him in the work. In June 1932, Fr. Joseph Shanley was appointed to Queen of Angels Parish. To make room for him, they moved from 63 Court Street to a larger house at 86 S. Tenth Street (Ahern to Duffy, Sept. 30, 1931).
23. Father Kelly, the moderator of the Montclair Mt. Carmel Guild, offered to defray half the cost of a bus from Montclair. Other arrangements were made to bus children from St. John's Mission on Albert Avenue, called the Down Neck section (now referred to as the Iron Bound section of Newark).
24. The one remaining black Portuguese man, Orlando E. Almeida, told the author that Queen of Angels was established to give the black Portuguese a place where they would be comfortable as a worshipping community. He also felt strongly that, because of their close involvement with the people, the Trinitarian sisters had the greatest and most lasting effect on the black community, as did the Oblate Sisters of Providence, who administered Queen of Angels School in the 1960s.

    He was the only remaining Portuguese parishioner at Queen of Angels until his death on November 24, 2000.
25. Ahern to Duffy, Sept. 30, 1931.
26. Ibid.
27. Ahern outlined the costs for the church in Ahern to Duffy, Oct. 6, Oct. 20, 1931. Ahern estimated that the removal of the chapel to the Queen of Angels' location would cost around $5,000. In the 1940 commemorative brochure for Queen of Angels' 10th anniversary an amount of $14,000 is quoted as the price for the church. The church's financial report for December 12, 1931, showed an amount of $3,188.34 from Monsignor Duffy for the new church. It is not clear where the remainder came from. In an interview with Sr. Peter Claver, May 6, 1995, she stated that the men who moved the church were "Black Portuguese" or Cape Verdeans.
28. Ahern to McLaughlin, Oct. 1, 1934.
29. Ahern to Duffy, Nov. 2, 1931.
30. Ahern to McLaughlin, Oct. 1, 1934.
31. Ibid., Dec. 1, 1934.
32. "April 1, 1935, Queen of Angels received authorization to erect a frame and brick building at 249 Academy Street, Newark. Loan from the bishop $10,000. William J. Waldron, contractor, 40 Park Pl. Mrs. Kelly died July 17, 1937, bequeathed over $15,000" (The actual address was 237 Academy St.) (Board of Trustee Minutes, QAPA).
33. At the end of June 1931, the Sisters of Charity donated property in Montclair on which to build an assembly hall for the black Catholics of the area.

34. Surrounding Newark are townships called Orange, East Orange, West Orange, and South Orange. A memorandum to Bishop Walsh from his secretary John G. Delaney discloses the controversy surrounding the location of a colored parish within the boundaries of Blessed Sacrament in East Orange. The pastor of Blessed Sacrament objected to the location on the grounds that his white parishioners would go to the colored parish just as some went to the national Italian parish of St. Joseph. Evidently, he felt whites would have no problem attending a black church, although from what we have seen, they did have a problem with blacks attending white churches. At the same time, both Catholic and non-Catholic residents of East Orange "bitterly opposed" extending the "colored belt in their city," fearing the decrease in their property values. Because of this the diocese moved the colored mission from East Orange to Orange, placing it in the middle of the neighborhood most populated with African Americans, on the border of Orange and East Orange (John G. Delaney to Bishop Walsh, Oct. 27, 1936. ADN, Carey Papers).
35. Ahern to Duffy, May 1, 1931.
36. The parish rented a storefront in Orange in May 1931 (letter to Duffy, June 4, 1931). Ahern to Duffy, Dec. 1, 1932.
37. Ahern to McLaughlin, May 2, 1934.
38. A discrepancy existed between the opening dates of the missions in the Tenth Year Anniversary Brochure and Ahern's letters. The difference between the initial startup dates and some kind of official opening may cause the inconsistency.
39. Ahern to McLaughlin, June 2, 1934.
40. Ibid.
41. Interview with Nathaniel Potts, Aug. 22, 1993.
42. See Dolan, *The American Catholic Experience,* 271–72.
43. Reilly, "Thomas J. Walsh," 104–5.
44. Walsh's attention to the Italian immigrant problem was well known from his days as bishop of Trenton prior to his appointment to the Newark diocese. Walsh brought more than twenty Italian *Maestre Pie Filippini* (religious teachers Filippini) from Italy, taught them English, and put them in the Catholic schools to induce Italians to send their children there. James Cox Brady funded the project with an initial $50,000 and $1,000 per month to continue permanently after his death. (See article in the *Jersey City Journal,* Monday, Aug. 12, 1929, ADN, Walsh Scrap Books.) In 1928, the entire Newark Diocese had 276 churches and missions. Of these the Official Catholic Directory listed the following national parishes: 28 Italian, 14 Polish, 12 German, 6 Lithuanian, 2 Spanish and Portuguese, 3 Slav, 3 Slovac, 2 Hungarian, and 1 Syrian. Of the 226 churches, 150 (66 percent) had their own parochial school with a total student population of 82,663. The total

Catholic population for the Newark diocese was 704,788 (*Official Catholic Directory,* 1928).

45. New Jersey Catholic Historical Records Commission, *The Bishops of Newark: 1853–1978*, 107.

46. He also found that Italian children outnumbered native-born Americans 30.5 percent to 26.4 percent in the public schools of Newark, and that the Catholic parochial school population was 47.8 percent native–born Americans and only 8.1 percent Italian. No doubt these facts, established by one of the diocese's priests, informed Walsh's drive to redirect Italians immigrants back into the fold of the church through his educational approach. See Ralph J. Glover, "Diocesan Social Welfare: A Study of the Diocese of Newark," (Ph.D. diss., Fordham Univ., 1929). (Walsh Papers, ADN).

47. Ahern cites "at least 12 inquiries regarding children attending grammar school. Referred all to their local pastors" (Ahern to Duffy, July 31, 1931). On Oct. 6, 1931, Ahern agonized over this issue to Duffy: "We are on the verge of losing a family of six converts, whom we have taken into the church, owing to the fact that Father Farrell has refused permission to two boys to enter his school. I was told last Wednesday that as we made the promise the youngsters would be taken care of and [since] conditions have turned out otherwise our converts are much offended."

48. Ahern to Duffy, Aug. 31, 1932.

49. See Sr. Patricia Margaret Judge, "The Negro in Queen of the Angels Parish, Newark, NJ: A Study of the Development of the Religious and Social Services Extended to the Negro by a Catholic Parish" (master's thesis, Fordham Univ., 1965), 67–68, 83–84.

50. They put 14,600 miles on the Ford after one year, traveling from one mission to another from 1930 to 1931. Their second car logged 17,000 miles from 1931 to 1932. The church bought a new car for them with $250 profit from the parish carnival (Ahern to Duffy, July 2, 1932, and Feb. 3, 1933). Ahern was making light of the situation, but the great interest that American Catholic missionaries had in foreign lands to the neglect of Americans was something that disturbed him immensely. In his sermon at The City of St. Jude he said, "Is it not true that we of America have paid more attention to the [conversion] of foreign lands, important though [they may be,] than those in our own home lands? Is it not true that the Colored man of South Africa has more glamor [*sic*], more appeal than our 13,000,000 here in our own United States[?] In our smug complacency of wealth and peace we have forgotten our own."

51. Ahern to Duffy, May 1, 1931.

52. Interview with Sr. Peter Claver, May 6, 1995; see also Missionary Report for Aug. 1931 (ADN: QAPP, Box 1).

53. Ahern mentioned their attendance at the Federation meetings twice in 1932, once under the heading of "outstanding events of the month" (Ahern to Duffy, Aug. 31 and Oct. 1, 1932).
54. Ahern to Duffy, Mar. 1, 1932.
55. Ahern to Duffy, Mar. 1, 1933.
56. In 1970, in his declaration in *Motu Proprio,* Pope Paul VI allowed mixed marriages to take place in church.
57. Interview with Walter P. Brown, Dec. 5, 1992.
58. Ibid.
59. Interview with Sr. Peter Claver, May 6, 1995.
60. Although dating back to the beginning of the Christian movement, the Corporal and Spiritual Works of Mercy were listed as such sometime in the Middle Ages. See *The Catholic Encyclopedia, Volume X,* (New York: Robert Appleton Co., 1911).
61. Ibid. In the Trinitarian missionary reports filed with the diocese from 1930 to 1935 the author of the reports divided the work between the Corporal Works of Charity and Spiritual Works of Charity (ADN: QAPP, Box 2–4).
62. Eldridge, *Max Weber,* 229–35.
63. Queen of Angels' tenth anniversary brochure, 1940, ADN: QAPP Files. Prudential Insurance Company had just built a housing complex in Newark.
64. Mission report to Duffy, Mar. 1932.
65. Ahern to McLaughlin, Feb. 3, 1934; interview with Sr. Francis Damien, May 6, 1995.
66. Ahern to McLaughlin, Feb. 3, 1934
67. Ahern to Duffy, Dec. 1, 1932.
68. Ibid., Apr. 4, 1932.
69. Ibid., Jan. 2, 1933.
70. Ahern to McLaughlin, Jan. 2, 1934.
71. Ibid., Dec. 2, 1934.
72. Ahern to Duffy, Dec. 1, 1932; Ahern to Duffy, Jan. 1, 1933. Private agencies like the Salvation Army and the Goodwill Mission refused assistance to blacks, and Roosevelt's New Deal Agencies discriminated as well. See *AACN,* 115, 124.
73. Ahern to McLaughlin, Sept. 3, 1934.
74. Ahern to McLaughlin, Jan. 31, 1935. Twenty-nine families were dropped from the ERA relief roles in January 1935. Ahern wrote: "We hope nothing like this happens again as we have some of the poorest and most helpless of God's creatures in our parish."
75. See *AACN* and Deleney, *The Interaction between Protestant Churches and Their Social Environment in the Inner City*, 22. Also see Dolan, *The Immigrant Church*.

76. Interracial Committee, 43–48.
77. Ibid., 48.
78. Ibid.
79. Interview with Sr. Francis Damien, May 6, 1995.
80. Ahern to Duffy, Apr. 4, 1932. Sr. Patricia Judge cites the date of the medical clinic as 1931 rather than 1932. Judge wrote, "One of the first social endeavors of Queen of Angels in conjunction with the Mount Carmel Guild was the establishment of a medical clinic in 1931. It was the first sub-clinic in the city of Newark and had the full recognition of Doctor Charles Craster, director of the Board of Health" (92). In 1940, Gillard had this comment about the medical clinic: "Two physicians and two nurses give a day a week in the clinic connected with Queen of Angels Missions. Last year 370 cases were treated (*CCIUS,* 230).
81. Ethel Wright to Duffy, May 13, 1930 (ADN: QAPP, Box 1).
82. Ahern to Duffy, May 1, 1933.
83. Ibid. Msgr. William Field, former director of Seton Hall Archives (now deceased) knew Ahern when Field was both a teenager and during his early years as a cleric. According to Field, Ahern's request for St. Bridget's was made directly to the bishop, and he hoped for it until his death. It seemed to him the ideal location and plant to carry on his African American parish (interview with Msgr. William Field, May 24, 1995).
84. Ahern letter to Duffy, June 1, 1933.
85. See *CCAN* and *CCIUS;* Dolan, *American Catholic Experience*.
86. There is nothing in the correspondence between Ahern and Duffy to indicate why the latter did not ask a religious order of priests to head the missions. Possibly Duffy's sense of personal destiny regarding the black work led him to the belief that the diocese should handle the missions themselves.
87. John LaFarge, *The Catholic Viewpoint on Race Relations* (Garden City, N.Y.: Hanover House, 1956), 60.
88. In his last letter to Duffy as vicar-general of Newark, Ahern said: "In case of any change in the work I will allot the necessary monies to the new pastor" (Ahern to Duffy, June 1, 1933).
89. John LaFarge, S.J., *Interracial Justice: A Study of the Catholic Doctrine of Race Relations* (New York: America Press, 1937), 163. Ahern describes the meetings with LaFarge and Kramer in a letter to Duffy, October 31, 1932, calling them "our conferences" or "inter-racial work."
90. John LaFarge, S.J., *The Manner Is Ordinary* (New York: Harcourt, Brace and Co., 1954), 339.
91. Minutes of Clergy Conference on Negro Welfare at Queen of Angels (undated). LaFarge credits Ahern with coining the term *colored conscious* in LaFarge, *The Catholic Viewpoint on Race Relations,* 64–65.

92. See both Coffman, *Build Me a City,* 117, and LaFarge, S.J., *The Manner Is Ordinary*, 339. LaFarge credits Ahern and Purcell with organizing the Clergy Conference on Negro Welfare. Also, William Osborne mentioned that in 1933, the Clergy Conference on Negro Welfare was started in Newark by "a group of white priests involved in the Church's apostolate to the Negro." Others were established in the Midwest, Mobile, Alabama, and in the dioceses of Richmond and Raleigh. Osborne states that the conference disbanded after a decade, but LaFarge and Coffman record that it existed until shortly after Ahern's death in 1945, which is more likely the case (Osborne, *The Segregated Covenant,* 36–37). Also see Ochs, *Desegregating the Altar,* 345–46. He states that the first meeting was held in Pennsylvania.
93. Ibid. Minutes of Clergy Conference on Negro Welfare at Queen of Angels (undated), QAPA.
94. Ibid.
95. Ibid.
96. Ibid.
97. Mentioned in the several interviews I had with Sr. Peter Claver from 1991 to 1995. In her nineties, she obviously was still distressed by Ahern's reaction to her departure.
98. *CCIUS,* 15.
99. William O'Laughlin started the Our Lady Queen of Angels Band, and also the Sons and Daughters of Saint Kitts. He was from Saint Kitts, British West Indies. Interview with Walter P. Brown, Dec. 5, 1992.
100. Sr. Francis Damien, Sept. 30, 1994.
101. Fr. Shanley was a cleric at Queen of Angels. Interview with Sr. Peter Claver, May 6, 1995. The parishioners from Ahern's time told Fr. Thomas Carey that Ahern died of a broken heart when he was not allowed to continue his work among African Americans at St. Bridget's Parish (interview with Thomas Carey, Dec. 15, 1995).
102. St. Columba's Parish Files, ADN. When Ahern left in 1940, Gillard's census for that year indicated a black Catholic population in the Newark diocese of 4,708, an increase of 3,608 in ten years (*CCIUS,* 16, 20).
103. Msgr. William Field recalls sitting in on meetings (probably those of the Clergy Conference on Negro Welfare) that Ahern held at St. Columba's with LaFarge and other priests concerning the black work (interview with Msgr. William Field, May 24, 1995).
104. Death Records, Queen of Angels Parish Records.

5. On Pilgrimage to Justice

1. Unfortunately, very little documentation survived Joseph Lenihan, the next pastor, severely limiting the ability to offer a critical history during that time. While the historical record of the first five years provides us with abundant resources to

reconstruct those seminal years, the period under the administration of Fr. Joseph Lenihan must be constructed with what little documentation we have.

2. Status Animarum, a statistical report submitted to the archdiocese for 1946, 1954, 1958, 1961–68, QAPA.
3. Years later, Msgr. John P. Lenihan wrote a letter requesting payment from the then administrator Thomas Carey. Carey had no documentation for the loan, nor did Queen of Angels have the funds to repay it (telephone interview with Thomas Carey, Oct. 21, 1997).
4. LaFarge, *The Catholic Viewpoint on Race Relations,* 60.
5. Interview with Walter P. Brown, Dec. 5, 1992.
6. Ibid.
7. Interview with Ruby Jones, May 2, 1997; interview with Nathaniel Potts on Aug. 22, 1993.
8. Although Walsh's interest was the Italian work, with Duffy as vicar-general in charge of the colored work, Queen of Angels was able to accomplish a great deal (interview with Sr. Francis Damien, Sept. 30, 1994). See also the 1953 Official Catholic Directory regarding Boland.
9. Queen of Angels Board of Trustees Record Book, QAPA. The Queen of Angels' rectory was at least partially financed by the sale of property in East Orange. The notation in the Queen of Angels Board of Trustees Record Book reads, "Property which had been donated by the late Mrs. Elizabeth Rothschild, 221 Amherst St., E[ast] O[range] was sold to Melvin Roe for $5,000. Evidently, the previous impediment to a Negro church in Orange no longer existed.
10. Sr. Patricia Judge, M.S.B.T., writing in 1963, stated that Lenihan closed St. Thomas and Mother Boniface Mission in 1940 and St. John's Mission in 1951. My dates follow the Official Catholic Directory for those years and the entry in the Queen of Angels Board of Trustees Record Book regarding the St. John's property.
11. Judge, "The Negro in Queen of the Angels Parish," 54. Also, see Lani Luciano, "A Dying Parish Comes to Life," *Sign Magazine,* Oct. 1976, for information on St. Peter Claver's revival under Fr. Charles McTague. As indicated above, St. Peter Claver had no resident priest, being ministered to by one of the priests from Holy Spirit. McTague lived in the basement of St. Peter Claver Church for several years and then lived at the local YMCA until the parish was able to build a rectory. It is an interesting phenomenon that the black parishes of the archdiocese were without schools or rectories for so many years. In their entire histories, St. Peter Claver and Holy Spirit were never able to afford parochial schools.
12. Over the years, Fr. Paul Hayes wrote extensively for black and white newspapers concerning interracial issues.

13. On June 24, 1954, Archbishop Thomas A. Boland declared Holy Spirit and St. Peter Claver officially separated from Queen of Angels, and Rev. David J. Price was appointed as administrator of both parishes (Queen of Angels Baptismal Records, 1954, QAPA).
14. Carey Papers.
15. Interview with Ruby Jones, May 2, 1997.
16. Lenihan refused to baptize Elma Bateman's children because she lived in Blessed Sacrament parish. The next pastor, Thomas Carey, did not adhere to that policy. Interview with Elma Bateman, May 1, 1996.
17. Ibid. Nathaniel Potts changed his parish to Blessed Sacrament but did become very active in civil rights activities and Operation Understanding at Queen of Angels in the 1960s and 1970s.
18. Ruby Jones, who was probably closer to Lenihan than any other parishioner, said he wanted to be "carried out of Queen of Angels," but knew he would not be allowed back to the parish if he went on vacation. When he returned to Newark, he was placed in St. Joseph's Parish (see the 1958 Official Catholic Directory).
19. Mar. 1, 1957, entry in the Queen of Angels Board of Trustees Record Book, QAPA.
20. According to Mrs. Jones, during the time that the pastor position was vacant, several priests covered the post.
21. Board of Trustee Record Book. Carey was born on April 4, 1917, in Jersey City to Irish American parents. He attended St. John's Elementary School and Dickenson High School, from which he graduated in 1938. Subsequently, he studied Greek and Latin at St. Peter's Prep and the following year entered St. Andrew-on-Hudson Jesuit novitiate in Poughkeepsie, New York. After two years he left there and entered Immaculate Conception Seminary in the Newark archdiocese. He was ordained in 1949 and was assigned to Christ the King Church in Jersey City. This fulfilled his wish to work with the black community that began when he volunteered at that parish while he was a high school student. After two years he was made procurator (administrator) of Immaculate Conception Seminary, where he remained for seven years. His request to return to parish work resulted in his assignment to Queen of Angels.
22. Interview with Thomas Carey, June 8, 1992.
23. 1958 Status Animarum report (QAPA).
24. I first learned of the archdiocese's action in calling in the loan from Thomas Carey (interview with Carey, June 8, 1992). In the financial report, June 30, 1975, from acting pastor Fr. John J. Maloney, the source of the money that Msgr. John Duffy dispersed to Christ the King in Jersey City and Queen of Angels in Newark is clarified. Maloney lists the current debt of Queen of Angels to the diocese and then ends with

this explanation: "This figure however is debatable because some of the monies received from the fire on Academy Street went directly to the diocese. Included in this would be a $60,000 grant from the Conservation of the Faith for the establishment of Queen of Angels Parish. A grant to my knowledge which was not expected to be repaid because of the mission nature of the parish today and in the 1930s" (ADN RG 10.7, Parish Files: Financial Reports [P.A.C.] Newark, Queen of Angels 6/2/75–6/9/81).

25. Telephone interview with Ruby Jones, Oct. 22, 1997.
26. Carey to Archbishop Thomas Boland, July 29, 1958, Carey Papers.
27. Ibid.
28. In direct contrast to Queen of Angels' history, St. Richard's black Catholic church in Boston closed in some measure because of the Civil Rights movement. Initially, the archdiocese of Boston resisted the idea of a separate black church, allowing one only after years of persistent petitions from laypeople and the involvement of religious orders. St. Richard's Church was established in 1945, but by the late 1950s, Cardinal Cushing was reevaluating the idea of a separate black church in light of the U.S. Supreme Court's *Brown* v. *Board of Education* decision outlawing segregated public schools. Eventually, when white flight left Catholic neighborhoods to blacks, largely black Catholic parishes evolved by demographic default. In spite of the objections of parishioners, the parish closed in 1964. See William C. Leonard, "A Parish for the Black Catholics of Boston," *Catholic Historical Review* 83, no. 1 (Jan. 1997): 51.
29. Judge, "The Negro in Queen of the Angels Parish," 58.
30. *Newark Sunday News,* Aug. 25, 1963; telephone interview with Carey, Dec. 15, 1997.
31. *Newark Sunday News,* Aug. 25, 1963.
32. *Understanding: The Communication Media for Operation Understanding* (Aug. 25, 1968), 8, Carey Papers.
33. *Star-Ledger,* Sept. 26, 1970.
34. Interview with Thomas Comerford, Aug. 24, 1996.
35. Interview with Joyce Smith Carter, Mar. 5, 1992.
36. Martin Luther King Jr., *Stride toward Freedom: The Montgomery Story* (New York: Harper & Brothers, 1958), 190.
37. In interviews with both Robert Curvin and Kenneth Gibson (the first black mayor of Newark), they stated that Queen of Angels was unique in its leadership position in the fight for civil rights in Newark. Not only was it in the forefront of the action, providing meeting space for activist organizations and developing its own solutions to the city's problems, but it shaped and trained blacks and whites for civil rights

and community leadership (interview with Robert Curvin, Sept. 16, 1997, and interview with Kenneth A. Gibson, Nov. 1, 1997). Parishioner Joyce Smith Carter named it a Mecca for civil rights (interview with Joyce Smith Carter, Mar. 15, 1992).

38. Austin Flannery, O.P., ed., *Vatican Council II: The Conciliar and Post Conciliar Documents* (Collegeville, Minn.: Liturgical Press, 1975), 946.
39. Gustavo Gutiérrez, *A Theology of Liberation: History, Politics, and Liberation,* 2d ed., trans. and ed. Sr. Caridad Inda and John Eagleson (Maryknoll, N.Y.: Orbis, 1988), xxix.
40. Carey's maxim, recalled by Thomas Comerford in a telephone interview, Jan. 27, 1998.
41. Luther D. Ivory, *Toward a Theology of Radical Involvement* (Nashville: Abingdon Press, 1997), 99–100. King's concept of the beloved community was appropriated from Walter Rauschenbusch and the social gospel. See William M. Ramsay, *Four Modern Prophets,* and Noel Leo Erskine, *King among the Theologians* (Cleveland, Ohio: Pilgrim Press, 1994). Within these works King's theology is compared to theologians Walter Rauschenbusch, Paul Tillich, Gustavo Gutiérrez, Rosemary Radford Reuther, Karl Barth, and James Cone. See also James Cone, *Martin Malcolm and America: A Dream or a Nightmare?* (New York: Maryknoll Press, 1991).
42. Thomas A. Carey, "The Spirit of Non-Violence and the Spirit of Freedom: What It Is and Why We Support It," n.d., ca. early 1960s. Carey Papers.
43. Msgr. John J. Egan, "Walking, Talking, and Listening," *Catholic Mind,* May 1966, as quoted in Msgr. Thomas Carey, "The Inner City Priest," n.d., Carey Papers. It is not certain, but there is evidence that Carey's essay was published in a clerical publication called *Fratres Unum,* ca. 1966.
44. *Newark News,* Oct. 26, 1966, quoting Carey at a forum entitled "What's Going on in Newark," sponsored by the North Reformed Church. Others on the panel were Rabbi Jonathan Prinz of Temple B'nai Abraham, Rev. James Scott of Bethany Baptist Church, and C. Willard Heckel, dean of the Rutgers University Law School.
45. Ibid.
46. Carey, "The Inner City Priest."
47. Lyke, "Black Catholics in America: A Documentation Overview," 3.
48. See chapter 3 for an in-depth analysis of Cornelius Ahern.
49. Elma Bateman repeated this phrase of Carey's to me several times, as did Carey himself.
50. I agree with Mrs. Fields that Ahern and Carey were similar in many ways, and I suspect that if Ahern lived during Carey's time he would have changed his approach to fit the era. Telephone interview with Bennie Fields, June 2, 2000.
51. Thomas A. Carey, "What Can Be Done by the Church for the Problems of the Inner City?" n.d., c.a. 1968. Carey Papers.

52. Ibid.
53. Thomas Carey, sermon at Queen of Angels Church on the occasion of the twenty-fifth anniversary of the Walk for Understanding, May 2, 1993.
54. Interview with Thomas Comerford, July 2, 1992.
55. César Chávez's union led a successful national boycott of California table grapes and lettuce on behalf of the workers who harvested the fruit and vegetables of California. Both Tom Carey and William Linder spoke of the parish's support of Chávez in our interviews. Linder remembered very clearly when Chávez stayed at Queen of Angels. For more on Chávez, see Richard Griswold del Castillo and Richard A. Garcia, *César Chávez: A Triumph of Spirit* (Norman: Univ. of Oklahoma Press, 1995); Jacques E. Levy, *César Chávez: Autobiography of La Causa* (New York: W. W. Norton, 1975); Peter Matthiessen, *Sal Si Puedes: César Chávez and the New American Revolution* (New York: Random House, 1969).
56. Stephen B. Oates, *Let the Trumpet Sound* (New York: HarperPerennial, 1994), 456–58, 460–62. King's plan was to have thousands of poor people of all races camp in Washington, demonstrate, boycott, and disrupt government operations with sit-ins. Bayard Rustin and others were afraid of the anger the Poor People's Campaign would inspire because of its attack on the national economic power structure, including "powerful corporations and business moguls of capitalism itself" (461). They would be doing, as Bernard Lee, a King adviser said, "what the powers of the country will kill you for" (462).
57. Interview with Msgr. William Linder, Jan. 23, 1998.
58. Ibid.
59. Martin Luther King Jr., "Interview," *Playboy Magazine* (Jan. 1965), 67.
60. Interview with Robert Curvin, Sept. 16, 1997; interview with Kenneth A. Gibson, Nov. 1, 1997, and interview with Joyce Smith Carter, Mar. 15, 1992.
61. Interview with Rev. James Scott, Dec. 12, 1994.
62. Joyce Smith Carter worked with Carey and Linder to bring discrimination cases to court (interview with Joyce Smith Carter, Mar. 15, 1992, and Thomas Carey, June 8, 1992).
63. Joyce Smith Carter speech at a luncheon honoring Martin Luther King Jr. at Queen of Angels auditorium, Jan. 11, 1998; follow-up telephone interview, Jan. 12, 1998.
64. King, "Interview," *Playboy Magazine* (Jan. 1965), 67. King acknowledged that his efforts to galvanize the support of white ministers, priests, and rabbis of the South from the Montgomery boycott effort onward failed. They either became "open adversaries," "cautiously shrank from the issue," or "hid behind silence." Consequently, he said, "My optimism about help from the white church was shattered; and on too many occasions since, my hopes for the white church have been dashed." In an annotated copy of the interview, Carey circled the statement following the above

quote of King's that read: "There are many signs that the judgment of God is upon the church as never before. Unless the early sacrificial spirit is recaptured, I am very much afraid that today's Christian church will lose its authenticity, forfeit the loyalty of millions, and we will see the Christian church dismissed as a social club with no meaning or effectiveness for our time, as a form without substance, as salt without savor."

65. *The Advocate*, Feb. 24, 1966.
66. Ibid. Carey was a sponsor of the American Committee on Africa that was co-chaired by Catholic priest and Scripture scholar Rev. Donald S. Harrington and A. Philip Randolph, who organized the Brotherhood of Sleeping Car Porters in 1925. Among the many notable sponsors were Thomas Merton, Harvey Cox, and Reinhold Niebuhr.
67. Interview with Robert Curvin, Sept. 16, 1997.
68. Before both Bethany Baptist and Queen of Angels moved to their present locations, they were only a block away from each other. Carey and Scott exchanged pulpits well before the ecumenical movement and Vatican II made such a practice acceptable. In a letter to Cary, Rev. Horace Hunt stated: "Every time I have the opportunity to work with you my admiration and respect for you only deepen. I covet the chance to work with you in the future and to share with you the fundamental concerns and convictions that unite us" (Horace H. Hunt to Thomas Carey, Aug. 3, 1964, Carey Papers).
69. For a long time Rev. James Scott of Bethany Baptist Church "did not know that Father Carey was white." He did not know until he finally met him, because "nobody ever said that he was white" (interview with James Scott, Dec. 12, 1994).
70. *Newark Sunday News,* Apr. 7, 1968. Carey was also advisor to the local Black Panthers. They rang the rectory door bell one day and asked to speak to him. They came weekly, asking for advice; they acted as guards on an ad hoc basis outside the church and at meetings, looking formidable in their black hats and sunglasses (interview with Thomas Carey, Oct. 27, 1997).
71. In a letter to Richard Cardinal Cushing of Boston, Carey mentioned that the parish had debt problems. From his "bed of pain," a seriously ill Cushing responded, "If you ever knew of the large debts on some of the large urban dioceses, Boston included, you would get the impression that those of us in charge of these great urban dioceses of the past suddenly cracked up" (Archbishop Richard Cardinal Cushing of Boston to Carey, Sept. 6, 1966).
72. Thomas A. Carey to the Rev. Msgr. Edward P. Looney, chairman of the Board for Retired Priests, n.d., ca. May 17, 1969, Carey Papers. I asked Carey if he had ever paid it; he said he never did. The parish did not have the money.
73. Interview with Thomas Carey, June 8, 1992.

74. *Star-Ledger*, Sept. 4, 1968. Interview with Dr. Leon Smith and Msgr. Thomas Carey.
75. Inner City Priests United for Christian Action, "The Present," Jan. 9, 1969, 1.
76. According to Dr. Leon Smith in *Star-Ledger,* Sept. 4, 1968.
77. *Star-Ledger,* Sept. 4, 1968.
78. "Higher Achievement Program: A Year Round Community Service of St. Peter's College and Queen of Angels Parish, Central Ward, Newark, New Jersey, 1965–1966," Carey Papers.
79. Ibid.
80. Ibid.
81. Ibid.
82. Ibid.
83. Summer Reading Improvement Program Proposal, Carey Papers.
84. Interview with Elma Bateman, May 1, 1996; interview with Thomas Carey, June 8, 1992. See also playbills and other articles from the productions, Carey Papers.
85. Judge, "The Negro in Queen of the Angels Parish," 94–97.
86. New Jersey State Advisory Committee to the United States Commission on Civil Rights, *Public Housing in Newark's Central Ward: A Report by the New Jersey State Advisor Committee to the United States Commission on Civil Rights* (Apr. 1968).
87. *National Catholic Reporter,* June 12, 1970.
88. *Public Housing in Newark's Central Ward,* Apr. 1968. The Committee was composed of Rabbi Gerson B. Chertoff, chairman; Mrs. Millicent H. Fenwick, vice chairman; and Donald F. Cameron, secretary; along with fifteen other New Jersey residents.
89. Newark Priests' Group, *The Needs of the People of Newark and the Resources of the Archdiocese* (privately published, 1967). Carey Papers. Priests listed as members of the committee: John P. Hourihan, chairman; Aloysius J. Welsh, editor; Francis J. Houghton; William J. Linder; John J. Maloney; John P. Nichas; and Joseph J. Sherer. Linder and Maloney were both assistants at Queen of Angels at the time.
90. Ibid.
91. *Newark Evening News,* July 14, 1967.
92. Tom Comerford wrote: "I don't like making enemies because I have to say that we had a rebellion last summer, and not a riot, and that I cannot now tell the people in the black community to "cool it" (*Negro Apostolate,* privately published article [May 7, 1968]: 2–3).
93. *Life Magazine,* July 28, 1967; *National Catholic Reporter,* June 12, 1970.
94. *Newark Sunday News,* Feb. 11, 1968.
95. Ibid. The commission's allusion to a conspiracy referred to a theory held by some in Newark government, especially in the police force. A 118-page report described the surveillance and phone tapping of activists Tom Hayden, LeRoi Jones, Willie Wright,

and others in an attempt to prove Communist and subversive actions against the U.S. government (Carey Papers).

96. *Life Magazine,* July 28, 1967. See also Tom Hayden's account of the riots, *Rebellion in Newark: Official Violence and Ghetto Response* (New York: Vintage Books, 1967), written shortly after the riots. Hayden details the cause of death of each person and several eyewitness accounts of police brutality.
97. *Newark Sunday News,* Feb. 11, 1968. As recorded in this article, the commission addressed the sniper situation with this statement: "The technique of employing heavy return fire at suspected sniper locations proved tragic and costly. The heavy firing by police elements against suspected snipers makes it difficult to determine the extensiveness of sniping. There may have been some organized sniping activity once the riot had reached its Friday peak."
98. Interview with Thomas Carey, June 8, 1992; *The Advocate*, July 27, 1967.
99. *The Advocate*, July 27, 1967.
100. Interview with Thomas Carey, Dec. 15, 1997.
101. *The Advocate,* July 20, 1967. The editorial was unsigned but was penned by Carey.
102. Unsigned letter to archbishop from "Priests of Riot-Torn Newark," July 29, 1967.
103. Ibid.
104. Ibid.

6. Moving beyond Pious Irrelevancies

1. Interview with William Linder, Jan. 23, 1998.
2. Former mayor Kenneth Gibson stated that nothing good came out of the riots (interview with Kenneth Gibson, Nov. 1, 1997). Bennie Fields told the author more than once that she believed the employment changes on the corporate level occurred because of the riots and, to a great extent, the work of Operation Understanding (interview with Bennie Fields, Apr. 27, 1994).
3. *New York Times,* July 22, 1967. Msgr. Frank Seymour, who was pastor of St. Charles Boromeo Parish in Newark, remembered the phenomenally rapid exodus of whites from his parish after the riots. Interview with Msgr. Frank Seymour, June 13, 1993.
4. *The Advocate,* July 20, 1968.
5. Interview with Thomas Comerford, June 2, 1992; Thomas Comerford, "The Negro Apostolate," 4.
6. As a result of the city council meeting, the Newark council rejected the canine corps. *Star-Ledger,* Apr. 1, 1968.

7. Linder mentioned the tremendous response of some white suburbanites to the situation in Newark in 1967.
8. "Proposal for Operation Understanding for One Year: Oct. 1, 1971–Sept. 30, 1972" (Pat Foley Private Papers).
9. Interview with Thomas Comerford, June 2, 1992.
10. See the 118-page police report that described the surveillance and phone tapping of activists in an attempt to prove Communist and subversive actions against the U.S. government (Carey Papers). Junius Williams, an African American Newarker who was just out of college at the time of the riots and connected with activist Tom Hayden, of Students for a Democratic Society, took a dim view of Willie Wright, as did Kenneth Gibson (interview with Junius Williams in Newark, Dec. 18, 1996, and interview with former Mayor Kenneth Gibson, Nov. 1, 1997).
11. Douglas Eldridge, *Newark News,* Feb. 26, 1968.
12. Interview with Tom Comerford, June 2, 1992.
13. Douglas Eldridge, *Newark News,* Feb. 26, 1968.
14. *Newark News,* Feb. 26, 1968.
15. Pat Foley Private Papers.
16. *Star-Ledger,* Friday, Apr. 5, 1968.
17. Ibid., Apr. 8, 1968.
18. Interview with Thomas Carey, Jan. 29, 1998.
19. Ibid. Although Carey demurred when asked if this was his strategy ("we weren't that smart"), he did believe that Addonizio could not be absent from such an event.
20. Greater Newark Chamber of Commerce, *The Exec,* a report dated Apr. 15, 1968.
21. Interview with Thomas Comerford, June 2, 1992.
22. The archdiocesan history *Bishops of Newark* states that Archbishop Boland did march in the Walk for Understanding, but several newspaper accounts do not mention his presence there, including the archdiocesan paper, *The Advocate*. It is highly unlikely that such an oversight would have occurred.
23. *New York Times,* Apr. 8, 1968.
24. Carey's speech delivered at the Walk for Understanding, Apr. 7, 1968. The reaction to the Walk for Understanding was sometimes hateful, as in one pointed note that said, "As a ROMAN CATHOLIC I think all your nonsense over a DAMN NIGGER is carrying things just a little too far. I SURE HOPE THEY NEVER CATCH THE KILLER —MORE POWER TO HIS ACT" (Carey Papers).
25. *Understanding: The Communication Media for Operation Understanding* (Oct. 13, 1968), 3, Pat Foley Private Papers. Deacon Bradsher has since moved away from Newark to a retirement community in southern New Jersey. A permanent deacon of the Roman Catholic Church is not allowed to remarry, but after his wife of many years

died of cancer, Bradsher sought special permission from the archbishop to do so. When permission was refused, he chose to remarry and, although it was a painful decision, left the Catholic Church to serve as a deacon in his wife's Baptist church.

26. *Understanding: The Communication Media for Operation Understanding* (Aug. 25, 1968), 7, Pat Foley Private Papers.
27. Ibid. (Oct. 13, 1968).
28. See Leon T. Mahon and Philip Berryman, "Priesthood," paper presented at a seminar along with Edward Schillebeeckx and Bernard Häring in Panama, Nov. 18, 1967, Carey Papers. The influence on Mahon and Carey by liberation theologians like Gustavo Gutiérrez can be inferred by their theology even though they did not explicitly use the terms *liberation theology* or *base communities* in this paper. Evidence of liberation theology's influence on Mahon, and therefore Carey, is that Mahon's co-writer on "Priesthood" was Philip Berryman, who published "Camilo Torres: Revolutionary Theologian," *Commonweal* 96 (Apr. 21, 1972). Torres, who was killed on Feb. 15, 1966, in Colombia as he was leading a group of guerrilla revolutionaries, was a priest and a close friend of Peruvian theology professor Gustavo Gutiérrez. In 1968, Gutiérrez helped draft a position paper for Latin American bishops that became a prototype of liberation theology. San Miguelito certainly anticipated that theology. See Ramsay, *Four Modern Prophets*. Also see Gustavo Gutiérrez, *A Theology of Liberation* (Maryknoll, N.Y.: Orbis Books, 1988).
29. Mahon and Berryman, "Priesthood," 10.
30. Ibid., 9.
31. Interview with Thomas Comerford, July 2, 1992. Of all the priests at Queen of Angels, Comerford felt most affected by base community theological praxis and implemented it systematically and effectively in the projects.
32. Junius Williams viewed the civil rights activities of Queen of Angels as compromised because of the integrated nature of its activities (interview with Junius Williams in Newark, Dec. 18, 1996). See Todd Gitlin, *The Sixties: Years of Hope, Days of Rage* (New York: Bantam, 1987), for more on the ethos of the period, and Tom Hayden's organizing of SDS's Newark Community Union Project. In reference to the SDS in Newark, Gitlin states: "At the same time three hundred northern students were flocking to Mississippi, SDS recruited a hundred more to move into the slums of Newark, Chicago, Cleveland, Philadelphia, and half a dozen other cities, looking to stir up an interracial movement of the poor" (165).
33. Inner City Priests United for Christian Action, "The Present," Jan. 9, 1969, 1.
34. Ibid.
35. Inner City Priests United for Christian Action, "The Past," Jan. 9, 1969, 2.
36. Ibid.

37. Tom Dente, "The Newark Twenty" (unpublished paper for Immaculate Conception Seminary, 1990), 7.
38. The designation *inner city* is not an exact one, and in fact is a euphemism for a racial or ethnic ghetto. The priests called themselves inner-city priests not to cloak a racial meaning but to identify themselves as those who worked and lived with blacks and Hispanics of the poor and marginalized people of Newark.
39. See appendix 3 for a reproduction of the "Letter to Archbishop Thomas Boland from the Newark 20."
40. Inner City Priests United for Christian Action to Archbishop Thomas A. Boland, Jan. 9, 1969, 1, Carey Papers.
41. Inner City Priests United for Christian Action, "Declaration of Brotherhood to Our People, A Statement for Public Release by Twenty Inner-City Priests of the Newark Archdiocese," Jan. 9, 1969, Carey Papers.
42. Ibid., 10–11.
43. "Declaration of Brotherhood to Our People," 11.
44. *Evening News,* Jan. 13, 1969.
45. Harold Baron, "The Web of Urban Racism," in *Institutional Racism in America,* ed. Louis L. Knowles and Kenneth Prewitt (Englewood Cliffs, N.J.: Prentice-Hall, 1969), 142–43.
46. Ibid.
47. Archbishop Thomas A. Boland to the Newark Twenty, n.d., released to the press on the evening of Jan. 9, 1969, Carey Papers.
48. Ibid.
49. United Black Catholics, "Press Release on Behalf of the Twenty Priests," Jan. 15, 1996, Carey Papers.
50. Ibid.
51. *Evening News,* Jan. 13, 1969.
52. Very Reverend John P. Hourihan to Thomas Carey, Jan. 14, 1969, Carey Papers.
53. Telephone interview with Msgr. William Linder, Jan. 23, 1998.
54. Carey Papers.
55. Interview with Elma Bateman, June 1, 2000. Interview with Bennie Fields, June 2, 2000. Mrs. Bateman and Mrs. Fields discussed the Newark Twenty incident many times over the past several years with me, basically stating the same point of view. I am grateful to one of the readers of the manuscript who urged me to clarify this point. Without having written documentation to prove this one way or the other, I asked Mrs. Bateman and Mrs. Fields the question, "Did any parishioner leave Queen of Angels because of the Newark Twenty?" This was their answer.
56. Interview with Thomas Carey, June 8, 1992.

57. Interview with Thomas Comerford, July 2, 1992.
58. Ibid.
59. Ibid. Also, updated information in telephone interview with Thomas Comerford, Jan. 27, 1998.
60. *The Advocate,* June 25, 1970.
61. Ibid.
62. *The Record,* Mar. 26, 1971.
63. *The Advocate,* July 9, 1970. Carey mentioned this in our first interview on June 8, 1992, but also in subsequent telephone conversations. In an interview, Msg. William Linder mentioned the terrible effect that the confrontation with Archbishop Boland had on Carey's health. I asked Carey on Jan. 29, 1998, if this were true. He told me that "those kinds of things take a lot out of a person." And that he was "not by nature a rebel."
64. *Star-Ledger,* Sept. 26, 1970.
65. Ibid.
66. Ibid.
67. We know the statement of the Black Clergy Caucus (see chapter 7) had a profound influence on Comerford from his essay *The Negro Apostolate* (May 7, 1968), in which he quotes Br. Joseph Davis to support his position.
68. Joyce Smith Carter quoted in *Star-Ledger,* Sept. 26, 1970.
69. Harris David and J. Michael Callen, "Newark's Public Housing Rent Strike: The High-Rise Ghetto Goes to Court," *Clearinghouse Review* (Feb. 1974): 583.
70. Ibid., 584.
71. *Understanding: The Communication Media for Operation Understanding* (Dec. 7, 1972), 2, Pat Foley Private Papers.
72. Ibid.
73. Thomas Comerford interview, July 2, 1992.
74. Harris David, "The Settlement of the Newark Public Housing Rent Strike: The Tenants Take Control," *Clearinghouse Review* (June 1976): 103.
75. Telephone interview with Msgr. William Linder, Jan. 23, 1998.
76. Telephone interview with Fr. Kevin Ashe, Feb. 26, 1998. "Fact Sheet" of New Community Corporation, Pat Foley Private Papers.
77. "Fact Sheet" of New Community Corporation, Pat Foley Private Papers.
78. *Evening News,* Aug. 19, 1970.
79. Telephone interview with Fr. Kevin Ashe, Feb. 26, 1998.
80. *Evening News,* Aug. 19, 1970.
81. Ibid.

82. NCC owns eighteen housing developments with almost 3,000 units for more than 7,000 residents and with assets of $300 million. NCC merged with Babyland and has extended its focus to a wide range of programs. In 1989 Babyland established the nation's first child care program for infants and toddlers infected and affected by AIDS and the HIV virus. The information on NCC and Babyland was obtained from NCC's official documentation (233 West Market St., Newark, N.J.).
83. *Understanding: The Communication Media for Operation Understanding* (Aug. 25, 1968), 2, Pat Foley Private Papers.
84. Much of this early story is from a telephone interview with Mrs. Jean Gibbons, one of the suburbanite women from the beginning of Babyland (Feb. 27, 1998).
85. Interview with Linder, also see *Star-Ledger,* Oct. 19, 1992.

7. The Mission Is Accomplished

1. On Aug. 5, 1966, in a protest march in Chicago, Dr. King was almost struck by a knife thrown from the large, barely restrained crowds of whites lining the streets screaming hatred at the marchers. The knife missed him and struck the shoulder of a white onlooker. Mayor Richard Daley's political maneuvering was quite effective against King's strategies, leading King to believe that his southern success could not be repeated in the diverse and more complex northern urban centers (Oates, *Let the Trumpet Sound,* 412–13). For various histories of SCLC see Taylor Branch, *Parting the Waters: America in the King Years, 1954–63* (New York: Simon and Schuster, 1988); David J. Garrow, *Bearing the Cross: Martin Luther King, Jr., and the Southern Christian Leadership Conference* (New York: William Morrow and Co., 1986). Also, see Oates, *Let the Trumpet Sound,* 412, for an explication of King's relationship to President Lyndon Johnson, the Black Power movement, and the fear and anxiety created among those close to him when he pushed for his Poor People's Campaign and against the Vietnam War. As strongly as even his staunchest supporters opposed the campaign, King just as strongly believed he had to see it through.
2. On March 23, 1968, a few days before King's last visit to New York and New Jersey, Adam Clayton Powell, minister of Abyssinian Baptist Church in Harlem and a New York congressman, proclaimed that the "day of Martin Luther King [had] come to an end." He declared that nonviolent activists would never again control the black movement. He rejected the NAACP and the Urban League and declared that "we are finished with Martin Luther King unless he comes back home—we'll make a good man out of him if he comes back home" (*New York Times,* Mar. 24, 1968).
3. Stokely Carmichael first used the term *black power* on June 12, 1966, at a SNCC rally in Mississippi when he emerged from prison; the crowd immediately picked up

his spontaneous utterance and it became the movement's title. At that time, SNCC and CORE began a policy of excluding whites from their ranks and their political activities (Oates, *Let the Trumpet Sound,* 398–406). According to Todd Gitlin, another SNCC member, Willie Rink promoted the slogan in Mississippi in 1966 (Gitlin, *The Sixties,* 278).

4. Brother Joseph M. Davis, S.M., vice-chairman of the Black Catholic Clergy Conference, "The Position of the Catholic Church in the Black Community," *Homiletic and Pastoral Review* LXIX, no. 9 (June 1969): 702.
5. Ibid., 703.
6. *New York Times,* July 21, 1967.
7. Davis, "African American Catholics," 17.
8. Ibid.
9. Ibid.
10. Davis, *The Position of the Catholic Church in the Black Community.*
11. In 1991, Msgr. William Linder received $330,000 from the John D. and Catherine T. MacArthur Award in recognition of his work. *New York Times,* Aug. 11, 1991.
12. Rev. Frank E. Hurtz, one of the Newark Twenty, was the only other African American priest to serve at Queen of Angels. He was a curate under Lenihan in 1956, and under Carey in 1961.
13. *The Advocate,* Sept. 10, 1980.
14. In 1950, 17 percent of the city was nonwhite. Years 1960 to 1967 saw an increase from 34 percent to about 60 percent (*New York Times,* July 22, 1967). According to the 1990 census, Newark's total population was 275,221, of which black (non-Hispanic) was 153,703; white (non-Hispanic) was 45,344; Hispanic of all origins was 71,761; American Indian and Eskimo was 649; and Asian, Pacific Islander, and other was 3,281.
15. *GRAFRICA,* May 10, 1981. In many conversations with the author, Joyce Smith Carter has insisted that, in the absence of any other such organization, one of QUEST's central reasons for being is to provide models for African American Catholic youth in the inner city.
16. On November 11, 1927, a Mr. Ray is listed in the minutes as attending the meeting on that day. But neither he nor any other man is mentioned anywhere else in the minutes.
17. In 1940, female church membership at Queen of Angels was only slightly larger than male: 2,260 women and 1,993 men; male and female organizations were equally represented (*CCIUS,* 15).
18. For more on the experience of African American women, see (among many other excellent resources) Higginbotham, *Righteous Discontent*; Cheryl Townsend Gilkes,

If It Wasn't for the Women: Black Women's Experience and Womanist Culture in Church and Community (Maryknoll, N.Y.: Orbis Books, 2000); Darlene Clark Hine, Wilma King, Linda Reed, eds., *"We Specialize in the Wholly Impossible": A Reader in Black Women's History* (New York: Carlson, 1995); Bettye Collier-Thomas, *Daughters of Thunder: Black Women Preachers and Their Sermons* (San Francisco: Jossey-Bass, 1997).

19. See Keith F. Pecklers, *The Unread Vision: The Liturgical Movement in the United States of America: 1926–1955* (Collegeville, Minn.: Liturgical Press, 1998), 40.
20. Most certainly Fr. John LaFarge had at least a supportive role in this development considering his relationship with Ahern, his prominent leadership in the interracial movement in the Catholic Church, and his experimentation with liturgical participation in another African American parish in Maryland (Pecklers, *The Unread Vision,* 57). Also, it is assumed that Ahern received permission from Bishop Thomas Walsh for the dialogue Mass since it was required of parishes to do so (55). However, at present no documentation is known to exist to support this assumption.
21. Pecklers, *The Unread Vision,* 55.
22. Secretariat for the Liturgy and Secretariat for Black Catholics, *Plenty Good Room: The Spirit and Truth of African American Catholic Worship* (Washington, D.C.: National Conference of Catholic Bishops, 1990), 49.
23. Interview with Elma Bateman and Bennie Fields, Apr. 27, 1994.
24. Ibid.
25. Interview with Ollie Pierce, Nov. 14, 1994.
26. McDonogh, *Black and Catholic in Savannah, Georgia,* 93.
27. In an interview with Cecilia Faulks, a present active member of Queen of Angels, she told me how deeply moved she was by Mrs. Gordon's public demonstration of her faith. Even though Mrs. Faulks is still inhibited to a certain extent by her own Catholic reticence to emote in church, Mrs. Gordon inspired her to discover a connection to her African American culture that she never had before (interview with Cecilia Faulks, Aug. 18, 1993).
28. Ibid.
29. Secretariat for the Liturgy and Secretariat for Black Catholics, *Plenty Good Room,* 52–53.
30. John Paul Muffler, "This Far by Faith: A History of St. Augustine's, The Mother Church for Black Catholics in the Nation's Capital" (Ph.D. diss., Columbia Univ. Teachers College, 1989), 63.
31. McDonogh, *Black and Catholic in Savannah, Georgia,* 89.
32. Elizabeth Houston interview with Msgr. William Field, June, 17, 1980.
33. McDonogh, *Black and Catholic in Savannah, Georgia,* 37.

34. Dean R. Hoge, *Conversion Theories—Converts Dropouts Returnees: A Study of Religious Change among Catholics* (New York: Pilgrim Press, 1981), 17.
35. Interview with Lucille Turner, Sept. 11, 1993.
36. Interview with James Scott, July 6, 1995.
37. Interview with Mary Watson, Apr. 19, 1991.
38. Interview with Cecilia Faulks, Aug. 18, 1992, and Lucille Turner, Sept. 11, 1993.
39. Interview with Deacon Albert Bradsher, June 27, 1993.
40. Will Herberg, *Protestant, Catholic, and Jew: An Essay in American Religious Sociology*, 2d ed. (Chicago: Univ. of Chicago Press, 1983), 4.
41. Interview with Sr. Mary Mathew, M.S.B.T., July 6, 1992.
42. See Gutiérrez, *A Theology of Liberation*.
43. Melodie M. Toby, "Bootstrap Ethics: Churches Helping Communities to Help Themselves" (paper presented at the Mid-Atlantic Regional Meeting of the American Academy of Religions, Mar. 2000), 13.
44. Ibid. Toby's entire paper is worth reading for the concept of bootstrap ethics. She advocates that the black church work to empower its members and those of the community within the venue of the church rather than outside of it, and by churches working together to achieve economic uplift.

Bibliography

Alstrom, Sidney E. *A Religious History of the American People.* New Haven: Yale Univ. Press, 1972.

Andrews, William L. *Sisters of the Spirit: Three Black Women's Autobiographies of the Nineteenth Century*. Bloomington: Indiana Univ. Press, 1986.

Atkinson, Joseph. *The History of Newark, New Jersey: Being a Narrative of Its Rise and Progress, from the Settlement in May, 1666, by Emigrants from Connecticut, to the Present Time*. Newark: William B. Guild, 1878.

Barnes, David M. *The Draft Riots in New York, July, 1863. The Metropolitan Police: Their Services during Riot Week*. New York: Baker & Godwin, 1863; reprint, Ann Arbor, Mich.: Univ. Microfilms International, 1978.

Bennett, Lerone, Jr. *Before the Mayflower: A History of Black America*. 6th ed. New York: Penguin Books, 1993.

Berlin, Ira. *Slaves without Masters*. New York: Pantheon Books, 1974.

Berry, Brewton. *Almost White*. New York: Macmillan, 1963.

Bilby, Joseph G. *Forgotten Warriors: New Jersey's African American Soldiers in the Civil War*. Hightstown, N.J.: Longstreet House, 1993.

Billington, Ray Allen. *The Protestant Crusade, 1800–1860: A Study of the Origins of American Nativism*. Chicago: Quadrangle Books, 1964.

Blackwell, Sr. Joseph Miriam, M.S.B.T. *Ecclesial People: A Study in the Life and Times of Thomas Augustine Judge, C.M.* 2d ed. Holy Trinity, Ala.: Missionary Cenacle Press, 1984.

Blassingame, John W. *Black New Orleans, 1860–1880*. Chicago: Univ. of Chicago Press, 1973.

———. *The Slave Community: Plantation Life in the Antebellum South*. New York: Oxford Univ. Press, 1979.

———, ed. *Slave Testimony: Two Centuries of Letters, Speeches, Interviews, and Autobiographies*. Baton Rouge: Louisiana State Univ. Press, 1977.

Blatnica, Dorothy Ann, V.S.C. *"At the Altar of Their God": African American Catholics in Cleveland, 1922–1961*. New York: Garland Publishing, 1995.

Bokenkotter, Thomas. *Church and Revolution: Catholics in the Struggle for Democracy and Social Justice.* New York: Doubleday, 1998.

Bibliography

Boxer, Charles R. *Race Relations in the Portuguese Colonial Empire, 1415–1825*. Oxford: Clarendon Press, 1963.

Brown, Richard D., and Stephen G. Rabe, eds. *Slavery in American Society*. 2d ed. Lexington, Mass.: D. C. Heath and Co., 1976.

Brox, Norbert. *A Concise History of the Early Church*. New York: Continuum Publishing Co., 1996.

Cahill, Thomas. *How the Irish Saved Civilization*. New York: Anchor Books, Doubleday, 1995.

Chestnut, Mary Boykin, and C. Vann Woodward, eds. *Mary Chesnut's Civil War*. New Haven: Yale Univ. Press, 1981.

Chinnici, Joseph P., O.F.M. *Living Stones: The History and Structure of Catholic Spiritual Life in the United States.* New York: Macmillan, 1989.

Coffman, Sr. Mary Ruth, O.S.B. *Build Me a City: The Life of Reverend Harold Purcell, Founder of the City of St. Jude.* Montgomery, Ala.: Pioneer Press, 1984.

Coll, George. *A Pioneer Church, Brief History of the Church of St. Benedict the Moor in the City of New York*. Elizabeth, N.J.: By the author, 1993.

Committee on African American Catholics, National Conference of Catholic Bishops. *Keep Your Hand on the Plow*. Washington, D.C.: Office of Research, 1996.

Cone, James. *Black Theology and Black Power*. New York: Harper & Row, 1968.

———. *God of the Oppressed*. Rev. ed. Maryknoll, N.Y.: Orbis Books, 1997.

———. *Martin Malcolm and America: A Dream or a Nightmare?* New York: Maryknoll Press, 1991.

Cooley, Henry Scofield. *A Study of Slavery in New Jersey*. Johns Hopkins University Studies in Historical and Political Science. Herbert B. Adams, ed. No. 14. Baltimore: Johns Hopkins Press, 1896.

Costen, Melva Wilson. *African American Christian Worship*. Nashville: Abingdon Press, 1993.

Cunningham, John. *Newark*. 2d ed. Trenton: New Jersey Historical Commission, 1988.

Davis, Cyprian, O.S.B. *The History of Black Catholics in the United States*. New York: Crossroad Publishing Co., 1990.

Davis, David Brion. *The Problem of Slavery in the Age of Revolution, 1770–1823*. Ithaca, N.Y.: Cornell Univ. Press, 1975.

———. *The Problem of Slavery in Western Culture*. Ithaca, N.Y.: Cornell Univ. Press, 1966.

Davis, Thurston N., S.J., and Joseph Small, S.J., eds. *A John LaFarge Reader*. New York: America Press, 1956.

Deleney, Moses. "The Interaction between Protestant Churches and Their Social Environment in the Inner City." Ph.D. diss., Drew Univ., 1959.

Desdunes, Rodolphe Lucien. *Our People and Our History*. Originally published in 1911 as *Nos Hommes et Notre Histoire*. Trans. and ed. Sr. Dorothea Olga McCants, Daughter of the Cross. Baton Rouge: Louisiana State Univ. Press, 1973.

Dolan, Jay P., ed. *The American Catholic Experience: A History from Colonial Times to the Present*. Garden City, N.Y.: Doubleday & Co., 1985; reprint, Notre Dame: Notre Dame Univ. Press, 1992.

———. *The American Catholic Parish*. Vol. 1, *The Northeast, Southeast, and South Central States*. New York: Paulist Press, 1987.

———. *The Immigrant Church: New York's Irish and German Catholics, 1815–1865*. Baltimore: Johns Hopkins Univ. Press, 1977; reprint, Notre Dame: Univ. of Notre Dame Press, 1983.

———, ed. The American Catholic Tradition Series. New York: Arno Press, 1978.

Dominguez, Virginia R. *White by Definition: Social Classification in Creole Louisiana*. Piscataway, N.J.: Rutgers Univ. Press, 1986.

DuBois, W. E. B. *The Souls of Black Folk*. New York: Fawcett Publications, 1967.

Eldridge, J. E. T., ed. *Max Weber: The Interpretation of Social Reality*. New York: Charles Scribner's Sons, 1971; reprint, New York: Schoken Books, 1980.

Erskine, Noel Leo. *King among the Theologians*. Cleveland: Pilgrim Press, 1994.

Federal Writers Project of the Work Projects Administration for the State of Connecticut. *History of Milford, Connecticut: 1639–1939*. Bridgeport, Conn.: Braunworth & Co., 1939.

Finkelman, Paul, ed. *Fugitive Slaves and American Courts*. Vol. 2, *Slavery, Race, and the American Legal System, 1700–1872*. 2d ser. New York: Garland Publishing, 1988.

———. *Articles on American Slavery*. Vol. 16, *Religion and Slavery*. New York: Garland Publishing, 1989.

Fischer, Roger A. *The Segregation Struggle in Louisiana, 1862–77*. Champaign: Univ. of Illinois Press, 1974.

Fishman, George. "The Struggle for Freedom and Equality: African-Americans in New Jersey, 1624–1849/50." Ph.D. diss., Temple Univ., 1990.

Flannery, Austin, O.P., ed. *Vatican Council II: The Conciliar and Post Conciliar Documents.* Collegeville, Minn.: Liturgical Press, 1975.

Flynn, Joseph M., M.R., V.F. *The Catholic Church in New Jersey*. New York: Publisher's Printing Co., 1904.

Foley, Albert S., S.J. *God's Men of Color: The Colored Catholic Priests of the United States, 1854–1954*. New York: Farrar, Straus & Co., 1955.

Fordham, Monroe. *Major Themes in Northern Black Religious Thought: 1800–1860*. Hicksville, N.Y.: Exposition Press, 1975.

Franklin, John Hope. *Race and History: Selected Essays, 1938–1988.* Baton Rouge: Louisiana State Univ. Press, 1989.

Frucht, Richard, ed. *Black Society in the New World*. New York: Random House, 1971.

Gannon, Michael V. *Rebel Bishop: The Life and Era of Augustin Verot*. Foreword by John Tracy Ellis. Milwaukee: Bruce Publishing Co., 1964.

———. *The Cross in the Sand: The Early Catholic Church in Florida, 1513–1870.* Gainesville: Univ. of Florida Press, 1965.

Genovese, Eugene D. *Roll, Jordan, Roll*. New York: Pantheon Books, 1974.

Georgia Writers' Project. *Drums and Shadows: Survival Studies among the Georgia Coastal Negroes*. Westport, Conn.: Greenwood Press, 1940.

Gillard, John Thomas. *The Catholic Church and the American Negro; Being an Investigation of the Past and Present Activities of the Catholic Church*. Baltimore: St. Joseph's Society Press, 1929.

———. *Colored Catholics in the United States: An Investigation of Catholic Activity in Behalf of the Negroes in the United States and a Survey of the Present Condition of the Colored Missions*. Baltimore: Josephite Press, 1941.

Glatthaar, Joseph T. *Forged in Battle: The Civil War Alliance of Black Soldiers and White Officers.* New York: Free Press, 1990.

Gleason, Philip. *Documentary Reports on Early American Catholicism*. Ed. Jay P. Dolan. The American Catholic Tradition Series. New York: Arno Press, 1978.

Glover, Ralph J. "Diocesan Social Welfare: A Study of the Diocese of Newark." Ph.D. diss., Fordham Univ., 1929.

Goodell, William. *The American Slave Code in Theory and Practice*. New York: American and Foreign Anti-Slavery Society, 1853; reprint, New York: Negro Universities Press, 1968.

Greenleaf, Richard E., ed. *The Roman Catholic Church in Colonial Latin America*. New York: Alfred A. Knopf, 1971.

Guttierez, Gustavo. *A Theology of Liberation*. Rev. ed. Maryknoll, N.Y.: Orbis Books, 1988.

Handy, Robert T. *A Christian America: Protestant Hopes and Historical Realities.* 2d ed. New York: Oxford Univ. Press, 1984.

Herskovits, Melville J. *The Myth of the Negro Past*. Boston: Beacon Press, 1958.

———. *The American Negro*. Bloomington: Indiana Univ. Press, 1928.

Higginbotham, Evelyn Brooks. *Righteous Discontent: The Women's Movement in the Black Baptist Church, 1880–1920*. Cambridge, Mass.: Harvard Univ. Press, 1993.

Hudson, Winthrop S. *Religion in America.* 4th ed. New York: Macmillan, 1987.

Ignatiev, Noel. *How the Irish Became White*. New York: Routledge, 1995.

Interracial Committee of the New Jersey Conference of Social Work and the State Dept. of Institutions and Agencies. *The Negro in New Jersey, Community Study XIX*. Newark: Dept. of Institutions and Agencies, 1932.

Ivory, Luther D. *Toward a Theology of Radical Involvement: The Theological Legacy of Martin Luther King Jr*. Nashville: Abingdon Press, 1997.

Jamison, Wallace N. *Religion in New Jersey: A Brief History*. Princeton, N.J.: D. Van Nostrand Co., 1964.

Johnson, Clifton H., ed. *God Struck Me Dead: Religious Conversion Experiences and Autobiographies of Ex-slaves*. Philadelphia: Pilgrim Press, 1969.

Judge, Sr. Patricia Margaret. "The Negro in Queen of the Angels Parish, Newark, N.J.: A Study of the Development of the Religious and Social Services Extended to the Negro by a Catholic Parish." Master's thesis, Fordham Univ., 1965.

Kolchin, Peter. *American Slavery, 1619–1877*. New York: Hill and Wang, 1993.

Labbe, Dolores Egger. *Jim Crow Comes to Church*. Ed. Jay P. Dolan. The American Catholic Tradition Series. New York: Arno Press, 1978.

LaFarge, John, S.J. *The Catholic Viewpoint on Race Relations*. Garden City, N.Y.: Hanover House, 1956.

———. *Interracial Justice: A Study of the Catholic Doctrine of Race Relations*. New York: America Press, 1937.

———. *The Manner Is Ordinary*. New York: Harcourt, Brace and Co., 1954.

Lemann, Nicholas. *The Promised Land: The Great Black Migration and How It Changed America*. New York: Alfred A. Knopf, 1991.

Lincoln, C. Eric, and Lawrence S. Mamiya. *The Black Church in the African American Experience*. Durham, N.C.: Duke Univ. Press, 1990.

Lucas, Lawrence. *Black Priest, White Church*. New York: Random House, 1970.

Lyman, Stanford M. *The Black American in Sociological Thought*. New York: Capricorn Books, 1972.

Madden, Richard C. *Catholics in South Carolina*. New York: Univ. Press of America, 1985.

Massa, Mark S., S.J. *Catholics and American Culture*. New York: Crossroad Publishing Co., 1999.

Mathews, Donald G. *Religion in the Old South*. Chicago History of American Religion Series. Ed. Martin Marty. Chicago: Univ. of Chicago Press, 1977.

Maxwell, John Francis. *Slavery and the Catholic Church: The History of Catholic Teaching Concerning the Moral Legitimacy of the Institution of Slavery*. London: Barry Rose Publishers, 1975.

McDonogh, Gary Wray. *Black and Catholic in Savannah, Georgia*. Knoxville: Univ. of Tennessee Press, 1993.

McGreevy, John T. *Parish Boundaries: The Catholic Encounter with Race in the Twentieth-Century Urban North*. Chicago: Univ. of Chicago Press, 1996.

Mencke, John G. *Mulattos and Race Mixture. Studies in American History and Culture*. No. 4. UMI Research Press, 1979.

Miller, Perry. *Errand into the Wilderness*. Cambridge, Mass.: Belknap Press of Harvard Univ. Press, 1956.

Miller, Randall M. "A Church in Cultural Captivity: Some Speculations on Catholic Identity in the Old South." In *Catholics in the Old South: Essays on Church and Culture,* ed. Randall M. Miller and Jon L. Wakelyn. Macon, Ga.: Mercer Univ. Press, 1983.

———. "The Failed Mission: The Catholic Church and Black Catholics in the Old South." In Randall M. Miller and Jon L. Wakelyn, eds. *Catholics in the Old South: Essays on Church and Culture*. Macon, Ga.: Mercer Univ. Press, 1983.

Misch, Edwardo J. "The American Bishops and the Negro from the Civil War to the Third Plenary Council of Baltimore (1865–1884)." Ph.D. diss., Pontifical Gregorian Univ., 1968.

Morgan, Edmund S. *The Puritan Dilemma: The Story of John Winthrop*. Boston: Little, Brown and Co., 1958.

———. *Visible Saints: The History of a Puritan Idea*. New York: New York Univ. Press, 1963.

Morris, Charles R. *American Catholic: The Saints and Sinners Who Built America's Most Powerful Church*. New York: Times Books, 1997.

Muffler, John Paul. "This Far by Faith: A History of St. Augustine's *The Mother Church for Black Catholics in the Nation's Capital.*" Ph.D. diss., Columbia Univ. Teachers College, 1989.

National Advisory Commission on Civil Disorders. *The Kerner Report*. New York: New York Times Co., 1968.

National Conference of Catholic Bishops. Secretariat for Black Catholics. *Many Rains Ago*. Washington. D.C.: United States Catholic Conference, 1990.

New Jersey Catholic Historical Records Commission. *The Bishops of Newark, 1853–1978*. South Orange, N.J.: Seton Hall Univ. Press, 1978.

Nickels, Marilyn Wenzke. *Black Catholic Protest and the Federated Colored Catholics, 1917–1933*. New York: Garland Publishing, 1988.

Northup, Solomon. *Twelve Years a Slave*. Ed. Sue Eakin and Joseph Logsdon. Baton Rouge: Louisiana State Univ. Press, 1968.

Oates, Stephen B. *Let the Trumpet Sound: A Life of Martin Luther King, Jr.* New York: HarperPerennial, 1994.

Ochs, Stephen J. *Desegregating the Altar: The Josephites and the Struggle for Black Priests*. Baton Rouge: Louisiana State Univ. Press, 1990.

Orsi, Robert Anthony. *Thank You, St. Jude: Women's Devotion to the Patron Saint of Hopeless Causes*. New Haven, Conn.: Yale Univ. Press, 1996.

———. *The Madonna of 115th Street: Faith and Community in Italian Harlem, 1880–1950*. New Haven, Conn.: Yale Univ. Press, 1985.

Osborne, William. *The Segregated Covenant: Race Relations and American Catholics.* New York: Herder and Herder, 1967.

Osofsky, Gilbert, ed. *Puttin' on Ole Massa*. New York: Harper & Row, 1969.

Pecklers, Keith F. *The Unread Vision the Liturgical Movement of the United States of America: 1926–1955*. Collegeville, Minn.: Liturgical Press, 1998.

Phelps, Jamie Theresa. "The Mission Ecclesiology of John R. Slattery: A Study of an African-American Mission of the Catholic Church in the Nineteenth Century." Ph.D. diss., Catholic Univ. of America, 1989.

Pingeon, Frances D. "Slavery in New Jersey on the Eve of Revolution." In *New Jersey in the American Revolution: Political and Social Conflict*, ed. William C. Wright. Rev. ed. Trenton: New Jersey Historical Commission, 1974.

Pitts, Walter F. *Old Ship of Zion: The Afro-Baptist Ritual in the African Diaspora.* New York: Oxford Univ. Press, 1993.

Price, Clement Alexander. "The Afro-American Community of Newark: 1917–1947: A Social History." Ph.D. diss., Rutgers Univ., 1975.

———, ed. *Freedom Not Far Distant: A Documentary History of Afro-Americans in New Jersey*. Newark: New Jersey Historical Society, 1980.

Quarles, Benjamin. *The Negro in the American Revolution*. New York: W. W. Norton & Co., 1961.

Raboteau, Albert J. *A Fire in the Bones: Reflections on African-American Religious History.* Boston: Beacon Press, 1995.

———. *Slave Religion: The "Invisible Institution" in the Antebellum South*. New York: Oxford Univ. Press, 1978.

Ramsay, William M. *Four Modern Prophets*. Atlanta: John Knox Press, 1986.

Randolph, Peter. *Slave Cabin to the Pulpit. The Autobiography of Reverend Peter Randolph: The Southern Question Illustrated and Sketches of Slave Life.* Boston: James H. Earle, 1893.

Rauschenbusch, Walter. *A Theology for the Social Gospel.* New York: Macmillan, 1917.

Rawick, George P. *From Sundown to Sunup: The Making of the Black Community*. Vol. 1, *The American Slave: A Composite Autobiography.* 1st ser. Westport, Conn.: Greenwood Publishing Co., 1972.

Reid, Whitelaw. *After the War: A Tour of the Southern States, 1865–1866*. New York: Moore, Wilstach & Baldwin, 1866; reprint, with an introduction and notes by C. Vann Woodward, New York: Harper & Row, 1965.

Rice, Madeleine Hooke. *American Catholic Opinion in the Slavery Controversy*. New York: Columbia Univ. Press, 1944.

Scott, William J. *History of Passaic and Its Environs.* New York: Lewis Historical Publishing Co., 1922.

Secretariat for the Liturgy and Secretariat for Black Catholics. *Plenty Good Room: The Spirit and Truth of African American Catholic Worship*. Washington, D.C.: National Conference of Catholic Bishops, 1990.

Sernett, Milton C., ed. *Afro-American Religious History: A Documentary Witness*. Durham: Duke Univ. Press, 1985.

Sidney E. Mead. *The Lively Experiment: The Shaping of Christianity in America.* New York: Harper & Row, 1976.

Sobel, Mechal. *Trabelin' On: A Slave Journey to an Afro-Baptist Faith*. 2d ed. Princeton, N.J.: Princeton Univ. Press, 1988.

Soule, Leon Cyprian. *The Know Nothing Party in New Orleans: A Reappraisal*. Baton Rouge: Louisiana State Univ. Press, 1961.

Stearns, Jonathan F. *Historical Discourses Relating to the First Presbyterian Church of Newark; Originally Delivered to the Congregation of First Church during the Month of January 1851*. Newark: Daily Advertiser Office, 1853.

Stewart, Alvan. *A Legal Argument before the Supreme Court of the State of New Jersey at the May Term, 1845, at Trenton for the Deliverance of 4,000 Persons from Bondage*. New York: Finch & Weed, 1845.

Stuckey, Sterling. *Slave Culture: Nationalist Theory and the Foundations of Black America.* New York: Oxford Univ. Press, 1987.

Swift, David E. *Black Prophets of Justice: Activist Clergy before the Civil War.* Baton Rouge: Louisiana State Univ. Press, 1989.

Tannenbaum, Frank. *Slave and Citizen.* New York: Alfred A. Knopf, 1946.

Wagley, Charles, and Marvin Harris. *Minorities in the New World*. New York: Columbia Univ. Press, 1958.

Weisenfeld, Judith, and Richard Newman, eds. *This Far by Faith.* New York: Routledge, 1996.

Weiss, Nancy J. *The National Urban League, 1910–1940*. New York: Oxford Univ. Press, 1974.

Whitehead, William A. "Documents Relating to the Colonial History of the State of New Jersey, 1631–1687." In *New Jersey Archives.* Vol. 1. Newark: New Jersey Historical Society, 1880.

Woods, Sr. Frances Jerome. *Marginality and Identity: A Colored Creole Family through Ten Generations*. Baton Rouge: Louisiana State Univ. Press, 1972.

Woodward, C. Vann. *American Counterpoint: Slavery and Racism in the North-South Dialogue*. Boston: Little, Brown and Co., 1964.

———, ed. *The Comparative Approach to American History*. New York: Basic Books, 1968.

Wright, Donald R. *African Americans in the Colonial Era: From African Origins through the American Revolution*. The American History Series. Ed. John Hope Franklin and Abraham S. Eisenstadt. Arlington Heights, Ill.: Harlan Davidson, 1990.

Wright, Marion T. "New Jersey Laws and the Negro." *Journal of Negro History* 27 (1943).

Zavala, Silvio. *The Defence of Human Rights in Latin America (Sixteenth to Eighteenth Centuries)*. Paris: United Nations, 1964.

Index

Index

Index

Index